D0941722

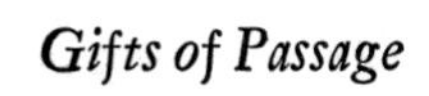
*Gifts of Passage*

*Books by Santha Rama Rau*

GIFTS OF PASSAGE
MY RUSSIAN JOURNEY
VIEW TO THE SOUTHEAST
REMEMBER THE HOUSE
THIS IS INDIA
EAST OF HOME
HOME TO INDIA

# GIFTS OF PASSAGE

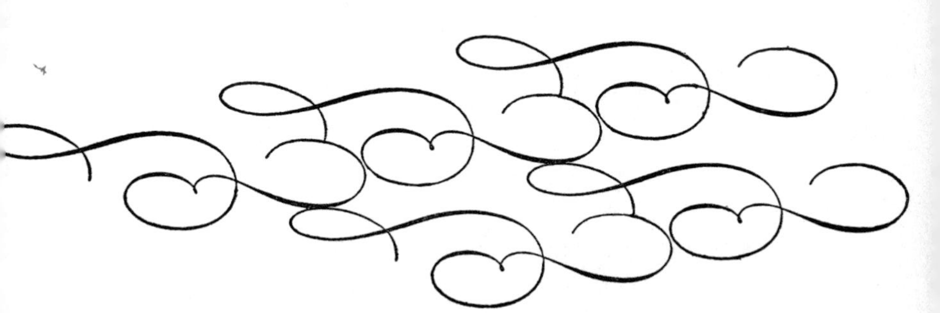

SANTHA
RAMA RAU

*Harper & Row, Publishers*

New York and Evanston

GIFTS OF PASSAGE



Printed in the United States of America



"By Any Other Name," "The Ghost in the Garden," "The Missionary," "The Friendship of Albert Hall," "The Spy," "Makassar Robbery," "The Laughing Dutchman and the Devil Dancers," and parts of Chapters Five and Six (in somewhat different form, under the titles "Letter from Madrid" and "Letter from Bombay") originally appeared in *The New Yorker*. "Who Cares?" originally appeared in *Good Housekeeping*. "The Ugly Face of Violence," "The Trial of Jomo Kenyatta," and "Return to India" originally appeared in *The Reporter*. "Stranded in Kabul" originally appeared in *Harper's Magazine*.

K-M

*Library of Congress catalog card number: 61-6440*

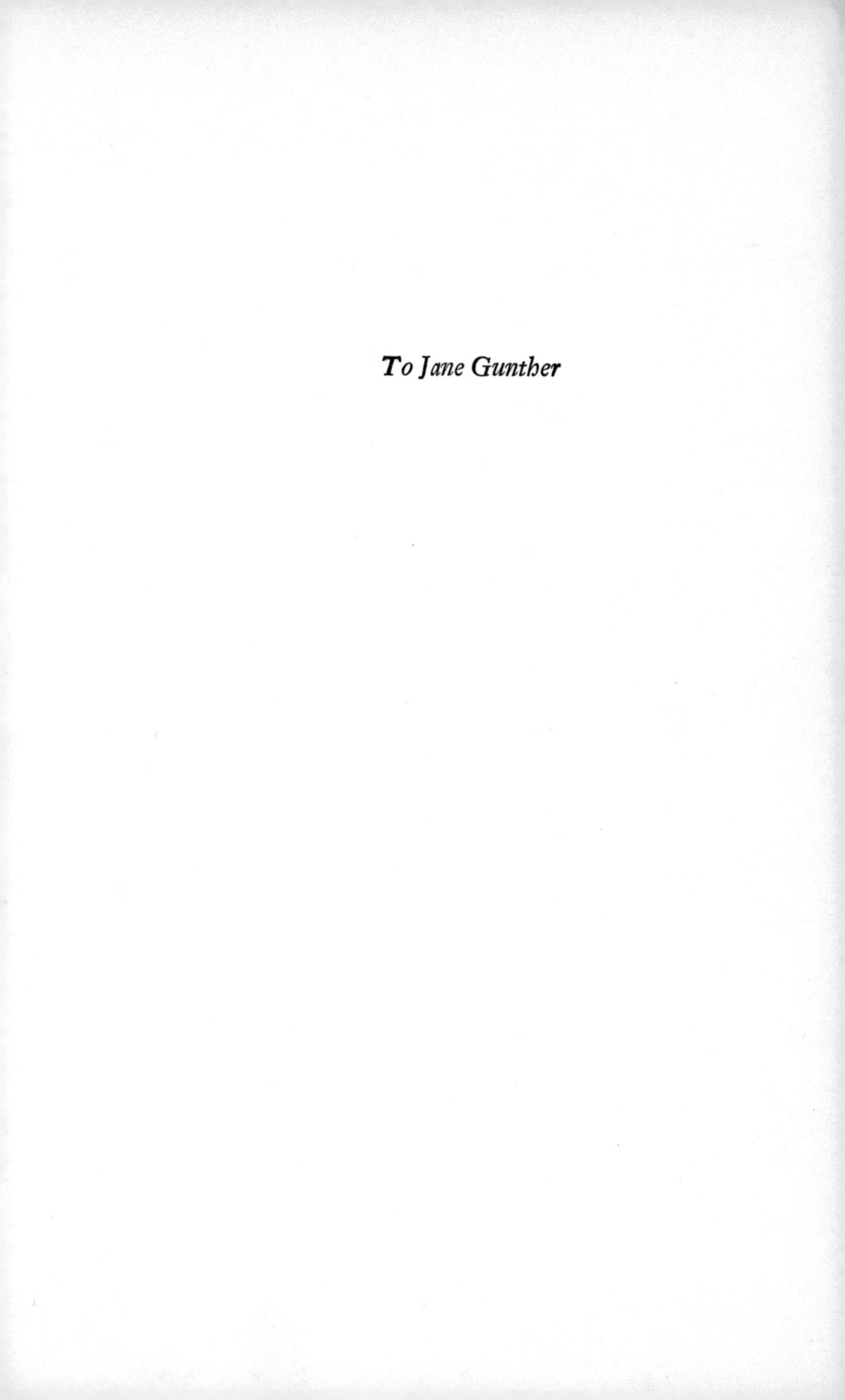

*To Jane Gunther*

*Contents*

## *Author's Note*

*The stories which form the body of this volume have appeared in various magazines over a number of years. In rereading them with a view to book publication, I was interested to discover that, taken in sequence, they provide a sort of rough outline of my life story. To me, my life has seemed ordinary enough, not usual perhaps as lives go but satisfactory to my needs. Yet I know that there are many people, including some of my best friends, who consider it odd, peculiar, even a little mad. Or exotic. So it occurred to me that it would be amusing to weld together these very personal stories—each of which has a basis in a true happening—with autobiographical comment. This I have done, prefacing each story or group of stories with such details of my wandering life as seemed relevant. The result is a curious kind of book, I suspect—a highly irregular self-exploratory essay which attempts to explain how the woman I am emerged from the child born thirty-odd years ago in Madras, India. In trying to recapture people and events, I have hoped to come upon the illuminating moments which have fixed the pattern.*

*Santha Rama Rau*

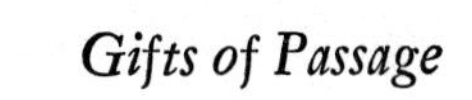

# ONE

My clearest memories of my childhood seem always to involve my grandmother's household in one way or another. That large, sprawling, diverse community with its surface casualness and its underlying, subtle organization, its warmth and expansiveness, its rigid rules, its eccentric members, its conventional structure, its latitude for people to be themselves (within certain boundaries), all live in my mind with that special clarity one associates with moments of intense experience, times that have a reality almost separate from the memories of the people concerned. It was, by Indian standards, a modest household—not rich, not poor—given the quality of excitement by the personalities and idiosyncrasies of its members. A glamorous, handsome uncle who was not only an excellent shot but who also knew, of all things, *how to drive a car!* A gentle, absent-minded great-grandmother, blind and almost deaf, who could still keep the small children enthralled with old stories, old legends, old fables. A splendid, teasing cousin who won all the tennis trophies in his class in the local university. An imaginative, highly strung cousin, only a couple of years older than I, who loved her music lessons and with whom I would dream away long afternoons inventing adventures that might someday happen to us. Aunts, second cousins, my sister, grandparents, distant relatives visiting for a week or six months, children that some member of the family had left to be taken care of while the parents were away on a trip, a pilgrimage, a job of work. It was in something of this sense that my sister and I came to know our grandmother's household well. Our father, in the course of his work, had to travel a great deal.

Much of the time we traveled with him, but when it was inconvenient, where the conditions were too rough for us, when it occurred to someone that we ought to have a "settled home," we would be shipped off to stay with our grandmother and would fall easily into the active, fascinating, absolutely ordinary life of that small family community. It was a source of absorbing normality to which we always returned.

My father was that curious, almost inexplicable creature known as an officer of the Indian Civil Service. This gave him a quite alarming degree of authority at a remarkably early age over thousands and thousands of people in whatever district he was stationed. He had, somehow, to produce the combined talents of an administrator, magistrate, family counselor, government representative, liaison between a dozen different fields and, on at least one occasion, game warden. In those beginning years of his career he was posted to a variety of districts ranging from the most primitive extremes of country living to the relative sophistication of India's governmental capital, New Delhi. I can remember, sometimes, being put to bed in a distant bungalow accompanied by the unearthly screech of wild peacocks in the jungle, and sometimes, protestingly, being dressed in velvet trousers and jacket, all decorated with gold braid, the formal wear for little Indian girls, to go to a fancy children's party in New Delhi. My mother had, in this sort of inconstant life, to use some of her many talents to maintain a fluid, accommodating kind of home, easily packed up and shifted from city to country, from small town to provincial touring, adaptable enough to produce a seven-course meal in the middle of the forest for women in their silk saris and brocades and men in full evening dress even though the dog had just uncovered a nest of cobras outside the kitchen door. Or she was equally well prepared to receive cotton-clad social workers asking for help in a much-needed educational or housing project.

It never occurred to my mother (and, possibly, as a result, to any of us) that this kind of life could present any problem to my sister or to me. My mother had a useful phrase that covered a multitude of bizarre situations—the right etiquette at a traditional Hindu wedding or my first attempt at British sports: "Of course you'll take it in your stride, darling." One way and another, of course we did. I never thought until much later that perhaps this was rather an odd upbringing. But, then, there was always the solid background to which we returned from time to time—my grandmother's household.

There the great, complex system of family and religion and custom that produced the old India still operated. There one's days were paced by the creaking of the wheel that drew water from the well, by the arrival and departure of the fish vendor, the vegetable seller, the butcher (the bread was all baked at home). There a new spark of interest would be kindled by the appearance of the sari merchant with special silks from, say, Benares or Bangalore or Madras. There the bangle seller would come around once a month with a dizzying selection of colored glass bangles and all the children would rush to rub soap on their hands and wrists so that the fragile glass circles would slip on more easily and each one could bask in the vanity of taking the smallest possible size. There the regular routine of the day was the core of human life—the cooking and cleaning and washing for the house, the cultivation and protection of the land, the human exchange that made sense of all the work. We had no entertainments in the modern sense. People were our only amusement—people and their inexhaustible activities, their endless divergencies. Our celebrations were almost all religious festivals, when special decorations were made for the house, oil lamps were lit and set along the line of the roof and in every window, when garlands of flowers were draped over religious paintings, elaborate food was cooked in the house and sweets were sent around to friends and neighbors. For the children it was a real holiday—first the painful business of having our hair washed and tightly braided with marigolds tucked into the braids to mark the day as different, best clothes, a scarlet spot in the center of the forehead, kohl around the eyes, sandalwood oil rubbed behind the ears, henna on our fingertips and the soles of our feet. Then—then, at last, we were free to enjoy ourselves, visit friends, eat too much, go through the gaudy, serious trip to the temple, making our offerings of flowers and fruit, but also gossiping with friends, dashing madly about among the worshipers, laughing and playing games—an Indian temple can be a marvelously social affair as well as a deep religious experience. Holi was our favorite festival, that exuberant burst of springtime when the children can go about the streets and to neighboring compounds with bicycle pumps full of red liquid, squirting acquaintances and strangers for the sheer fun of spring.

Then there were family celebrations—birthdays, betrothals, weddings—which came along often enough to make us unconscious of "parties" in the Western sense. I remember particularly the wedding of my uncle (the one who could drive a car) and the guests and the feasting that continued in the house every day for a week, the unfamiliar but imposing look of his tall figure dressed in gold brocade turban and jacket over tight white trousers, the long upward-curling toes of his gold-embroidered sandals as he wandered among relatives and friends gathered in the garden, and his bare feet neatly placed in the center of a painted design in the prayer-room floor for the ritual blessings, the solemn exchange of garlands of flowers between bride and groom. I remember the utter fascination of comparing the various wedding presents (Cousin So-and-so was known to be stingy though he could well afford more than the basic minimum of a gift; Second Cousin Something-else could be counted on for generosity though he was much too shy to appear for the festivities).

It was then that I learned that money is a perfectly appropriate present on any joyous occasion in India—a golden sovereign or a single silver rupee may be tucked into the tiny fist of a newborn baby, or five thousand and one rupees (never an even number, the money must have a new beginning to grow on) may be sent to a bride and bridegroom. My grandmother used to keep meticulous accounts of exactly how much money was given to any member of the family on any such occasion. A comparable amount had to be correctly returned when a similar celebration occurred in the donor's family.

It was also at this time that I learned the rights, privileges, duties, responsibilities of being a daughter of a decent Hindu family, learned that the oldest married woman of an orthodox household has unquestioned power, manages the finances, determines the organization of the life, rules her small empire with dignity and, if possible, with unobtrusive grace. "No Hindu woman worth her salt," my grandmother used to announce imperiously, "ever gives an order to a servant that she cannot carry out herself." In many ways this was the heart of our training. It was supposed to give us a sense of accomplishment in our daily life as well as teach us the value of human labor. We were taught to cook, sew, clean, tend the small children, manage the house, cope with people of wildly different personalities without ever considering ourselves martyrized. We might never have to use these talents, but to conduct ourselves properly it was assumed that we had to know them.

In retrospect I have often wondered that so many foreigners think of Indian women as "backward," without a grasp of "civil liberties," with little to recommend their position and with a genuine grievance against the world. To me, that childhood seemed like a reasonable—and engrossing—preparation for a kind of life. The currents of change were already moving in India, currents that were eventually to blossom in monumental social and political upheavals, but my sister and I didn't feel them until much later when my grandmother and grandfather were both dead, the household disbanded, the family scattered, the compound, the house, the orchards, the tennis court all sold.

Before this, when I was six years old, my father was sent to London for the first of the Round Table Conferences that were supposed to decide India's future as somewhere between complete independence and old-fashioned colonialism. My mother dutifully packed us all up for this unpredictable foreign excursion. I can still recall the arguments at home: Should we take my father's riding clothes? No, probably not. Where would one ride in London? What about my mother's precious Persian carpets? Better not risk it. They wouldn't be appreciated in London and the climate was likely to be too damp for their proper care. The problem of my mother's clothes—she refused flatly to wear the barbaric Western outfits which she had seen on Englishwomen in India. So, lots of saris, enough to last several years because, of course, Western materials were impossible for a self-respecting Indian woman. "What's more," she insisted, "I refuse to make myself ridiculous by curtsying in a sari." But what should one do about the children's clothes? Well, some dresses made by the family tailor in case . . . And some Indian clothes in case . . . Plenty of reading material for all of us for the long ship voyage. Household equipment? This aspect of our journey struck me as the most extraordinary. Were we really going to live in a *furnished* flat? Were we to live with *other people's* furniture, cooking utensils, pictures, curtains? What would happen to the people who *really* lived there? How kind of them to simply give us their house and make do with lodgings at some relative's house.

I didn't return to India until I was ten years old, when my father went back for a year to his district work. It was with a deep sense of recognition and comfort that once again I lived in my grandmother's house, caught up on family gossip, saw my changed, grown cousins, reacquainted myself with the older members of the family. The two strong strains of my childhood—the shifting life of district touring and the unshakable little universe of the family—were both vividly a part of my experience again. It is hardly surprising that the first stories should deal with these two aspects of my early years in India.

## *By any other name*

At the Anglo-Indian day school in Zorinabad to which my sister and I were sent when she was eight and I was five and a half, they changed our names. On the first day of school, a hot, windless morning of a north Indian September, we stood in the headmistress's study and she said, "Now you're the *new* girls. What are your names?"

My sister answered for us. "I am Premila, and she"—nodding in my direction—"is Santha."

The headmistress had been in India, I suppose, fifteen years or so, but she still smiled her helpless inability to cope with Indian names. Her rimless half-glasses glittered, and the precarious bun on the top of her head trembled as she shook her head. "Oh, my dears, those are much too hard for me. Suppose we give you pretty English names. Wouldn't that be more jolly? Let's see, now—Pamela for you, I think." She shrugged in a baffled way at my sister. "That's as close as I can get. And for *you*," she said to me, "how about Cynthia? Isn't that nice?"

My sister was always less easily intimidated than I was, and while she kept a stubborn silence, I said, "Thank you," in a very tiny voice.

We had been sent to that school because my father, among his responsibilities as an officer of the civil service, had a tour of duty to perform in the villages around that steamy little provincial town, where he had his headquarters at that time. He used to make his shorter inspection tours on horseback, and a week before, in the stale heat of a typically postmonsoon day, we had waved good-by to him and a little procession—an assistant, a secretary, two bearers, and the man to look after the bedding rolls and luggage. They rode away through our large garden, still bright green from the rains, and we turned back into the twilight of the house and the sound of fans whispering in every room.

Up to then, my mother had refused to send Premila to school in the British-run establishments of that time, because, she used to say, "you can bury a dog's tail for seven years and it still comes out curly, and you can take a Britisher away from his home for a lifetime and he still remains insular." The examinations and degrees from entirely Indian schools were not, in those days, considered valid. In my case, the question had never come up, and probably never would have come up if Mother's extraordinary good health had not broken down. For the first time in my life, she was not able to continue the lessons she had been giving us every morning. So our Hindi books were put away, the stories of the Lord Krishna as a little boy were left in mid-air, and we were sent to the Anglo-Indian school.

That first day at school is still, when I think of it, a remarkable one. At that age, if one's name is changed, one develops a curious form of dual personality. I remember having a certain detached and disbelieving concern in the actions of "Cynthia," but certainly no responsibility. Accordingly, I followed the thin, erect back of the headmistress down the veranda to my classroom feeling, at most, a passing interest in what was going to happen to me in this strange, new atmosphere of School.

The building was Indian in design, with wide verandas opening onto a central courtyard, but Indian verandas are usually white-washed, with stone floors. These, in the tradition of British schools, were painted dark brown and had matting on the floors. It gave a feeling of extra intensity to the heat.

I suppose there were about a dozen Indian children in the school—which contained perhaps forty children in all—and four of them were in my class. They were all sitting at the back of the room, and I went to join them. I sat next to a small, solemn girl who didn't smile at me. She had long, glossy-black braids and wore a cotton dress, but she still kept on her Indian jewelry—a gold chain around her neck, thin gold bracelets, and tiny ruby studs in her ears. Like most Indian children, she had a rim of black kohl around her eyes. The cotton dress should have looked strange, but all I could think of was that I should ask my mother if I couldn't wear a dress to school, too, instead of my Indian clothes.

I can't remember too much about the proceedings in class that day, except for the beginning. The teacher pointed to me and asked me to stand up. "Now, dear, tell the class your name."

I said nothing.

"Come along," she said, frowning slightly. "What's your name, dear?"

"I don't know," I said, finally.

The English children in the front of the class—there were about eight or ten of them—giggled and twisted around in their chairs to look at me. I sat down quickly and opened my eyes very wide, hoping in that way to dry them off. The little girl with the braids put out her hand and very lightly touched my arm. She still didn't smile.

Most of that morning I was rather bored. I looked briefly at the children's drawings pinned to the wall, and then concentrated on a lizard clinging to the ledge of the high, barred window behind the teacher's head. Occasionally it would shoot out its long yellow tongue for a fly, and then it would rest, with its eyes closed and its belly palpitating, as though it were swallowing several times quickly. The lessons were mostly concerned with reading and writing and simple numbers—things that my mother had already taught me—and I paid very little attention. The teacher wrote on the easel blackboard words like "bat" and "cat," which seemed babyish to me; only "apple" was new and incomprehensible.

When it was time for the lunch recess, I followed the girl with braids out onto the veranda. There the children from the other classes were assembled. I saw Premila at once and ran over to her, as she had charge of our lunchbox. The children were all opening packages and sitting down to eat sandwiches. Premila and I were the only ones who had Indian food—thin wheat chapatties, some vegetable curry, and a bottle of buttermilk. Premila thrust half of it into my hand and whispered fiercely that I should go and sit with my class, because that was what the others seemed to be doing.

The enormous black eyes of the little Indian girl from my class looked at my food longingly, so I offered her some. But she only shook her head and plowed her way solemnly through her sandwiches.

I was very sleepy after lunch, because at home we always took a siesta. It was usually a pleasant time of day, with the bedroom darkened against the harsh afternoon sun, the drifting off into sleep with the sound of Mother's voice reading a story in one's mind, and, finally, the shrill, fussy voice of the ayah waking one for tea.

At school, we rested for a short time on low, folding cots on the veranda, and then we were expected to play games. During the hot part of the afternoon we played indoors, and after the shadows had begun to lengthen and the slight breeze of the evening had come up we moved outside to the wide courtyard.

I had never really grasped the system of competitive games. At home, whenever we played tag or guessing games, I was always allowed to "win"—"because," Mother used to tell Premila, "she is the youngest, and we have to allow for that." I had often heard her say it, and it seemed quite reasonable to me, but the result was that I had no clear idea of what "winning" meant.

When we played twos-and-threes that afternoon at school, in accordance with my training, I let one of the small English boys catch me, but was naturally rather puzzled when the other children did not return the courtesy. I ran about for what seemed like hours without ever catching anyone, until it was time for school to close. Much later I learned that my attitude was called "not being a good sport," and I stopped allowing myself to be caught, but it was not for years that I really learned the spirit of the thing.

When I saw our car come up to the school gate, I broke away from my classmates and rushed toward it yelling, "Ayah! Ayah!" It seemed like an eternity since I had seen her that morning—a wizened, affectionate figure in her white cotton sari, giving me dozens of urgent and useless instructions on how to be a good girl at school. Premila followed more sedately, and she told me on the way home never to do that again in front of the other children.

When we got home we went straight to Mother's high, white room to have tea with her, and I immediately climbed onto the bed and bounced gently up and down on the springs. Mother asked how we had liked our first day in school. I was so pleased to be home and to have left that peculiar Cynthia behind that I had nothing whatever to say about school, except to ask what "apple" meant. But Premila told Mother about the classes, and added that in her class they had weekly tests to see if they had learned their lessons well.

I asked, "What's a test?"

Premila said, "You're too small to have them. You won't have them in your class for donkey's years." She had learned the expression that day and was using it for the first time. We all laughed enormously at her wit. She also told Mother, in an aside, that we should take sandwiches to school the next day. Not, she said, that *she* minded. But they would be simpler for me to handle.

That whole lovely evening I didn't think about school at all. I sprinted barefoot across the lawns with my favorite playmate, the cook's son, to the stream at the end of the garden. We quarreled in our usual way, waded in the tepid water under the lime trees, and waited for the night to bring out the smell of the jasmine. I listened with fascination to his stories of ghosts and demons, until I was too frightened to cross the garden alone in the semidarkness. The ayah found me, shouted at the cook's son, scolded me, hurried me in to supper—it was an entirely usual, wonderful evening.

It was a week later, the day of Premila's first test, that our lives changed rather abruptly. I was sitting at the back of my class, in my usual inattentive way, only half listening to the teacher. I had started a rather guarded friendship with the girl with the braids, whose name turned out to be Nalini (Nancy, in school). The three other Indian children were already fast friends. Even at that age it was apparent to all of us that friendship with the English or Anglo-Indian children was out of the question. Occasionally, during the class, my new friend and I would draw pictures and show them to each other secretly.

The door opened sharply and Premila marched in. At first, the teacher smiled at her in a kindly and encouraging way and said, "Now, you're little Cynthia's sister?"

Premila didn't even look at her. She stood with her feet planted firmly apart and her shoulders rigid, and addressed herself directly to me. "Get up," she said. "We're going home."

I didn't know what had happened, but I was aware that it was a crisis of some sort. I rose obediently and started to walk toward my sister.

"Bring your pencils and your notebook," she said.

I went back for them, and together we left the room. The teacher started to say something just as Premila closed the door, but we didn't wait to hear what it was.

In complete silence we left the school grounds and started to walk home. Then I asked Premila what the matter was. All she would say was "We're going home for good."

It was a very tiring walk for a child of five and a half, and I dragged along behind Premila with my pencils growing sticky in my hand. I can still remember looking at the dusty hedges, and the tangles of thorns in the ditches by the side of the road, smelling the faint fragrance from the eucalyptus trees and wondering whether we would ever reach home. Occasionally a horse-drawn tonga passed us, and the women, in their pink or green silks, stared at Premila and me trudging along on the side of the road. A few coolies and a line of women carrying baskets of vegetables on their heads smiled at us. But it was nearing the hottest time of day, and the road was almost deserted. I walked more and more slowly, and shouted to Premila, from time to time, "Wait for me!" with increasing peevishness. She spoke to me only once, and that was to tell me to carry my notebook on my head, because of the sun.

When we got to our house the ayah was just taking a tray of lunch into Mother's room. She immediately started a long, worried questioning about what are you children doing back here at this hour of the day.

Mother looked very startled and very concerned, and asked Premila what had happened.

Premila said, "We had our test today, and She made me and the other Indians sit at the back of the room, with a desk between each one."

Mother said, "Why was that, darling?"

"She said it was because Indians cheat," Premila added. "So I don't think we should go back to that school."

Mother looked very distant, and was silent a long time. At last she said, "Of course not, darling." She sounded displeased.

We all shared the curry she was having for lunch, and afterward I was sent off to the beautifully familiar bedroom for my siesta. I could hear Mother and Premila talking through the open door.

Mother said, "Do you suppose she understood all that?"

Premila said, "I shouldn't think so. She's a baby."

Mother said, "Well, I hope it won't bother her."

Of course, they were both wrong. I understood it perfectly, and I remember it all very clearly. But I put it happily away, because it had all happened to a girl called Cynthia, and I never was really particularly interested in her.

## *The ghost in the garden*

In India you can always recognize a ghost by his feet, which are attached to his ankles the wrong way around, with the heels in front and the toes pointing backward. The rest of his appearance may be entirely normal, and, of course, since a ghost doesn't wish to be recognized, he usually takes the trouble to hide his feet. Indian clothes are particularly well suited to this purpose. The loose pajamas of a northern Indian man, the southern man's *mundu* (a sort of long sarong), a woman's sari, and the robes of a holy man—a *sanyasi*—are all floor-length, all excellent disguises.

The problem of recognizing a ghost by somehow persuading him to expose his feet occupied a great deal of my time the spring I was ten. My mother, my sister, and I spent some months in my mother's family home, just outside Allahabad, while my father traveled in south India, and I learned a few days after we arrived that the house—or, rather, the garden—was haunted.

It wasn't a particularly big house, but it was full of people. My great-grandmother was alive, at that time, very old, incredibly frail, almost deaf, and quite blind. In the late afternoons, she used to sit cross-legged on a wooden platform out in the courtyard behind the house, her white hair turned luminous and pink by the declining sun, her maid beside her, from time to time wrapping her special concoction of tobacco and lime in betel leaves and handing her the little bright-green packages.

The platform—platforms are the chief items of furniture in Indian homes—was about the size of a low double bed, and was the only thing to sit on in the courtyard. Occasionally, my grandfather would join my great-grandmother on it, but since he was very jolly and loved to talk, he soon became bored with so remote an audience, and would call the children to him. My four cousins, my sister, and I—or as many of us as were in the courtyard—would then collect around him and listen while, accompanied by the gentle bubbling of his hookah, he told us stories of kings and battles, or fragments of his childhood, or bits of family history. One of his favorites, I remember, concerned an ancestor of ours, a man who was deplored by his family and mocked by his acquaintances because he would never work. He would only sit in his garden, watch the brilliant flights of birds, and write poetry. This was in the early eighteenth century, during the days of the Mogul rule of India, and one day, when the court of the Great Mogul announced a poetry competition, our family wastrel decided to travel to the capital and read his poems to the Emperor. When he arrived, the Muslim courtiers laughed at the impudence of a Hindu who thought he could compete with the great Persian tradition of poetry, and declared that he should be the last of the contestants to appear before the Mogul.

"It was well known," my grandfather used to say, "that Hindus could not hear the song that lies within the simplest words of our daily language. But *he* had studied the music of the birds, he had listened to the leaves in his trees, and had heard the fall of the dew. His poetry was far more beautiful than anything the Mogul court could write. The Emperor was so deeply moved that at the end of the reading he exclaimed, 'I cannot simply say that you are the best poet, for you are the king, the shah, of poets!' "

From that time on our ancestor was called Shah. "Your second cousins," my grandfather would invariably conclude, "are still named Shah. Has it never struck you as strange that there should be a *Muslim* name in our family?"

If I hadn't been worried about the ghost, those last couple of hours before sunset would have been a pleasant time of day, with the great violet shadows moving across the courtyard and the old lady sitting, nodding in silence. Back and forth, from the storerooms to the kitchen—a separate building, opening off the courtyard—my grandmother and one or another of my aunts would go, busy about their household duties. On the kitchen doorstep the servants would be squatting with shallow brass pans before them, cleaning the rice and vegetables for the evening meal. My oldest cousin, Radha, would return from her classes at the Allahabad University. Another of my cousins, Mohan, younger than Radha but also at the university, would wheel in later on his bicycle, sweaty from playing tennis with his friends. My grandfather would pause for a second to greet each new arrival, and then continue with his stories.

Most of the time I only half listened to my grandfather, because this was also the time of the day when my anxiety about the ghost began to intensify. Actually, the story of the ghost was a good deal more banal than most of my grandfather's stories. All of us had been forbidden to talk about it—not so much because the family disapproved of superstition as because the story was not considered suitable for young children.

It concerned a gardener who had worked in the family's compound a generation before. He was a widower, but in the last years of his life he decided to marry again. He had saved enough money, he felt, to command the best, and, in fact, he did secure as his wife the prettiest girl in his native village, a few miles the other side of Allahabad, and brought her to live in his house near the compound. I don't suppose he was in love with her—I don't suppose he thought in such terms—but she was undeniably his most cherished possession. She was a beautiful ornament, and even if she wasn't a particularly talented or economical housekeeper, still, he didn't seem to mind, although he made quite a point of chiding or disparaging her in public.

She, it later turned out, was resentful of her old and bossy husband, and rather repelled by him, but most of all she felt lonely and homesick, for her husband's friends were old and her own seemed far away. So, when a distant relative of hers, a young man, found a job (through her husband's recommendation) in a neighboring compound, she saw a lot of him, and inevitably they became lovers. For some months they managed their affair with remarkable discretion, but nothing is secret very long in India, and eventually the gardener heard about it. He was angry, of course, at his wife's ingratitude, and jealous of her beauty, and he returned home unexpectedly one afternoon when he was supposed to be working in the orchards, and discovered the lovers together. He hadn't, the story goes, expected to find so great a fury in himself—an old man, past the age for such emotions.

His wife saw his face and ran screaming from the house. He followed her, waving the long stick with a hooked knife on the end that he used in cleaning the springy undergrowth from around the fruit trees. He caught her as she reached the well just outside the courtyard of our house. He tried to hold her—or did he try to push her? Anyway, in the confusion of his anger and her fear, she fell down the well—a huge, old-fashioned well, bricked on the inside, with an old wooden scaffold above it, a rope, and a winding handle—and was drowned.

The gardener went back to his house, bewildered and in despair. He never went to work again but merely sat in his one room staring at the mud walls, the uneven floor, the litter of cooking pans and discarded clothes. The wives of the other servants brought him food every day, and sometimes he ate it and sometimes he didn't. But he needed something more than food to keep him alive, and he never recaptured it. He died a few months later, alone and still bewildered, without having talked to anyone after his wife's death.

As for the lover, he fled, and was never seen again. My cousins and I believed, for some reason, that he had been in a ghastly accident soon afterward, and that, although nobody had ever seen his ghost, it lurked in the branches of the huge neem tree that shaded our courtyard. The wife was a less cautious ghost, and several people had seen her. Mohan, for instance, claimed, with entirely convincing detail, that he had watched her wandering disconsolately under the mango trees beyond the well—searching, he assumed, for her lover. (Her husband, to whom we assigned no guilt, wasn't driven to return by the traditional restlessness of ghosts.) Mohan said he had come home after dark from the house of one of his college friends and was getting off his bicycle just outside the courtyard when he saw her, a faint, fugitive figure in the deep shadows. He assured us that the starlight caught an occasional gleam of silver from her sari or her jewelry—and why, he demanded, would she be wearing her wedding finery except to delight her lover? Certainly she had never worn it for her husband after the day of her ceremonial arrival at his house.

We might have doubted Mohan's unsupported word. He loved to tease us. He would tell us to rush out to the garden and see an airplane—one of our greatest excitements at that time—when there was nothing in the sky but the high, hovering hawks and the mist of dust over the town. Once he made us crouch for a long time staring into the eye of a cobra that had been killed in the garden and watching for a picture of the man who had killed him to form. This, Mohan told us, was how the mate of the cobra would know whom to strike for her revenge. But in the case of the ghost, a couple of the servants corroborated Mohan's story. They, too, had glimpsed the mysterious white figure, and there was much agitated discussion among them of why, after so many years, the ghost had chosen this time to appear. Was it a portent? A warning? Should they, perhaps, be less confident of the fidelity of their wives? And then a friend who came to call on the family after dinner one evening asked casually if it wasn't rather late for one of the girls to be walking alone in the garden. My grandmother quickly and sternly said that it was probably just the sweeper's wife returning home. The friend began to protest that she was too well dressed, but he dropped the matter in the face of my grandmother's obvious annoyance.

My youngest cousin, Gita—Mohan's sister—and I talked endlessly about what we would do if we should happen to meet the ghost. Gita, who was eleven, was both braver and more skeptical than I was, and felt very strongly that it would be silly and rude to assume that any mysterious woman in the garden after dark was a ghost until we had made sure by looking at her feet. Suppose, Gita said, it really *was* the sweeper's wife. She would think we had gone off our heads if we ran away from her without even a word of greeting.

In the slow, hot hours of the afternoon, when the grownups were resting indoors and the house was closed tight against the sun, Gita and I used to walk down to the guava orchard, each carrying a small package of salt. There we would lie in the dusty shade of the trees, eating unripe guavas dipped in the salt and making pleased, sour faces at the taste. Daily we discussed the ghost. We had several ingenious schemes for getting her to show her feet. We thought, for instance, of suggesting that she come with us to a mosque or temple, where she would have to remove her shoes before she entered. That would undoubtedly give us an opportunity to look at her feet. But there were flaws in this plan. A ghost would be sure to refuse to go with us in the first place. Besides, there were no mosques or temples closer than the town itself, and neither of us really had the courage to walk for nearly an hour with a possible ghost.

We thought of trying to find her footprints, too. Most of the garden was too dry and the ground baked too hard, at that time of year, to hold a print, but there was always a muddy patch near the well, where water was spilled or the damp seeped up from below. Conveniently enough, this was the part of the garden where the servants said the ghost liked to walk, but so many other people came to the well in the course of the day that we were sure we would never be able to distinguish her footprints from the hundreds of others, especially since–it occurred to us–they would probably look like natural ones.

We even considered the possibility of using mice. Were ghosts afraid of them? we wondered. If we released one suddenly, would she, without thinking, raise her sari in alarm? We thought she probably would, but we would have the inconvenience of going around every evening of our lives armed with a mouse for the emergency.

It was all very complicated and usually, after some time, we would revert to our other major topic of conversation–whom our cousin Radha would marry when she graduated from college. He would have to be a Brahmin, and preferably a Kashmiri Brahmin, because that was the community to which we all belonged. It was a large, very cliquish minority in the town; all its members were descended from the Brahmins who had fled into voluntary exile when Kashmir was invaded by the Muslims and had settled in Allahabad. Almost all of them were related, in one way or another, so Radha's match had to be carefully planned; the man must be one whose connection with our family was distant enough to be religiously acceptable but who was still within the community.

Radha's should have been an extremely easy marriage to arrange, because she was very beautiful in a way that is much admired by Kashmiris. She was tall and slender, with wavy reddish hair, a white skin, and rather startling gray eyes set with a slight tilt up toward her temples. In every way, she was most eligible, but Radha herself said disdainfully that she had no intention of getting married, that she wanted to get a job, and that people could think what they wished but she wasn't going to discuss the matter further.

None of the family took this announcement seriously. My grandmother didn't believe the part about the job at all, but she was, on the whole, rather pleased that Radha could afford to be so offhand about her marriage. Too great an eagerness for a husband was scarcely becoming in a girl, and, besides, having a marriageable daughter sought after rather than seeking put the family in a strong position.

Gita and I knew that negotiations had already been begun. The parents of various young men had, in the conventional way, sent the horoscopes of their sons for the family priest and astrologer to compare with Radha's horoscope and see if the combination augured well for the young couple. Actually, the main purpose of this practice was to give the girl's family a graceful way of refusing proposals and selecting the most desirable suitor.

Gita and I had already chosen our favorite. We had borrowed the horoscopes from their hiding place in my grandmother's big metal trunk, which contained the household linen, and had decided on the one whose owner would be "a leader of men" whose fame was to spread beyond the province. We interpreted this to mean that he would somehow become a prince, and we were very taken with the idea of a real shah in the family, instead of only the namesakes of the old poet. It was a great relief, in the long afternoons, to forget the ghost for a while and daydream about visiting Radha in her palace after she became a queen.

Mohan, typically, used to tease Radha to a fury about her admirers in college, the students who sat and stared at her during lectures, when they should have been taking notes. "Ridiculous!" Radha would say. "What nonsense you talk!"

But Mohan would go on, in his plaguing singsong, and talk about Radha's "special"–a most unsuitable admirer, wrong in both caste and community, who was so much in love with her that his college work had gone to pot and nobody thought he would pass his final examinations.

Radha, caught between anger and tears, once shouted, "You fool! What do *you* know about anything? It's because of politics. He spends all his time on *politics!*" And she ran weeping from the room. My grandmother scolded Mohan, and afterward Radha was more scornful than ever about the proposals and suggestions for her marriage.

This mention of politics worried my grandmother. At that time the Indian independence movement had caught fire all across the country, and we heard a lot about *Swaraj* and civil disobedience. In the colleges, particularly, groups of fervent nationalists were forming, ready to lead strikes, carry flags bearing anti-British slogans, or go to jail, like Gandhi. My grandmother forbade Radha to meddle in such things, and Radha was sulky and silent, but she defiantly had the borders of her white muslin saris dyed orange and green, and so went to college every day wearing the nationalist colors.

Gita and I were generally on Radha's side, but, talking lazily in the shade of the guava trees, we worried a good deal lest she remain stubborn for so long that her chances might slide away until she had grown too old to be desirable. Eventually, the salt and the sour guavas would make us so thirsty that we'd wander back to the courtyard to get a drink from the big terra-cotta jar that stood in one corner, in the shade. The water in it always tasted of the smell of earth after rain. Soon tea would be served, my great-grandmother would take up her place on the platform, my grandfather would emerge with his hookah, and the evening would begin.

At night the servants carried the family's beds–light wooden frames crisscrossed with a webbing of tape–out into the courtyard, put the thin mattresses and the bedclothes on them, and set mosquito nets over them. The whole family slept outdoors, in a long column of beds, in the tepid darkness. Gita and I usually went to bed only a little while before the grownups. From within our white cubes of netting, we whispered to each other, identifying the members of the family as they passed us–indistinct shapes accompanied by the soft flapping of sandals. After they had all been accounted for, we often stayed awake a little longer to be sure that no additional figure was moving about the courtyard—that the ghost had in fact stayed safely outside the wall.

We would wake, in the sweet chill of the early morning, to the sound of my grandmother singing hymns in her prayer room, to the smell of the first wood smoke from the kitchen fire, and to the creaking of the winding rope of the well, where two blindfolded oxen with painted foreheads and silver-tipped horns were walking round and round, turning the wheel and raising the day's supply of water. The only reminder of the ghost came when we broke off twigs of the neem tree to brush our teeth with. I used to wonder briefly then about the man that haunted its branches, and decide that I needn't think about it until evening came again.

The night I saw the ghost must have been at the end of April. I remember that the first mangoes had arrived, and that the corroding heat of the last two months before the monsoon had already set in. Those nights we dined later and stayed up later than we had been doing, not wanting to lose the few comfortable hours of the day. On one such evening, when the grownups were deep in uninteresting family talk, when Radha had gone indoors saying she had to study for her examinations, and Mohan and my other cousins were playing a complicated card game, which they told us we were too young for, Gita and I decided to watch the moonrise.

We climbed the courtyard wall and seated ourselves precariously on top of it, looking over the dusty fruit trees beyond the well to the paleness on the horizon where the moon would appear. We had a theory that if we could catch the exact moment when the rim of the moon was level with the rim of the earth, we would see a vivid green flash leap from the horizon. We had never actually managed to prove this, either because we blinked or because something distracted us, but still we hopefully watched the moonrise from time to time. That night, we missed the green flash once more because we both turned at the same instant, aware of some slight stirring under the mango trees. We couldn't see anything there, but by the time we turned back, the edge of the moon was already showing, and it was rising, in the way of the Indian moon, almost visibly.

Again there was a stirring in the shadows, this time more distinct, and when we stared, we could make out a pale figure walking away from us and see the first, slanting glitter of moonlight on the silver at her wrists.

I think I must have made a movement to get down from the wall, for something just then loosened a piece of the old mortar, which fell whispering down the bricks and landed with an alarmingly loud noise on the ground. The ghost must have heard it. At once, she vanished into the deeper darkness. Then Gita and I, still staring, saw that the taller figure of a man was still standing, entirely motionless and all in white, under the trees where we had seen the other.

We scrambled down the inside of the wall and stood breathless in the courtyard. It had not, of course, occurred to either of us to check on the figures' feet. We held on to each other, unable to speak, for what must, I suppose, have been several minutes. It was only after we had got back to the family, still sitting and talking in an ordinary way, to the security of the oil lamp with the big, stupid moths bumping into it, to the quarrels of the cardplayers, that our excitement exploded and we gabbled the story over and over. My cousins dropped their cards, the grownups began to protest. We had made it all up, they said, or we were dreaming.

Radha came out of the house looking flushed and worried.

"We *saw* them! We *saw* them!" Gita shouted. "We were–"

"Shut *up!*" Radha said, her face tense with anger.

"But it's true! We saw the ghosts–*both* of them!"

"Ghosts?" Radha said, and then, with a sudden change of tone, "Oh, ghosts." Almost vaguely she added, "You foolish children, can't you ever think of anything but that boring old ghost? I thought the world was coming to an end the way you were yelling out here." She shook back her bangles, gleaming silver in the lamplight, glanced out into the dark reaches of the courtyard, and went back indoors.

"She's studying too hard," her mother said. "She's nervous."

But my grandmother was looking very thoughtful. Slowly she got to her feet and followed Radha into the house.

# TWO

It was not until I was sixteen years old that we returned to India. The intervening years had been spent in English schools and in holidays on the Continent, sometimes joining our parents in one or another of the European capitals, sometimes staying quietly on the Brittany coast with French friends of the family. In London we could not, of course, help knowing a good deal about what was going on in India. My father, as Deputy High Commissioner for India, was inextricably involved in many of the developments, and conversation at home was full of references to the growing power of the nationalist movement, of the imprisoning of Indian leaders, of the vast changes that were altering the face and temper of India, of Mahatma Gandhi's revolutionary ideas–imagine a leader who could tell his people that the only way to fight was *not* to fight, to convince them and then to make a success of his principle. We talked about Gandhi, Nehru, Sapru, Rajagopalachari, and countless other names that became great in Indian history in their own time. Some of them were related to our family, many were personal friends. It was a curiously intimate yet distant view of India's progress.

Meanwhile, all around us in Europe, we got a similarly personal though far less exalted view of the events that were shaping our generation. On French beaches we might meet groups of Hitler Youth on some kind of organized walking tour. At school in England we might be asked to support the international youth camps of the League of Nations. Like so many of our friends, we took in refugees from Dachau and other concentration camps until they could find places of their own in London or get a work permit or a visa to America. My sister, with thousands of idealistic people of her age, felt strongly about the Spanish Civil War, and I, deeply impressed by her sentiments, fell in love with a young man I had never met only because he wrote beautiful poetry and was killed in Spain.

All this was, naturally, quite typical of the generation that grew up in Europe between the wars. The only thing that set us apart in our own minds was that we would return to India to live, that eventually our loyalties would be tied to a country that was growing daily less familiar. My mother, more than anyone else, kept this principle in our minds. In her years in England she had plunged, with her usual inexhaustible energy, into committee work of a semisocial, semipolitical nature, arguing, explaining, pestering, persuading any group that would listen to facts about India's changing position and demands, clearing away, as far as she could, the fog of misunderstandings and semantics, of half-grasped psychology and prejudice, that surrounded the whole question of India in the land of its rulers. She organized her own bands of workers from among the Indian community in London, and hours every day were spent in conferences, discussions of programs and issues, liaisons with British women's organizations. I sometimes think that the first long words I ever learned in English were "committee meeting" and "emancipation." I heard them every day at home. To my mother her ten years abroad were a kind of challenging exile. She coped easily with her diplomatic commitments—parties, receptions, remembering the protocol-determined pattern of who should sit next to whom at dinner—worked at expressing her own convictions through her committees and informal groups, but she never had a doubt in her mind that one glorious day we would all return to India to live there for the rest of our lives. Things didn't turn out quite that way.

The year before the war broke out in Europe, my father was sent, as High Commissioner, to South Africa. Following our usual pattern, my sister and I spent our summer holidays from school in 1939 with our parents. We found out only after we arrived in Capetown that this was our father's trickiest and most disagreeable assignment. This segment of our education began at the moment when he came to meet us at the ship. My father, who has never, before or since, noticed how we dressed or cared what we wore, suddenly demanded that we change into saris before landing in South Africa. Assuming that we were perhaps to go straight to a party or something and intimidated by his grim expression, we asked no questions but simply took off our ugly English gym tunics and black woolen stockings and rather awkwardly (we hadn't had much occasion to wear them in England) draped our saris. We soon learned the reason. The segregation policy of South Africa extends to the Indians as well as the Africans. My father wanted no one to think that his daughters might be trying to appear as something they were not.

We soon learned, too, the extent of this prejudice. One afternoon when my sister and I had decided to go to the movies, we phoned our father at his office, hoping that he might be free to join us. Rather cautiously he inquired about exactly which movie we wanted to see and what time we planned to be there. He sounded preoccupied and busy, but said he would try to join us. In fact, we later discovered, he had been so precise about times and places only because he wanted to be sure that we would not, in our saris, be turned away from the theater, for theaters, like restaurants, hotels, bars, wayside inns, clubs, were all forbidden to Indians. We were pleased by the courtesy with which we were received at the movie house, but puzzled by the fact that in a crowded theater all the seats each side of us for an entire row were left vacant. When we asked the reason for this we were told, with embarrassment, that none of the usual patrons would wish to sit with us. It was only because we as daughters of a diplomatic representative were immune from the usual rules that we could enter the auditorium at all. We never went to the movies again in South Africa.

During our months there we toured extensively, through the Cape Province, Natal (where the largest part of the Indian community lives), through the Transvaal and up into the Rhodesias. There was no question about it—South Africa is a magnificent country, full of variety, breath-takingly beautiful, studded with flowers, sights, animals I had never seen before, extraordinary in its scope and grandeur. And I never hope to see it again. My father, in one of his rare moments of quiet bitterness, after we had driven from

Johannesburg to Pretoria along avenues lined with jacaranda trees in full bloom, the clouds of unimaginably blue flowers throwing a light as cool as snow on the road, and had stopped to see the equally unimaginably inhuman conditions of life in the African compounds along the way, remarked, "Of this country that old cliché is really true: 'Every prospect pleases, and only man is vile.' "

With mingled horror and resignation we heard, that summer, that war had broken out in Europe. Between hearing the blaring announcements on the radio and reading the increasingly sickening headlines in the newspapers, we had to settle the insignificant details of our own lives for the next few weeks . . . months . . . years, as it finally turned out. My mother and sister and I were not sorry to leave South Africa, even though my father's work would keep him there—indeed it almost seemed that my mother's dream of returning to India to live might, by this world-wide catastrophe, actually come about. In any case, since my sister and I could not, under the circumstances, return to England to finish our education, at least my mother could take us back to India—not just to relearn what we had known before we left but to learn afresh a new country, new conditions and situations and ways of living. A new world.

So much had changed. My mother's parents were both dead. Three of my cousins and all my uncles were married. Two of my aunts were widowed. The big, busy, much-loved household in Allahabad had dispersed, leaving us with only strong family ties and strong family memories. And all around us the social and political pressures in India were reaching their peak.

One factor that added an element of fantasy to an already unusual situation was that we spent our first months in India with my father's parents. They were both more orthodox and more rigid in the observance of family rules than the household in Allahabad. They were more formal in the observance of religious ritual—not merely, say, vegetarian, but even concerned about eating eggs because you couldn't tell until the egg was broken whether it was really unfertilized. Rather than risk taking even embryonic life you didn't eat eggs at all. Since your fellow feeling with all forms of life included birds, it was better to let the pigeons nest in the rafters of your bedroom than to drive them away and possibly leave them homeless. "You might," my grandmother assured me, "have been a pigeon in your last birth." You dressed formally before your elders, waited until you were spoken to before you spoke, respected their wishes in every way. Yet this island of time, isolated against the country's turbulent shifts and developments, was not enough to insulate us from the new life of India.

My mother very sensibly decided that my sister and I should make an educational circuit of this new-old land which was both our home and so very foreign. Most of that voyage of exploration, which took us all over India with relatives, friends, strangers, and involved us in innumerable situations and lives, I recorded some years ago in a book called *Home to India.* In retrospect, although I was at no regular school, they seem to me the two most important years of my education. Even though they ended in my going to college in America, they left with me an indelible engagement with India—an engagement that even now, when I am married to an American, have a child who divides his allegiance between America and India, have lived so many more years outside my own country, never entirely leaves me, and never allows me escape from an almost automatic concern with India. I make a very poor expatriate.

My four years in America were spent mostly at Wellesley College, with vacation intervals of working for the Office of War Information. It was a strange time for me—half in love with America, with its driving energy, its earnestness, its kindness, and its extraordinary beauty, half deploring its ignorance of conditions in the rest of the world, its smug self-righteousness, and its assumption of privilege. Anyway, out of the whole experience emerged two things that have plagued me all my life. I realized that I wanted to be a writer (my first book was written while I was at Wellesley) and I had somehow learned to work—not simply to *work* but to *want* to work. The phrase "career girl" was already unfashionable by then, but by the time I returned, once again, to India it was clear that a "career girl" was what I was going to be. America gave me not only the freedom but the compulsion to feel in this way, and also a kind of sadness that a whole era of my early life was irretrievably lost. The world—and I with it—had moved too fast.

As soon as I got back to Bombay, the year the war ended, I set about looking for a job. My family didn't mind my *working*, but they were worried about the idea of my *earning money*. It wasn't considered entirely respectable for a girl whose family could afford to support her until she got married to be actually picking up a paycheck. By then I felt rather militant about the whole situation and insisted with many specious and cheeky arguments that work should be *paid* for. It is to this period of my life that the following two stories belong. It says a lot for the broad-mindedness of my parents that they indulged me in this unconventional quirk and allowed me to take a job on a magazine in Bombay.

## *Who cares?*

The only thing, really, that Anand and I had in common was that both of us had been to college in America. Not that we saw much of each other during those four years abroad—he was studying business management or some such thing in Boston and I was taking the usual liberal arts course at Wellesley, and on the rare occasions we met, we hadn't much to say—but when we got back to Bombay, the sense of dislocation we shared was a bond. In our parents' generation that whole malaise was covered by the comprehensive phrase "England-returned," which held good even if you had been studying in Munich or Edinburgh, both popular with Indian students in those days. The term was used as a qualification (for jobs and marriages) and as an explanation of the familiar problems of readjustment. Even after the war, in a particular kind of newspaper, you could find, in the personal columns, advertisements like this: "Wanted: young, fair, educated girl, high caste essential, for England-returned boy. Send photograph." The point is that she would have to prove herself—or rather, her family would have to demonstrate her desirability—but "England-returned" would tell her just about everything she needed to know about the boy: that his family was rich enough to send him abroad for his education; that his chances for a government job or a good job in business were better than most; that his wife could probably expect an unorthodox household in which she might be asked to serve meat at meals, entertain foreigners, speak English, and even have liquor on the premises. She would also know that it would be a "good" (desirable, that is) marriage.

"England-returned," like that other much-quoted phrase, "Failed B.A.," was the kind of Indianism that used to amuse the British very much when it turned up on a job application. To Indians, naturally, it had a serious and precise meaning. Even "Failed B.A.," after all, meant to us not that a young man had flunked one examination, but that he had been through all the years of school and college that led to a degree—an important consideration in a country where illiteracy is the norm and education a luxury.

In the course of a generation that became increasingly sensitive to ridicule, those useful phrases had fallen out of fashion, and by the time Anand and I returned to Bombay we had to find our own descriptions for our uneasy state. We usually picked rather fancy ones, about how our ideas were too advanced for Bombay, or how enterprise could never flourish in India within the deadly grip of the family system, or we made ill-digested psychological comments on the effects of acceptance as a way of life. What we meant, of course, was that we were suffering from the England-returned blues. Mine was a milder case than Anand's, partly because my parents were "liberal"—not orthodox Hindus, that is—and, after fifteen years of wandering about the world in the diplomatic service, were prepared to accept with equanimity and even a certain doubtful approval the idea of my getting a job on a magazine in Bombay. Partly, things were easier for me because I had been through the worst of my readjustments six years before, when I had returned from ten years in English boarding schools.

Anand's England-returned misery was more virulent, because his family was orthodox, his mother spoke no English and distrusted foreign ways, he had been educated entirely in Bombay until he had gone to America for postgraduate courses, and worst of all, his father, an impressively successful contractor in Bombay, insisted that Anand, as the only son, enter the family business and work under the supervision not only of the father but of various uncles.

Our families lived on the same street, not more than half a dozen houses from each other, but led very different lives. Among the members of our generation, however, the differences were fading, and Anand and I belonged to the same set, although we had never particularly liked each other. It was a moment of boredom, of feeling at a loose end, and a fragmentary reminder that both of us had been in America that brought Anand and me together in Bombay.

It was during the monsoon, I remember, and the rain had pelted down all morning. About noon it cleared up, and I decided to spend my lunch hour shopping instead of having something sent up to eat at my desk. I started down the street toward Flora Fountain, the hideous monument that is the center of downtown Bombay, and had gone about halfway when I realized I had guessed wrong about the weather. The rain began again, ominously gentle at first, then quickly changing into a typical monsoon downpour. I ducked into the first doorway I saw, and ran slap into Anand, a rather short, slender young man, dressed with a certain nattiness. It was the building in which his father's firm had its offices, and Anand stood there staring glumly at the streaming street and scurrying pedestrians. We greeted each other with reserve. Neither was in the mood for a cheery exchange of news. We continued to gaze at the rain, at the tangle of traffic, the wet and shiny cars moving slowly through the dirty water on the road.

At last, with an obvious effort and without much interest, Anand said, "And what are you up to these days?"

"I *was* going to go shopping," I said coolly, "but I don't see how I can, in this."

"Damn rain," he muttered. I could hardly hear him over the sound of the water rushing along the gutters.

I said, "Mm," and, as a return of politeness, added, "And you? What are you doing?"

"Heaven knows," he said, with a world of depression in his voice. "Working, I suppose." After another long pause, he said, "Well, look, since you can't shop and I can't get to the garage for my car, suppose we nip around the corner for a bite of lunch."

"Okay," I said, not knowing quite how to refuse.

Anand looked full at me for the first time and began to smile. " 'Okay,' " he repeated. "Haven't heard *that* in some time."

We raced recklessly down the street, splashing through puddles and dodging people's umbrellas, until we arrived, soaked and laughing, at the nearest restaurant. It was no more than a snack bar, really, with a counter and stools on one side of the small room and a few tables on the other. We stood between them, breathless, mopping our faces ineffectually with handkerchiefs and slicking back wet hair, still laughing with the silly exhilaration such moments produce. We decided to sit at a table, because Anand said the hard little cakes with pink icing, neatly piled on the counter, looked too unappetizing to be faced all through lunch.

Our explosive entrance had made the other customers turn to stare; but as we settled down at our table, the four or five young men at the counter—clerks, probably, from nearby offices, self-effacing and pathetically tidy in their white drill trousers and white shirts (the inescapable look of Indian clerks)—turned their attention back to their cups of milky coffee and their curry puffs. The Sikhs at the next table, brightly turbaned and expansive of manner, resumed their cheerful conversation. The two Anglo-Indian typists in flowered dresses returned to their whispers and giggles and soda pop.

When the waiter brought us the menu, we discovered that the restaurant was called the Laxmi and Gold Medal Café. This sent Anand into a fresh spasm of laughter, and while we waited for our sandwiches and coffee, he entertained himself by inventing equally unlikely combinations for restaurant names—the Venus and Sun Yat-sen Coffee Shoppe, the Cadillac and Red Devil Ice-Cream Parlor, and so on—not very clever, but by that time we were in a good mood and prepared to be amused by almost anything.

At some point, I remember, one of us said, "Well, how do you *really* feel about Bombay?" and the other replied, "Let's face it. Bombay *is* utter hell," and we were launched on the first of our interminable conversations about ourselves, our surroundings, our families, our gloomy predictions for the future. We had a lovely time.

Before we left, Anand had taken down the number of my office telephone, and only a couple of days later he called to invite me to lunch again. "I'll make up for the horrors of the Laxmi and Gold Medal," he said. "We'll go to the Taj, which is at least air-conditioned, even if it isn't the Pavillon."

He had reserved a table by the windows in the dining room of the

Taj Mahal Hotel, where we could sit and look out over the gray, forbidding water of the harbor and watch the massed monsoon clouds above the scattered islands. Cool against the steamy rain outside, we drank a bottle of wine, ate the local *pâté de foie gras*, and felt sorry for ourselves.

Anand said, "I can't think why my father bothered to send me to America, since he doesn't seem interested in anything I learned there."

"Oh, I know, I know," I said, longing to talk about my own concerns.

"Can you believe it, the whole business is run *exactly* the way it was fifty years ago?"

"Of course I can. I mean, take the magazine–"

"I mean, everything done by vague verbal arrangements. Nothing properly filed and accounted for. And such enormous reliance on pull, and influence, and knowing someone in the government who will arrange licenses and import permits and whatever."

"For a consideration, naturally?"

"Or for old friendship or past favors exchanged or–"

"Well, it's a miracle to me that we ever get an issue of the magazine out, considering that none of the typesetters speaks English, and they have to make up the forms in a language they don't know, mirrorwise and by hand."

"Oh, it's all hopelessly behind the times."

"You can see that what we really need is an enormous staff of proofreaders and only a *tiny* editorial–"

"But at least you don't have to deal with the family as well. The *amount* of deadwood in the form of aged great-uncles, dim-witted second cousins, who *have* to be employed!"

"Can't you suggest they be pensioned off?"

"Don't think I haven't. My father just smiles and says I'll settle down soon. Oh, what's the use?"

Our discussions nearly always ended with one or the other of us saying, with exaggerated weariness, "Well, so it goes. Back to the salt mines now, I suppose?" I never added that I enjoyed my job.

That day we didn't realize until we were on the point of leaving the Taj how many people were lunching in the big dining room whom we knew or who knew one or the other of our families. On our way out, we smiled and nodded to a number of people and stopped at several tables to exchange greetings. With rising irritation, both of us were aware of the speculative glances, the carefully unexpressed curiosity behind the pleasant formalities of speech. Anand and I sauntered in silence down the wide, shallow staircase of the hotel. I think he was trying to seem unconcerned.

It was only when we reached the road that he exploded into angry speech. "Damn them," he said. "The prying old cats! What business is it of theirs, anyway?"

"It was the wine," I suggested. "Even people who have been abroad a lot don't drink wine at lunchtime."

"So? What's it to them?"

"Well, Dissolute Foreign Ways, and besides—"

"And besides, they have nothing to do but gossip."

"That, of course, but besides, you're what they call a catch, so it's only natural that they wonder."

Anand frowned as we crossed the road to where his car was parked against the sea wall. He opened the door for me and then climbed in behind the steering wheel. He didn't start the car for a moment or two, but sat with his hands on the wheel and his head turned away from me, looking at the threatening light of the early afternoon, which would darken into rain any minute. I thought he was about to tell me something—about a disappointment or a love affair—but instead, he clenched his fingers suddenly and said, "Well, the devil with them. Let them talk, if they have nothing better to do."

"Yes. Anyway, who cares?" I said, hoping it didn't sound as though *I* did.

He smiled at me. "That's the spirit. We'll show them."

We lunched at the Taj several times after that, but on each occasion a bit more defiantly, a bit more conscious of the appraising looks, always knowing we were the only "unattacheds" lunching together. The others were businessmen, or married couples doing duty entertaining, which, for some reason, they couldn't do at home, or ladies in groups, or foreigners.

As we stood inside the doors of the dining room, Anand would pause for a second, and then grip my elbow and say something like, "Well, come along. Let's strike a blow for freedom," or, "Throw away the blindfold. I'll face the firing squad like a man." He didn't deceive me—or, I suppose, anyone else.

Bombay is a big city—something over two million people—but in its life it is more like a conglomeration of villages. In our set, for instance, everyone knew everyone else at least by sight. At any of the hotels or restaurants we normally went to we were certain to meet a friend, a relative, an acquaintance. We all went to the same sort of party, belonged to the same clubs. People knew even each other's cars, and a quick glance at a row of parked cars would tell you that Mrs. Something was shopping for jewelry for her daughter's wedding, or that Mr. Something-else was attending a Willingdon Club committee meeting. So, of course, everyone knew that Anand and I lunched together a couple of times a week, and certainly our families must have been told we had been seen together.

My parents never mentioned the matter to me, though there was a certain wariness in their manner whenever Anand's name came up in conversation. (It's a sad moment, really, when parents first become a bit frightened of their child.) Privately, they must have put up with a good deal of questioning and comment from friends and relatives. Even to me people would sometimes say, "Can you come to a party on Saturday? Anand will be there." If Anand's mother ever lectured him on getting talked about, he evidently didn't think it worth repeating. Of them all, I dare say she was the most troubled, being orthodox, wanting a good, conservative marriage for her only son, being bewildered by what must have appeared to her—it seems astonishing in retrospect—sophistication.

Occasionally Anand would take me home to tea after our offices had closed. I think he did this out of an unadmitted consideration for his mother, to set her mind at rest about the company he was keeping, to show her that I was not a Fast Girl even if I did work on a magazine. I don't know how much I reassured her, with my short hair and lipstick, no *tika* in the middle of my forehead. But she always greeted me politely, bringing her hands together in a *namaskar*, and gave me canny looks when she thought I wasn't noticing. We couldn't even speak to each other, since we came from different communities and she spoke only Gujerati, while my language was Hindi. She would always wait with us in the drawing room until one of the servants brought the tea; then she would lift her comfortable figure out of her chair, nod to me, and leave us alone. We were always conscious of her presence in the next room beyond the curtained archway, and every now and then we would hear her teacup clink on the saucer. Our conversation, even if she didn't understand it, was bound to be pretty stilted.

Perhaps it was this silent pressure, perhaps it was only a sort of restlessness, that made Anand and me leave the usual haunts of our set and look for more obscure restaurants for our lunch dates. Liberal as we considered ourselves, we still couldn't help being affected by the knowing curiosity. There's no point in denying it (predictably, I always *did* deny it to Anand); I was concerned about public opinion. I suppose I was beginning to lose my England-returned brashness and intractability. I was not, however, prepared to stop meeting Anand for lunch. I liked him and waited with some impatience for his telephone calls, the rather pleasant voice saying things like "Hello? Is this the career girl?" (This was one of Anand's favorite phrases of defiance—a career girl was still something of a peculiarity in Bombay in those days. If you came from a respectable family that could support you, you weren't supposed to work for money. Social work would have been all right, but not something as shady as journalism.) Sometimes he would say, "This is underground agent 507. Are you a fellow resistance fighter?" or, "Am I speaking to Miss Emancipation?"

In any case, I would laugh and say, "Yes," and he would suggest that we try some Chinese food, or eat dry curried chicken at a certain Irani shop, or, if it was one of the steamy, rainless days near the end of the monsoon, go to Chowpatty beach and eat odds and ends of the delicious, highly spiced mixtures the vendors there concoct. By tacit agreement, he no longer picked me up at the office. Instead, we either met at the corner taxi rank (leaving Anand's car parked in the alley behind his office building) or arrived separately at our rendezvous.

Once, when we were driving to Colaba, the southernmost point of the island, Anand suddenly leaned forward and asked the taxi driver to stop. On an otherwise uninspired-looking street, lined with dingy middle-class houses, he had seen a sign that said "Joe's Place." Anand was entranced, and certainly the sign did look exotic among the bungalows and hibiscus. Joe's Place—named by some homesick

American soldier, who had found his way there during the war—quickly became our favorite restaurant. We felt it was our discovery, for one thing, and then it had a Goan cook, which meant that, unlike some of the other Indian restaurants, you could order beef. Most Hindus will not eat beef, cook it, or allow it on the premises; it is, as a result, the cheapest meat in Bombay. We ate a lot of beef at Joe's Place, and I often thought that Anand, at home in the evening, probably got rather a kick out of imagining how horrified his mother would be if she knew he had a rare steak inside him.

The proprietor, whom Anand insisted on calling Joe, even though he was a fat and jolly Indian, soon got used to seeing us almost every other day. We couldn't imagine how he made any money, since there never seemed to be anyone there besides Anand and me. Joe waited on table, so there weren't even waiters. Anand said that it was probably a front for black-market activities and that you could expect anything of a man who ran a Joe's Place in Bombay. More likely, the real, prosaic reason was that most of Joe's business was in cooking meals to send out.

We came to feel so much at home at Joe's that we bought him a checkered tablecloth, to lend the place a bit of class, and he would spread it ceremoniously over the corner table, invariably pointing out that it had been laundered since our last meal. We kept a bottle of gin at Joe's and taught him to make fresh-lime gimlets with it, so that we could have a cocktail before lunch. He hadn't a license to sell liquor, so he always shook our cocktails in an opaque bottle labeled Stone Ginger, in case anyone came in. He probably watered the gin; but we didn't much care, because it was the idea that pleased us.

We would sit at our table between the windows, glancing out occasionally at the patch of straggly garden, the jasmine bush, the desultory traffic, and talk. How we talked! On and on and on. Sometimes it was "In the States, did you ever—" or "Do you remember—" kind of talk. Sometimes it was about incidents at home or in our offices. We talked a lot about Them—a flexible term, including any relatives or friends we considered old-fashioned, interfering, lacking in understanding. We often discussed Their iniquities, and many of our conversations began, "Do you *know* what They've gone and done *now?*" All through the sticky postmonsoon months, into the cooler, brilliant days of early winter, we talked. It seems a miracle to me now that we could have found so much to say about the details of our reasonably pedestrian lives.

If we'd been a bit older or more observant, we would certainly have known that this state of affairs couldn't last much longer. I was dimly aware that every day of life in Bombay relaxed our antagonism a tiny bit and blurred the outlines of our American years. However, I never guessed what Anand's family's counterattack to his England-returned discontent would be. Anand's mother was a direct, uncomplicated woman, and in her view there was one obvious and effective way to cure the whole disease without waiting for the slower methods of time.

It was at Joe's Place that Anand announced the arrival of Janaki. I had got there early, I remember, and was sitting at our table when Anand came in. He always had a certain tension in his walk, but that day it seemed more pronounced. He held his narrow shoulders stiffly and carried an air of trouble, so I asked him at once whether anything was the matter.

"Matter?" he asked sharply, as though it were an archaic word. "Why should anything be the matter?"

"Well, I don't know. You just look funny."

"Well, I don't feel funny," he said, deliberately misunderstanding.

Joe brought him his gimlet and inquired rather despairingly if we wanted steak *again.*

Anand waved a hand at him impatiently and said, "Later. We'll decide later." Then he looked at me in silence, with a portentous frown. At last he said, "Do you *know* what They've gone and done *now?* They've invited a cousin—a *distant* cousin—to stay."

This didn't seem to me any great disaster. Cousins, invited or not, were eternally coming to visit. Any relatives had the right to turn up whenever it was convenient for them and stay as long as they liked. His announcement came as an anticlimax; but since he did seem so distressed, I asked carefully, "And I suppose you'll be expected to fit him into the firm in some capacity?"

"Her," Anand said. "It's a girl."

"A *girl?* Is *she* going to work in the business?" This was really cataclysmic news.

"Oh, of *course* not. Can't you see what They're up to?"

"Well, no, I can't."

"Don't you *see?*" he said, looking helpless before such stupidity. "They're trying to arrange a marriage for me."

I could think of nothing to say except an unconvincing "Surely not."

He went on without paying any attention. "I dare say They think They're being subtle. Throwing us together, you know, so that my incomprehensible, *foreign*–" he emphasized the word bitterly– "preference for making up my own mind about these things will not be offended. We are to grow imperceptibly fond of each other. Oh, I see the whole plot."

"You must be imagining it all."

"She arrived last night. They didn't even tell me she was coming."

"But people are forever dropping in."

"I know. But she was *invited*. She told me so."

"Poor Anand." I was sorry for him, and angry on his behalf. There had never been any romantic exchanges between Anand and me, so the girl didn't represent any personal threat; but I honestly thought that a matter of principle was involved and that one should stand by the principle. We had so often agreed that the system of arranged marriages was the ultimate insult to one's rights as a human being, the final, insupportable interference of domineering families. I tried to think of something comforting to say, but could only produce, feebly, "Well, all you have to do is sit it out."

"And watch her doing little chores around the house? Making herself quietly indispensable?" He added with a sour smile, "As the years roll by. Do you suppose we will grow old gracefully together?"

"Oh, don't be such a fool," I said, laughing. "She'll have to go, sooner or later."

"But will I live that long?" He seemed to be cheering up.

"It's rather unfair to the poor thing," I said, thinking for the first time of the girl. "I mean, if they've got her hopes up."

"Now, don't start sympathizing with *her*. The only way to finish the thing once and for all–to make my position clear–is to marry someone else immediately. I suppose you wouldn't consider marrying me, would you?"

"Heavens, no," I said, startled. "I don't think you need to be as drastic as that."

"Well, perhaps not. We'll see."

At last I thought to ask, "What's she called?"

"Janaki."

"Pretty name."

"It makes me vomit."

I could hardly wait for our next lunch date, and when we met a couple of days later at Joe's Place I started questioning Anand eagerly. "Well, how are things? How are you making out with Janaki?"

Anand seemed remote, a bit bored with the subject. "Joe!" he called. "More ice, for Pete's sake. Gimlets aren't supposed to be *mulled*." He tapped his fingers on the table in a familiar, nervous movement. "He'll never learn," he said resignedly. Then, after a pause. "Janaki? Oh, she's all right, I suppose. A minor pest."

"Is she being *terribly* sweet to you?"

"Oh, you know. I will say this for her, she manages to be pretty unobtrusive."

"Oh." I was obscurely disappointed.

"It's just knowing she's always *there* that's so infuriating."

"It would drive me crazy."

In a voice that was suddenly cross, he said, "She's so *womanly*."

"Hovers about, you mean?"

"Not that, so much, but I can see her *hoping* I'll eat a good dinner or have had a good day at the office, or some damn thing."

"It sounds rather flattering."

"I dare say that's the strategy. It's pathetic, really, how little They know me if They think she's the sort of girl I'd want to marry."

"What sort of girl *would* you want to marry?"

"Heaven knows," Anand said in a hopeless voice. "Someone quite different, anyway. I knew one once."

"Was there a girl in America?" I asked with interest.

"Isn't there always a girl in America? A sort of tradition. In our fathers' time, it used to be the daughter of the landlady somewhere in Earl's Court. Usually blonde, always accommodating."

"And yours?"

"Accommodating. But several cuts above the landlady's daughter. She was a senior in college. And she had quite a nice family, if you can stand families, rather timid, but determined to believe that a

Good Home Environment was a girl's best protection. I don't think they would have raised many objections if we'd got married."

"Why didn't you marry her, then?"

"Oh, I don't know. Do those things work? I really don't know."

"I expect your parents would have raised the devil."

"Before—if I'd told them. Not after. By then the particular alchemy that turns a girl into a daughter-in-law would have done its work. That was really the trouble. I couldn't see her being an Indian daughter-in-law living in a Bombay family—and what a mess that would have made. Hurt feelings and recriminations and disappointment all around. I'm not sentimental about her," he said earnestly, as if it were an important point. "I mean, I know she wasn't particularly good-looking or anything, but I had a separate identity in her mind. I wasn't just somebody's son, or someone to marry, or someone with good business connections."

"And all that is what you are to Janaki?"

"I suppose so. What else could I be?"

As we left Joe's Place after lunch, he said, "I think you'd better come to tea to meet her. Would you like to?"

"I was hoping you'd ask me."

"Okay, then. Tomorrow?"

Full of excitement, the next day, I met Anand after work and drove home with him. "Is your mother going to be cross about your asking me?"

"Why should she be cross? You've been to tea with us before."

"But that was different."

"I can't see why," he said, refusing to accept the situation.

"Oh, don't be so dense," I said, thinking, Poor girl, it's going to be very frustrating for her if he insists on treating her as a casual cousin come for a holiday. "Does your mother tactfully leave you alone with her for tea?"

"Never. The two of them chatter about domestic details. It's really very boring."

To me it was far from boring. For one thing, Anand's mother was far more cordial to me than she had been on previous visits, and I wondered whether she could already be so sure of the success of her plan that I was no longer a danger. And then there was the suspense of waiting to see what Janaki would be like.

She came in with the servant who carried the tea tray, holding back the curtain of the dining-room archway so that he could manage more easily. A plump, graceful girl with a very pretty face and a tentative, vulnerable smile, which she seemed ready to cancel at once if you weren't going to smile with her. I saw, instantly, that she was any mother-in-law's ideal—quiet, obedient, helpful. Her hair was drawn back into the conventional knot at the nape of her neck; she had a *tika* on her forehead, wore no make-up except for the faintest touch of lipstick, and even that, I decided, was probably a new experiment for her, a concession to Anand's Westernized tastes.

She spoke mostly to Anand's mother, in Gujerati, and I noticed that she had already assumed some of the duties of a hostess. She poured the tea and asked, in clear, lilting English, whether I took milk and sugar, handed around the plates of Indian savories and sweets.

After the first mouthful, I remarked formally, "This is delicious."

Anand's mother caught the tone, even if she didn't understand the words, and said something in Gujerati to Anand.

He translated, without much interest, "Janaki made them."

Janaki, in embarrassment, wiped her mouth on her napkin with the thorough gesture that someone unused to wearing lipstick makes, and then gazed in surprise and alarm at the pink smear on the linen. She saw me watching and gave me one of her diffident smiles.

I quickly said the first thing that came into my head. "How clever you are. I wish I could cook."

"It is very easy to learn," she replied.

"There never seems to be any time for it."

Entirely without sarcasm or envy she said, "That is true for someone like you who leads such a busy and interesting life."

I felt ashamed of myself, for no reason I could quite put my finger on.

We continued to talk banalities, and Janaki kept up her end admirably, managing to seem interested in the most ordinary comments and still keeping a watchful eye out to see that cups and plates were filled. The conversation gradually fell entirely to Janaki and me, because Anand retreated into a sulky silence. I remember thinking that one couldn't really blame him. It must have been maddening to have to face this sweet and vapid politeness every day after work. At last he jumped up, said abruptly that he had some papers to go through, and left the room. I left soon after.

Janaki saw me to the front door and, with an unexpected spontaneity, put her hand on my arm. "Please come to tea again," she said. "I mean, if you are not too occupied. I should so much like it. I have no friends in Bombay."

"I'd be delighted, and you must come to tea with me."

"Oh, no, thank you very much. Perhaps later on, but I must learn the ways of this house first. You see that, don't you?"

I walked home, wondering at her mixture of nervousness and confidence, at the fact that she already felt certain she had a permanent place in that house.

At our next lunch date, it was Anand who asked the eager questions. "Well? What did you think of her?"

And I replied noncommittally, "She seemed very pleasant."

"Quite the little housewife, do you mean?"

"No. Sweet and anxious to please, I meant."

"You sound like my mother. She says, 'A good-natured girl. You should count yourself fortunate.' I suppose she asked you to be her friend?"

"How did you know?"

"She's not as stupid as she looks. She said the same to me. 'Will you not allow us to be friendly, Anand?' " He attempted a saccharin, unconvincing falsetto. He frowned. "The thin end of the wedge, don't you see? It would be funny if it weren't so sad."

"Well, at least she's very good-looking," I said defensively.

"She's too fat."

"I think it rather suits her."

"A strong point in her favor, my mother says, to make up for my puniness." Anand was sensitive about his height. He said, in a touchy voice, daring one to sympathize with him, "Eugenically very sound. Strong, healthy girl like Janaki married to a weakling like me, and we have a chance of strong, healthy children that take after her. The children, you see, are the whole point of this stratagem. I'm an only son and must produce some. My mother has a rather simple approach to these things."

"You must admit," I said rather uncomfortably, "that she'd make a very good mother."

"Not a doubt in the world. She's a natural for the part of the Great Earth Mother. But I rather resent being viewed in such an agricultural light."

In the weeks that followed, Janaki dominated our conversation at lunchtime, and I had tea with them quite frequently. Sometimes, if Anand was kept late at his office or had to attend a board meeting, Janaki and I would have tea alone, and she would ask hundreds of questions about America, trying, I thought, to build up a picture of Anand's life there and the background that seemed to influence him so much. She claimed to be uniformly enthusiastic about everything American, and for me it was rather fun, because it made me feel so superior in experience. Once she asked me to teach her to dance, and I was unexpectedly disconcerted. There was something very refreshing about her lack of Westernization, and I didn't want to see her lose it.

"I will if you really want me to, but—"

"Anand likes dancing, doesn't he?"

"Yes, but wouldn't it be better if he taught you himself, after you —I mean, when he—what I mean is, a little later on?"

"You think that would be best?" She meant, of course, "The best way of handling Anand."

"Yes, I do," I said, meaning, "You don't want to seem too eager."

"Very well." She nodded, accepting my opinion as final. On this level of unspoken frankness we understood each other perfectly.

She would question me, sometimes openly and sometimes indirectly, about Anand's tastes and preferences. We had a long session, I remember, about her looks. Should she wear make-up? Should she cut her hair? What about her clothes? I told her she was fine the way she was, but she insisted, "Has he *never* said anything? He must have made *some* remark?"

"Well," I said reluctantly, "he did once mention that he thought you were just a fraction on the chubby side."

Without a trace of rancor, Janaki said, "I will quickly become thin."

"Heavens! Don't take the remark so seriously."

"It is nothing," Janaki assured me. "One need only avoid rice and ghee." She did, too. I noticed the difference in a couple of weeks.

When Anand was there, the atmosphere was much more strained. From the frigid politeness of his early days with Janaki, his manner gradually changed to irritation, which expressed itself in angry silence and later in a kind of undercover teasing sometimes laced with malice. For instance, he would greet her with something like, "What have you been up to today? Hemstitching the sheets? Crocheting for the hope chest?" and Janaki would look puzzled and smile, as though she had missed the point of a clever joke. Actually, she was a beautiful needlewoman and did a good deal of exquisitely neat embroidery on all kinds of things—antimacassars, doilies, face towels—infallibly choosing hideous designs of women, in enormous crinolines, watering the flowers in an English garden, or bunches of roses with ribbons streaming from them. Once Janaki answered Anand's inquiry quite seriously with an account of her day, the household jobs she had done, the women who had called on his mother in the morning and had been served coffee, and even produced the embroidery she had been working on.

"Wonderfully appropriate for India, don't you think?" Anand remarked to me with rather labored irony.

"I think it's lovely," I said unconvincingly.

Janaki seemed unruffled. "Men do not appreciate embroidery," she said quietly.

Anand leaned back in his chair, stared at the ceiling, and gave an exaggerated sigh.

One couldn't help disliking him in this role of tormentor. The fact was, of course, that, in Anand's phrase, *I* was getting imperceptibly fonder of Janaki as his impatience with her grew more overt. There was, to me, both gallantry and an appealing innocence in her undaunted conviction that everything would turn out all right. What I didn't recognize was the solid realism behind her attitude. I started to suspect the calculation in her nature one day when Anand had been particularly difficult. He had insisted on talking about books she hadn't read and, with apparent courtesy, addressing remarks to her he knew she couldn't answer.

Janaki said nothing for a long time and then admitted, with a becoming lack of pretension, "I'm afraid I read only the stories in the *Illustrated Weekly*. But, Anand, if you would bring me some books you think good, I would read them."

"I'll see if I can find the time," he replied in a surly voice.

When Janaki showed me to the door that evening, I said in considerable exasperation, "Why do you put up with it? He needn't be so disagreeable when he talks to you."

"It is natural that there should be difficulties at first. After his life in America, there are bound to be resentments here."

"Well, I think you are altogether too forbearing. I wouldn't stand it for a second." Privately, I had begun to think she must, after all, be stupid.

Then Janaki said, "What would you do?"

"Leave, of course. Go back." And at that moment I realized what she meant. Go back to what? To another betrothal arranged by her elders? Learning to please some other man? Here, at least, she liked her future mother-in-law.

"And besides," she said, "I know that really he is kind."

In the end, Janaki turned out to be the wisest of us all, and I have often thought how lucky it was that she didn't follow my advice then. Not that Anand capitulated all at once, or that one extraordinary morning he suddenly saw her with new eyes, or anything like that. He remained irritable and carping; but gradually he became enmeshed in that most satisfactory of roles, a reluctant Pygmalion.

I noticed it first one day when he finished his lunch rather hurriedly and said, as we were going back to our offices, "That girl's conversation is driving me nuts. I think I really had better buy her some books. As long as I'm stuck with her company," he added awkwardly.

We parted at the bookshop, and in later conversations I learned that Janaki was doing her homework with diligence and pleasure.

From then on things moved fairly rapidly. I began to anticipate Anand's frequent suggestions that we spend part of the lunch hour shopping—usually rather ungraciously expressed: "We've got to get that girl into some less provincial-looking saris." "That girl listens to nothing but film music. I really must get her some decent classical stuff. What do you suggest as a beginning? Kesarbai? Subbaluxmi?"

"No Western music?" I asked pointedly.

"She wouldn't understand it," Anand replied.

All the same, at home he continued to be offhand or overbearing with her. She remained calm and accepting, a willing pupil who knew that her stupidity was a great trial to her teacher. Still, there wasn't a doubt in my mind about the change of attitude going on in Anand. I wanted a lived-happily-ever-after conclusion for Janaki; but mostly I was certain that the Pygmalion story could have only one ending, whatever the minor variations might be.

Anand's parents were evidently equally confident of the outcome, for one day at tea he announced, with an exuberance no amount of careful casualness could disguise, that his father was going to send him to New York on a business trip. He was pleased, he insisted, largely because it meant that at last he was to be trusted with some real responsibility.

I said, "And it will be such wonderful fun to be back in America."

"Oh, yes. That, too, naturally. But I don't know how much time I'll have for the bright lights and parties." He had moved so smoothly into the correct businessman's viewpoint that I wanted to laugh.

We were absorbed in discussing the details of the trip, and besides, by then Janaki had become such an accepted—and pleasing—part of the scenery of the house that we assumed she was listening with her usual attention and, as always, trying to fit in with Anand's mood.

So it came as quite a shock when she suddenly spoke in a flat, decisive voice. "I, too, am leaving. I am going back to my home." Dead silence for a moment. "Tomorrow," she said.

"But *why*—" I began.

"It is my decision," she said, and wouldn't look at either of us.

Anand didn't say anything, just stood up, with all his bright, important planning gone, and walked out of the room. We waited to hear his study door slam.

Then my affection for Janaki (and, of course, curiosity) made me ask, "But why *now*, just when things are going so well?"

"It was your advice, don't you remember?"

"But things were different then."

"Yes." She nodded as though we both recognized some particular truth.

At the time I thought she believed herself defeated. I was surprised and concerned that what seemed so plain to me should remain obscure to her. "Listen," I said cautiously, "don't you see that he—that in spite of everything, he has fallen in love with you?"

I don't know quite what I had expected her response to be—a radiant smile, perhaps, or even a sense of triumph. I hadn't expected her to glare at me as though I were an enemy and say, "Oh, love. I don't want him to *love* me. I want him to marry me."

"It's different for him," I said, as persuasively as I could. "For him it is important."

She looked at me shrewdly, making up her mind about something. "You are sure?" she asked.

"Absolutely sure."

Her voice was hard and impatient. "Love, what books you read, whether you like music, your 'taste'—whatever that may mean. As if all that has anything to do with marriage."

"Well," I said ineffectually.

How can one make the idea of romantic love attractive to someone who wants only a home, a husband, and children? Even if nothing could be done about that, I thought I knew the reason for her sudden despair. The renewing of Anand's American experiences must have seemed to her an overwhelming menace. I tried to reassure her, reminded her that Anand would be gone only a matter of weeks, that he would miss her, that America would look quite different to him now, that he had changed a lot in the past year—more than a year, actually.

But she wouldn't listen, and she kept repeating, "I must pack my things and leave the house tomorrow."

I thought, Poor Janaki. I can see that the tedious business of starting all over again on the unraveling of Anand's England-returned tangles might well seem to be too much to face. It didn't occur to me that I might equally have thought, Clever Janaki, the only one of us who knows exactly what she wants. Leave the house? She would have slit her throat first.

When I think of it, I can't help wondering at the extent of my naïveté then. The fact is that women—or perhaps I mean just the women of a certain kind of world, Janaki's world—have inherited, through bitter centuries, a ruthless sense of self-preservation. It still seems to me ghastly that they should need it; but it would be silly to deny that, in most places on earth, they still do. That cool, subtle determination to find her security and hang on to it, that all's-fair attitude—not in love, which she discounted, but in war, for it *was* war, the gaining or losing of a kingdom—was really no more than the world deserved from Janaki. As in war, victory, conquest, success, call it what you will, was the only virtue. And, of course, the really absurd thing was that nobody would have been more appalled than Janaki if you had called her a feminist.

As it was, I heard with anxiety Anand on the phone the next day, saying, "Let's lunch. I want to talk to you. Joe's Place? One o'clock?"

I was certain that Janaki had gone home, with only the indignities of a few new clothes and a lot of tiresome talk to remember.

As soon as I saw him, I knew I was wrong. He had the conventionally sheepish look that makes the announcing of good news quite pointless. He said, "An eventful evening, wasn't it?"

"Yes, it was, rather."

Then there was a long pause while he looked embarrassed and I could think of no way to help him out. At last he said, all in a rush, "Look, this is going to seem ridiculous. I mean—well, Janaki and I are going to be married."

"You couldn't do a more sensible thing," I said, much relieved.

He looked startled. "Sensible? Perhaps it seems that way to you. Actually, we're in love with each other."

"With *each other?*" I echoed incredulously, and regretted it immediately.

"I knew it would seem peculiar to you. I dare say you've thought I hated her all this time." He smiled at me in a rather superior way. "I thought so myself for a while. And Janaki, as you well imagine, had every reason to think so. And I must say it certainly took a lot of courage on her part. I mean, when you think—"

"You'd better start at the beginning," I said, suddenly feeling depressed.

"Okay. I heard you leave yesterday, and then I heard Janaki come into the hall—you know that timid way she has of walking—and stand outside my study door. I was in quite a state; but I dare say that I wouldn't have done anything about anything if she hadn't—I mean, if someone hadn't taken the initiative."

"Yes," I said, knowing what was coming but unable to shake off my gloom. "She came to explain why she was going home."

"She said—you see, she isn't the passive, orthodox girl you think—

she told me that quite against her plans or anything she's expected, she'd—I know this will seem silly—but she'd fallen in love with me."

"I see. And that accounted for her behavior. Trying all the time to please you, I mean."

"Well, yes. Then I realized that—"

"All your resentment and bad manners were just that—" I wanted to hurry him through the story.

"Well, yes."

"Well, yes," I repeated, and couldn't look at him. We were silent for a while. "Well, congratulations," I said uneasily.

"It's funny, isn't it," he said in a confident voice, "that Their plans should have worked out—but so differently. I don't suppose They'll ever understand."

"It wouldn't be worth trying to explain."

"Heavens, no. Look, I'm taking Janaki out to lunch tomorrow. Will you join us?"

"Oh, no, surely—"

"She asked particularly that you come. She likes you very much, you know, and besides, she doesn't feel quite comfortable going out without a chaperon."

"In *that* case—" I said, with a nastiness lost on Anand. And all the time I was thinking, Have we all been made use of? A sympathetic mother-in-law, a man you can flatter, a gullible friend from whom you can learn background and fighting conditions, with whom you can check tactics and their effects. Now that she has won, she must have nothing but contempt for all of us. But simultaneously I was wondering, Is she, after all, really in love? It was a state she didn't know how to cope with, and she could hope only to use the weapon she knew, an ability to please or try to please. Why should she, or how could she, tell me all that herself—a realm of which she was so unsure, which was so far out of her experience?

Now that I have met so many Janakis of the world, I think I know which explanation was right.

"So we'll meet," Anand was saying, "at the Taj, if that's all right with you?"

He had reserved a table by the windows. Janaki was a bit late, to be sure—she explained breathlessly—that we would be there before her, because it would have been agony to sit alone.

We ordered from the Indian menu, and Anand said, with only a fleeting, questioning glance at me, "No wine, I think. There really isn't any wine at all that goes with Indian food, is there?"

## *The ugly face of violence*

In the spring of 1946 I was working for a Bombay magazine called *Trend*, subtitled (with the hope of attracting a larger audience) *The National Pictorial.* The summer after I was graduated from Wellesley and returned to Bombay, Sharouk Sabavala and another friend, Frene Talyarkhan, a competent and determined girl who had started the magazine, asked me to join their staff.

I accepted at once and with some excitement because this was the first "real" job I had ever had. My only other job had been with the Office of War Information during vacations, and that had seemed to me anything but "real" from the beginning. I was, besides, rather impressed with my new title, Associate Editor. Actually that meant very little, because apart from two photographers and the stenographer who appeared on the masthead as Editorial Assistant, the editorial staff included only Editor in Chief Frene, Sharouk, a slight, quiet young man who was the managing editor and was also supposed to understand the business end of the magazine, and me.

The three of us did all the writing for *Trend* except the book reviews, which were handled by John Rowdon, a young Englishman of considerable charm and talent. I thought his work was the best in the magazine, but at that time, although he was a friend of all of us, the feeling between the British and the Indians as a whole was pretty tense, and John used to sign his reviews only with his initials.

The *Trend* office, with all its disadvantages of stuffiness and noise, was at least cozy. We had one room on the second floor of a good building in the center of the business section of the city. We had partitioned this into two smaller sections. In the half without windows sat the accountant-circulation manager and an office boy surrounded by files and reference books. In the half with the windows, Frene, Sharouk, the stenographer, and I had our desks, and since this arrangement left room for only one extra straight chair, we could never have more than one visitor at a time.

Frene had to see important clients at the Taj Majal Hotel. We shared our telephone with the man in the next office. A small hatch had been cut in the wall, and the telephone sat in it, and while this left neither office much privacy, at least our phone bill was smaller that it would otherwise have been.

Of course the magazine was constantly in debt, and friends and families were called on for assistance. We had bullied as many people as we knew into taking annual subscriptions, but that didn't nearly meet our costs. Our advertising manager (part-time) tried his best to make up the deficit, but a circulation of 2,500 was not much to offer prospective clients.

In spite of the rather limited scope of *Trend*, my job there was as pleasant as any I could hope for. Between stories we used to chat and drink coffee and plan spectacular issues once the magazine was out of the red, and after every issue we would make firm resolutions to get the next one out on time—well, if not on time, at least not more than a week late.

The morning of the day on which the Indian naval enlisted men went on strike, my father and I left the house, as usual, in his car. As usual he had read the *Times of India* all through breakfast, and in the car on the way to his office he read the Bombay *Chronicle*, and handed me the *Times*. Both papers were full of the news that the sailors were protesting the discrimination in pay, food, and treatment between them and their British colleagues. That morning they were to hold a parade through the streets of Bombay.

In those days the struggle for independence was reaching its last stages, and tempers were taut all over India. One never knew when a relatively minor grievance might snap into widespread rioting. In the bigger cities, bands of *goondas* (unemployed looters) would attach themselves to any cause or disturbance and turn it into a mob action, attacking Indians and Britishers alike. But we had no way of knowing that the naval strike would serve as a suitable springboard.

As usual, my father left me at the *Trend* office with his daily formula of "Pick you up at five-thirty." The early part of the morning was quiet—a little too quiet. Frene had gone out to see someone and had taken one of the photographers with her. The rest of the staff, with the exception of Sharouk and Samel, the other photographer, had not come to work at all. They lived in the suburbs, where apparently the underground vibrations of trouble were felt sooner and more accurately. Someone phoned up from our printers in Kalbadevi and said that there, too, work had stopped.

Sharouk, Samel, and I sat about gossiping. At about ten o'clock we thought we might ask the elevator operator to order us some coffee from the restaurant downstairs, but we discovered that he had left the building too, and the elevator stood empty at the ground floor, with its light on and the doors open. The restaurant hadn't opened that day at all. The J. Walter Thompson advertising agency had offices across the hall from us. Its receptionist told us that all the Thompson employees had been given permission to go home, because the office was closing for the day.

The building was strangely quiet that morning, so we heard the commotion of feet and voices when it first began on the stairs. Fists banged on doors, there was the sound of breaking glass, and then the voices were on our floor and hands were hammering on the doors of J. Walter Thompson. We listened tensely, but there was no further sound. Either the J. Walter Thompson people had managed to get out or they were sitting silently in their rooms behind locked doors.

A couple of minutes later the *goondas* reached our office. Five or six young men wearing loose white pajamas and white shirts pushed in. The one in front must have been in his early twenties; the rest were not much more than boys. We stared at each other.

Samel, who had been sitting on Frene's desk and fiddling with his camera, was the first to move. He slithered off the desk and stood up. Then one of the boys at the back of the group in the door pushed forward to get in the room. The oldest one asked, "What office is this?"

Sharouk said, "*Trend* magazine."

"Do you work for the British?"

"No, of course not. We run the magazine ourselves."

There was more shuffling in the rear. "Do you employ any Britishers?"

"No."

There was a pause. The boys looked vaguely disappointed. Then one of them said, "How do we know you don't work for the British?"

"Well, we don't."

"But how do we know?"

Samel picked up a letterhead from Frene's desk and took it over to the group. "Look," he said, pointing to the red-and-black type. "It says *Trend, The National Pictorial.* National, do you understand?"

The boys peered over each other's shoulders, shoving to see the piece of paper.

Samel said with conviction, "Would any British magazine call itself national?"

I wondered nervously whether any of them could read, and even if they could, whether they could make out the English letters. It didn't occur to me until afterwards that "national" might not be close enough to "nationalist" to convince them.

The group seemed undecided. Samel picked up some more sheets of paper. "Here," he said grandly, "I'll give each of you one to look at."

As he was handing out the letterheads, somewhere in the building a door slammed. The boys turned at once, and, shouting and pushing, rushed toward the sound. We watched them sprint up the steps by the elevator, waving the *Trend* letterheads.

"What," I asked Samel, "would they have done if we had employed Britishers?"

"Oh, broken the place up, probably," he said casually.

"Well," I said, "I suppose we had really better go home now."

But by then it had become impossible to leave the building. Through the windows we could hear the gathering sound of shouting crowds from Hornby Road, the main road that runs through the business section of Bombay and crosses Pherozeshah Mehta Road, where our office was. The sailors' parade was passing, and from there the trouble spilled outward until most of our section of the city was involved. A couple of trucks full of policemen hurtled down our road toward the swelling noise. Shops had slammed their shutters across show windows. Traffic had stopped. There were no people on the street. Such emptiness in the bright sunlight was far more ominous than the distant noise.

When our office door closed sharply, we all turned from the windows at once. John Rowdon walked in, carrying a large envelope and looking rather peeved.

"Do you know," he said, "someone threw a brick at me!"

There was silence for a couple of seconds, and then Sharouk began to laugh. I said, "My God, John, what are *you* doing out today?"

"Well," he replied reasonably, "I brought my book reviews over," and with some annoyance, "and as I was walking here someone chucked a brick at me."

"But there's a riot on."

"Oh?" he said vaguely, "What about? I haven't seen today's paper."

"It's the sailors' strike, but it's going to turn into a riot. Didn't you notice the crowds on Hornby Road?"

John said crossly, "There are always crowds on Hornby Road."

He came over to join us at the windows just as more trucks raced along the road. Gradually from the bazaars, the docks, and the narrow side alleys people were pouring into our road. They looked much like any India crowd, dressed mostly in white dhotis or pajamas. The glistening black heads and the brown limbs clotted together in couples and groups and finally a surging crowd. Some carried the Congress tricolor; others had sticks and stones. The shouts and slogans were indistinguishable in the general noise as the crowd moved toward Hornby Road, but we could tell the change in tone when the policemen returned to meet this mob on our road.

The movement of the crowd slowed slightly, and suddenly a couple of the cars parked along the curb were on fire. I discovered then that one of the first things that happens when a car burns is that the horn short circuits. All through the rest of that morning the noise of the riots was cut from time to time by the screaming of car horns.

The pressing of the crowd stopped unexpectedly because the policemen at the far end of the street had set up machine guns across the road and had fired a couple of rounds at the ground in front of the people. At the corner of our block there was a sudden fountain of excitement. Some of the men had broken into a bank, and in a weird, incredible scene were standing on the window ledge flinging currency out to the crowd. Five- and ten-rupee notes fluttered about. People were laughing and grabbing at them. Samel turned from beside me and reached for his camera. Sharouk phoned a friend of his on a newspaper and came back with the rumor that the sailors had seized control of the vessels in Bombay harbor, trained the guns on the city, and announced that unless their grievances were redressed they would open fire.

It was just about then that a truck loaded with bottles of soda came down the street. Why the policemen let it through I shall never understand, but one of them, an Anglo-Indian in a white uniform and sun helmet, had jumped on a running board to escort the driver through the mob.

With a ghastly sense of anticipation I knew what was about to happen. Of course the crowd stopped the truck, and the driver, terrified, ducked under the steering wheel. Within a few seconds there were people climbing all over it. Cases of soda were distributed among the crowd, and immediately the real action started. It is extraordinary how much damage an exploding bottle of soda can do. Glass crashed against buildings and on the pavements; windows shattered; people twisted away from the explosions with torn faces and bloody clothes.

The Anglo-Indian policeman was lynched. It seemed to happen quite slowly. He had tried to back away from the truck toward the police line with his revolver in his hand. When the first soda bottle hit the road just in front of him, he fired at the crowd. He held his revolver low, aiming at the legs of the people. The noise had suddenly dropped alarmingly; there was not the menacing roar one had vaguely imagined from a scene of violence, but the crowd advanced steadily toward the isolated figure.

He was almost directly under our window when he ran out of bullets. We all heard quite distinctly the flat clicking of the hammer as he jerked on the trigger. Everyone must have realized at almost the same second that he hadn't a chance. Panic gripped him like a fit of malarial shivering. We saw his contorted face as he turned to

run, the pale-brown knees churning under the white drill shorts. But the crowd, with a sound that was almost like a gasp of relief, was on him at once and literally tore him to pieces.

We all moved away from the window with a frightened sort of calmness as the noise from the street swelled again.

"We've got to get out of here," I said at last, thinking foggily that they might decide to search the building again.

Samel said something about pictures. Sharouk, John, and I walked down the deserted, silent corridor to the stairs. The lobby was crowded. People had dragged the wounded and bleeding men from the street, and they lay moaning on the stone floor with their heads covered. A number of other people had crowded in. Leaning against one wall were two policemen.

Rather hysterically I shouted to them, "Why don't you *do* something? Why don't you take these men to hospital?"

One of the policemen looked at me with considerable amusement. He nodded toward the crowd outside the iron grille. "For fifty rupees a month would you go out in that?"

We found Sharouk's mother's chauffeur crouching in a corner of the lobby. "We are going home," Sharouk said. "Where is the car?"

The chauffeur looked doubtfully at John and said slowly, "In the alley."

Behind the office building there was a narrow crescent of an alley that opened at both ends into Pherozeshah Mehta Road. There we got into the car. Sharouk and I sat in the back. John looked acutely embarrassed. Sharouk said briskly, "You'd better get down on the floor." We draped part of my sari over John, and a shawl that Sharouk's mother had left in the car.

At the entrance to the alley, of course, the car was stopped. Faces and fists pressed up against the windows. The men outside shouted, "*Jai Hind!*"

"*Jai Hind!*" Sharouk and I replied enthusiastically.

"Success to the sailors!"

I noticed that we were both smiling brightly. "Success, success!"

We were allowed to proceed.

In the ten-minute drive to the undisturbed residential section of Marine Drive we were stopped several times more in the same way to respond to the same shouts.

When we dropped John at home we all felt rather foolish. "Well," I said senselessly, "I'm sorry."

"Not at all, not at all," John said, and added vaguely, "The sins of the fathers or something."

The city was tense all the rest of that day, but the next day it looked as if the demands of the sailors would be met. The city relaxed to its normal life. The rubble and glass from Pherozeshah Mehta Road had already been cleared away when we went to work the next morning.

Samel's pictures came out very well, and we gave a large part of the next issue to them. That was the first month that *Trend* broke even.

# THREE

In 1947 my father was appointed free India's first ambassador to Japan. This, rather abruptly, changed my life. The previous two years had been filled with occasions to learn about the new India that was emerging from a century and a half of colonialism and the last stages of a struggle for independence that was most gracefully accepted by the British in the postwar years. There were, of course, the horrifying evidences of the cost of that independence, the slaughter and bitterness that accompanied the partition of the country into the Indian Union and Pakistan, but the principle of self-determination had been established for us. I wasn't in India to see the fireworks and excitement, to hear the great speeches by our leaders and the celebrations of the crowds. That summer I was in Japan with my father because my sister was already married, had children, and was living in Bombay; my mother was, that year, President of the All-India Women's Conference, the largest association of women's organizations in India, and her work and duties compelled her to stay in the country. I was the only unattached member of the family who could go to Japan with my father to keep house and be hostess for him.

As it turned out I didn't have much to do in either capacity. Tokyo had been so extensively bombed during the war that housing was painfully short and my father and I lived at the Imperial Hotel. Army protocol (these were the years of the Japanese Occupation) was so inflexible, as were the rules about conduct and fraternization with the Japanese, that I found our social life largely determined for us. We were even given our appropriate military ranks (I discovered that I was technically the wife of a three-star general) and expected to live within those limitations. We, as occupation personnel, were barred from Japanese restaurants, hotels, inns, theaters, movies, and so on. At the time it seemed to me the most frustrating sort of situation—to see the Japanese only as passers-by on the streets when I wanted to get to *know* them—but later I realized that there were many good reasons for the rules. The Japanese supply of food and housing had to be protected from foreign encroachment, the theater was still under censorship regulations, the Japanese themselves were still, officially, enemies. Anyway, as a result, I got a job teaching English in a Japanese school partly because the Japanese were very short of English teachers and could use even my very slender qualifications, partly because it seemed to be the only way to meet and work with some of the people of a country that was already beginning to enchant me.

It was a combination of my first excursion as a schoolteacher and my perennial interest in the theater that introduced me to Faubion Bowers—the man who was then the official censor of the Japanese theater. He was the occupation authority to whom I had to apply to be allowed to get sixty—when I think about it that seems an absurd number, but it *was* sixty—tickets to the Japanese classical theater for my students who, because of the wartime closing of Tokyo theaters and because of the high cost of the tickets, had never in their lives been to the theater at all. It was a moment that left two indelible influences on my life: an enduring love of the kabuki theater, and Faubion Bowers himself to whom I became engaged three years later in New York and married the year after that in France.

Meanwhile Faubion and I, after my year in Japan and after my father had been posted as ambassador to Washington, decided to take a brief trip through Asia. We persuaded two friends of ours, one American and one English, to accompany us on the tour which was supposed to last two months. It lasted closer to two years. Most of that journey, as well as my life in Japan, is described in a book that was published in 1950 called *East of Home*. One of the sad things about life in colonial Asia was that most of us never got to know our neighbors in fellow Asian countries. When we thought of travel it was usually in terms of Europe, the homelands of our conquerors and rulers. We were much more familiar with, say, English, French, Dutch than with any Asian language except our own. The education of "Westernized" Asians had given them at least a passing knowledge of European art and letters—for instance, if we found ourselves in France we could have remembered the names of a few French kings, a few historical episodes. It was more than we could have done if we had visited our neighboring country, Burma. There is a moment from my childhood which I recall with all the isolated clarity of a good photograph: my mother and I standing on Westminster Bridge when we first arrived in London, her voice quoting, "Earth has not anything to show more fair: Dull would he be of soul who could pass by a sight so touching in its majesty." And both of us stared at the famous Thames, astonished that, compared with Indian rivers, it should be so small. We could never have captured a similar moment or a comparable quotation standing on a bridge over the Sumida River in Tokyo—although Japanese literature abounds with such references. I, at least, had never heard of the Sumida River until I lived in Tokyo.

Our journey through Asia was, therefore, another exploration for me. Partly through seeing a new Asia just emerging from colonial rule—Indo-China, Malaya, Burma, Indonesia, Ceylon—and much of its accompanying struggles, partly through learning everywhere we traveled the cultural or religious or linguistic or political ties with India in so many Asian countries, I was beginning to acquire a new sense of identity as an *Asian* as well as an Indian. My education took on a different dimension altogether.

Although the major part of this adventure appears in *East of Home*, one or two moments and experiences that particularly impressed me by crystallizing aspects of what I was discovering about the East and the West were not included in the book. The next story is among them.

## *The missionary*

I hadn't expected to find another foreigner in the town of Ching-si. Actually, it was hardly a town but a fairly large village on the edge of the Gobi Desert, square, enclosed by high walls, and built in the compact geometric pattern of all villages in the northwest of China. It had an inn, several shops selling furs and felts, because it was on the only road connecting China with Sinkiang and Tibet, and some good restaurants to accommodate the travelers along that road. This slight edge of prosperity over yet more remote villages gave Shing-si animation and made it a logical place for the weekly mail truck to halt overnight.

I had been riding for some days on the mail truck, returning from Mongolia to Lanchow to rejoin friends with whom I was traveling in China. I have an amateurish interest in caves (preferably old, always with either painting or sculpture inside) and had spent the previous few weeks on a side trip of my own, journeying to the famous and fabulous Buddhist caves of northwest China, at Tunhwang, which are certainly old (fourth to eleventh century A.D.) and were decorated with both painting and sculpture by the Buddhist pilgrims to ensure their safety when they traveled the old silk route to Persia, centuries ago.

By the time I reached Ching-si, an interest in caves had begun to seem a feeble reason for being in that part of the world in midwinter, although when I had first decided to make the trip it had seemed silly to miss so good an opportunity. With the encroaching Communist armies taking over more of the country every day, when would there be another chance?

I was exhausted from the ride over the raw roads, frozen from the bitter blizzards of December, and my knowledge of Chinese, scanty at the best of times, had begun to desert me entirely. In the hope of finding something even slightly familiar in the village, and because

I felt very far from the places I knew, surrounded by strangers, I asked the driver of the mail truck, as we neared the village, if there were any foreigners in the town—"*Wai-guo ren yo mei-yo?*"—in an appalling accent. There was the usual delay while my question was relayed to the mechanic, the postal official who traveled with the truck, and a couple of passengers who, like me, had bribed their way into a ride. Finally, one of them answered, "There is one woman."

At the Ching-si post office I asked again, and there the matter took on the proportions of a theatrical performance. The postmaster chattered to the driver of the truck in northwestern dialect, and the passengers stood about making comments and occasionally smiling encouragingly at me. Then the postmaster invited us all to have a cup of tea with him. He occupied a little house behind the post office, and it was arranged in the usual Chinese way. Across one side of the mud-walled main room was the *k'ang*, a low, earthen platform that serves as a communal bed and that can be heated by lighting a fire underneath it. There was no *k'ang* fire now, because of the shortage of fuel in that barren part of the country. Our hosts were waiting for the extreme cold of January before they lit it; instead, there was a charcoal brazier on top of the *k'ang*. We all clustered around it. There were no decorations on the walls and, apart from a rickety table in one corner, there was no furniture. Stacked against the walls were sacks of meal; strings of garlic and red peppers hung from the ceiling.

The postmaster's wife brought in tea. She was much younger than her husband, wore the usual padded blue cotton trousers and jacket, and seemed intensely amused by the sheepskins and rough peasants' clothes of my two fellow travelers on the truck, and, I suppose, by their countrified manners, which must have seemed to her, a citizen of a town, hopelessly provincial. She served no food —it was too hard to come by in that area—but we had plenty of tea, in bowls we all held in both hands, and discussed the problem of my going to see the foreigner. Eventually the postmaster's young son was assigned to take me to the foreigner's house.

The two of us walked down the main street of the town. People standing in doorways of shops and behind road stalls watched our progress and stared at me. The boy was kept busy shouting explanations of who I was and what I was doing in Ching-si, while I dodged around the lines of donkeys and the yak trains that were coming into the town in the evening.

The foreigner's house was mud-walled, like any other, and had a scarlet door opening onto a courtyard. From a shack at the side of this yard came smoke and the smell of something cooking. It was then that brilliant-purple moment of a desert evening when light rises all around you and the night will come suddenly in a few minutes. The cook stood at the door of the shack and shouted at my small escort. He shouted back. The cook shouted again, and the small boy looked at me and pointed to the front door of the house. I gave him some money and smiled at the cook. He, too, pointed to the door. It was too cold to stand about outside, so I walked straight in.

In front of a tiny charcoal brazier a woman sat with a Bible in her lap, her finger marking the place she had evidently stopped reading when she heard the shouting outside. She must have been somewhere in her sixties; she was wearing an old tweed suit and had a black knitted shawl wrapped about her head. It took her a second to focus her eyes and see that I was a stranger. Then she jumped up and came toward me, a stocky, graceless figure, with her hand out.

"Do forgive me," I said, "for marching in on you like this with no warning—"

"Oh, please!" she said in the breathless voice of a little girl. "Such a pleasure—and a fellow *American*—"

"No," I said, "I'm—"

"But at least you speak *English*. Why, come in, child. Look at the state this room is in! You look chilled to the bone. Come close to the fire."

"Thank you. I'm just in Ching-si for the night, on my way to Lanchow. They told me there was a foreigner in town, so I thought—" I stopped, partly because I wasn't very clear *what* I had thought (that I would find some vague reassurance, perhaps, from speaking a language I knew) and partly because the woman wasn't listening to me at all. She was busily putting more charcoal on the brazier, straightening a lace doily in the center of her table, and trimming the oil lamp. In her manner there was a curious combination of absent-mindedness and fussiness.

"Please don't bother," I said, "I just came–"

She looked up. "You're *not* American."

"No. I was saying–"

"Then you're English. I might have guessed by the accent."

"No, I'm Indian." I told her my name.

She told me her name, which, for the purposes of this account, I shall say was Mildred Wiltsey. Then she sat down slowly, smoothed her skirt over her knees, leaned forward, and said, "Tell me–" she paused, and her fussiness vanished, a look of calm intensity coming into her face–"have you been washed in the Blood of the Lamb?"

"I beg your pardon?"

She had the wide, beautifully dreamy eyes of myopia. She gazed at me in silence.

I wondered if I had heard her correctly, but, to be on the safe side, I said, "I am a Hindu."

"Oh, my dear!" she said, with all the warmth and sympathy in the world. "You poor child!"

"Well . . ." I said.

Miss Wiltsey patted my knee comfortingly. "The good Lord never gives a burden without the strength to bear it." Almost without a change of tone, she went on, "How too bad that you are only staying the night. People visit such a short time these days. When I was a child, in *my* part of the country we never did look on it as a visit unless folks stayed a month–unless, of course, we were just calling on acquaintances in the afternoon. Why don't you just sit and warm yourself while I fix the spare room for you?"

"Please," I said quickly. "You really mustn't bother. I'm going to stay at the inn."

She turned sharply in the doorway. "Why, I never heard of such a thing! You'll be sharing a room with *Chinese!* Chinese *men,* I mean."

"Yes, but the inn is outside the town walls, and the mail truck leaves before dawn, so I can't stay inside Ching-si, because the gates won't be open in time."

Miss Wiltsey wasn't exactly satisfied, but she decided to let the matter drop, saying only that she would pray for me. With a return to her former concern, she asked if I had eaten.

During the walk from the post office to Miss Wiltsey's house, I had planned in my mind that if the foreigner was at all congenial, I would ask her to dine with me at one of the local restaurants. I had thought it would be nice to chat casually and pleasantly—two strangers together in a cold and foreign country—about the desert, the people, the vagaries of the Chinese character, the delights of Chinese food, with, possibly, a few reminiscences of home and background.

I said to Miss Wiltsey, "I was thinking of eating at a restaurant. Is there a specially good one?"

"I have never eaten at a restaurant here." She turned away modestly. "My digestion—I don't think it could stand Chinese food."

Astonished, I asked, "But what do you live on out here?"

She smiled. "You mustn't feel sorry for me. I can buy chickens, and eggs. I've taught my cook how to prepare them. I wonder, have you visited in America ever? In the South, we have wonderful ways of fixing chicken. Of course it's not the same here, but I ask the good Lord to give me patience. My cook tries his very best. Chinese carrots and cabbage are almost the same as at home, but bamboo shoots . . ." She shuddered.

Somehow the vision of Southern fried chicken in northwest China was too much for me. I said, "I wouldn't dream of bothering you. Can't I persuade you to join me for dinner?"

I sensed that something else was on her mind. At last, with some embarrassment, she said, "I wonder if it will be all right for two ladies to dine alone in a public restaurant?"

"I think that when one is traveling, it is permissible," I said carefully.

Finally, Miss Wiltsey agreed to sit with me in a restaurant while I ate. She bustled off on thick legs to collect her outdoor clothes and left me to gaze around the room. She had made it as nearly American as she could. Coarse blue Chinese cotton hung over the small, high window as a curtain. The round table in the center of the room was covered with a dark-green plush cloth with a fringe of tassels around the edge. In the middle was the lace doily, and on it the lamp. The two chairs were straight and wooden, and obviously had been made by local carpenters, but each had an embroidered thing like a pillowcase covering its back, as some dim reminder that, in another country and another generation, upholstery had to be saved from the brilliantine on the hair of gentlemen callers. On one wall hung a large framed print of a haloed shepherd and a lamb. Opposite it was a sampler on which was picked out, in faded cross-stitch, "AGATHA WILTSEY. 123456789. JULY 1870. GOD IS GOOD."

Miss Wiltsey returned wearing a heavy coat and carrying a small parcel. Outside it was now dark, and we set off at a rapid pace. In the evening the life of Chinese families turns inward. Shops are shuttered and present blank wooden surfaces to the street. Children are called into the courtyards of their houses. The bright doors are closed and only an occasional gleam of light shows where a fire is burning for the evening meal, or a stray shout or burst of laughter announces that children are still awake. The restaurants are the only inviting, active places. When we entered the first one we came to, the Chinese diners gave us their usual stare of unconcerned inquisitiveness. Although Miss Wiltsey's face was bright red from the biting cold, I could tell that she was blushing.

The restaurant consisted of one large room with mud walls and floor, rather more open to the street than is usual in Chinese buildings. There were about eight bare wooden tables, each surrounded by stools. Along one side of the room was a long cooking bench, and on it were four charcoal braziers and several trays of sliced vegetables and meat. Hanging from the ceiling above it were strings of dark-brown dried chickens, sausages, dried vegetables, and ginger and other roots.

The tables near the cooking bench—and the heat from the braziers—were monopolized by families with children, all eating earnestly and silently. In one corner, there was a large group of soldiers drinking and gambling, and talking in shrill, excited voices. And, of course, there was the inevitable quota of the mangy dogs that cower through the streets and houses of every Chinese village, screaming hysterically when they get kicked, fighting over any scrap of food that is dropped, and even lapping at the dregs from teacups, which people casually dump on the floors of restaurants.

The restaurant keeper and an assistant were busy behind the bench. When Miss Wiltsey and I sat down at a table on the cold side of the room, the proprietor came over and asked what we wanted to eat. I ordered rice, chicken, and peppers, and a cup of the strong liquor distilled from kaoliang.

The man had just begun to ask the familiar questions about where

I came from and what I was doing in Ching-si when Miss Wiltsey cut him off politely, saying, "I will not be eating, thank you." She produced her parcel from her lap, unwrapped it, and placed neatly on the table four boiled Chinese carrots, brilliantly red and somehow out of place in that dingy room, two hard-boiled eggs, and a boiled onion. Next to them she set out, with care and obvious pride, a silver spoon and fork. She then sat back to wait until my food was served.

I picked up the spoon and examined its ornate, scrolled-and-flowered handle. "How pretty," I said.

"They were my mother's. They were sent to me when she passed on, nearly twenty-five years ago."

"You were in China then?"

"Yes, indeed. I've been here thirty-three years. But at that time I was in the Mukden area. Of course, when *They* came we had to leave." She closed her eyes and placed her fingers on the bridge of her nose, as if she had a headache.

"The Communists?"

"We stayed as long as we could. It was terribly discouraging to think that all our work should be lost just because of a few wild heathen."

"I can imagine," I said, impressed that the Communist armies should be dismissed like that.

"But I managed to save some of my mother's things—the silver she was given for her wedding and her big lace tablecloth. I don't have much occasion to use it here. I just about never have company." She looked at me almost shyly. "I guess it seems worldly to think about those things when I am engaged in the Lord's work, but a person likes to have a few familiar things around, just to remind them of home."

There was wistfulness in Miss Wiltsey's voice, but no self-pity. I asked whether she ever got lonely, and she replied, "The Chinese don't seem to believe in calling at people's houses. But perhaps it is all to the good. A Chinese oven is mighty hard to bake in."

"I mean don't you ever want to go back to America?"

She said with surprise, "Why, we get to go home every few years. But China is my *life* now. I just can't imagine leaving." She seemed embarrassed, and I certainly was. One's social training gives no formula for dealing with courage in chance acquaintances. One can't congratulate them, and at the same time one feels that it shouldn't go unsaluted.

To change the subject, I asked whether Miss Wiltsey's mission had made many converts around Mukden.

"Many Chinese came to our little hospital," she answered, "but the Chinese peasants are like children. So easily frightened. We couldn't persuade them to stay with us, to carry on our work. We tried with all our hearts, and when we asked them to keep the school and the clinic open after we left, they said why of course they would. But you can't trust them any more than you can trust a child. I used to teach them just as I would Sunday-school children at home. We treated them in the clinic, and when they were well enough to be convalescing, I used to tell them stories from the Bible."

"Really?" I asked, fascinated. "Did they have trouble understanding any of them?"

"Well, they certainly never said so, but I could never be sure that they really understood. Only once, a man—and he was a grown man, too—asked questions about the story of the Good Shepherd. He said that no good shepherd would leave a flock to search for one sheep. He said he was a shepherd himself, and he would never do it. He might send his son."

The food and the liquor were beginning to take effect. I was feeling warmer and was more than willing to dawdle over the last stages of the meal listening to Miss Wiltsey's story.

She told me about the day when they first received the news that the Communists had surrounded Mukden. "For a whole night I sat up praying and hoping for guidance. By the morning the Lord still had not spoken to me." In the end, the decision was made for her by the mission, which sent instructions for all the workers to leave. "I still felt that I should stay and teach the godless and the wicked. Finally, it was the way the Chinese behaved that made me content to leave. One by one they stopped coming to prayer meetings, and even to the clinic. Even workers we *trusted*, who had heard the Word and had been Washed, made excuses and left us." When Miss Wiltsey had been told that she would be evacuated by plane, she gathered a few of her mother's possessions and a few of her own.

"There is very little a person needs besides a knife and fork and spoon and something to wear."

"And then?"

"Why, then I made some sandwiches and went to join my brothers and sisters," she said.

The Chinese didn't show much interest either way when they left. At first she and some of her co-workers were stationed at Shansi. From there she came up alone to Ching-si.

"It's a frightfully desolate part of the country," I said, wondering whether, in a crisis, I would have enough presence of mind to make sandwiches.

"Our Lord suffered far greater tribulations," Miss Wiltsey assured me. "I, too, am a voice crying in the wilderness, but I must tell the Word to as many of these people as I can. It is their only chance of salvation."

"What about those who don't hear you?"

"You must remember, child, that God is *kind*. The Bible tells us that those who have not heard the gospel cannot be to blame. They will be beaten in hell with *few* strokes. It is those who hear and will not listen that will be beaten with many strokes."

There is the question that is traditionally asked of prostitutes and of people who have chosen evangelism for their career, because, I suppose, both in their different ways are objects of surprise and sympathy, and one assumes that some drama must have brought them to their present pass. Accordingly, I asked Miss Wiltsey how it happened that she had become a missionary.

"Why," she said, "I knew I had to pursue the work of the Lord from the time I was a child. One night I had a dream. We had been swimming that afternoon—the Williams girls, who lived next door, and I had gone down to the creek. It was against our mothers' orders, because we weren't supposed to go where the village boys might see us. That night I dreamed about it. I dreamed that I swam and was caught in a mighty whirlpool, and I sank and sank, and I drowned. All was blackness and swirling water, and then, after I was dead, I came face to face with God. There He sat, in His great radiance, and I was very scared. 'Please,' I said, 'let me go back to earth.' And in a great, shaking voice, God said, 'A mortal lives but once.' 'Please,' I begged, 'I promise I will be good. I promise I will do whatever You say.' Again the great voice said, 'A mortal lives but once.' Again I begged and promised to devote my life to His service, and again the reply came back, 'A mortal lives but once.' At last, when I thought there would be no answer to my pleading, God gave me another chance and sent me back to the world. Since then I have done everything in my power to prove worthy of His kindness. When I was a child I could only help by saving my pennies for other missionaries, but now I can give my life to the Lord's work."

So far Miss Wiltsey's story had had the flowing ease that constant repetition in her own mind must have given it. But now her voice caught. "I have tried," she said, deeply moved by her narrative, "oh, I have tried so hard to be a Christian. But it is so difficult to be sure that your work is pleasing." Tears came smoothly down her face. "How can you be sure that you are worthy? God has never appeared to me again. Is it because He is too displeased with me? How can I ask His indulgence again?"

I pushed my bowl of rice away from me. There was a burst of laughter from the soldiers who were drinking in the corner, and I looked nervously at the faces of the Chinese diners. "You mustn't be so upset, Miss Wiltsey," I said. "I'm sure God understands the difficulties under which you work."

She caught her breath. "You are right," she said. "I must believe in His mercy. Why should I, who have received the greatest gift of all—the gift of a return to life—why should I expect to be comforted as well?"

"Come," I said, in the voice of a trained nurse, "have a cup of tea with me and then we will go."

"How stupid of me," she said briskly. "I didn't bring it—my tea, I mean." It was almost without surprise that I heard her explanation. "My friends at the mission in Shanghai are very kind and keep me supplied with Lipton's whenever they can. They feel that anyone in this post deserves a few luxuries," she added apologetically. "They don't realize that I *want* the hardest jobs. I *choose* the most difficult places because I have so much to repay, and nothing but my greatest effort can repay my Lord. I will spread His word into the farthest deserts."

I quickly poured out a cup of tea and passed it across the table. "Try it. You'll find it's not as bad as you think."

She took a sip doubtfully and said, "Well-l-l," and then, "Mmm! It doesn't have much taste, but it *is* warm." She smiled. "You were at school in England? Was it a Christian school?"

"Yes."

"Was it Baptist?"

"Well, no. Actually, it wasn't."

"But you have heard the gospel of the Lord and you are not a Christian?" she asked, more severely.

"I'm not." I added, with an attempt at flippancy, "I suppose that means that I get the full quota of strokes in hell."

"Yes, I'm sorry to tell you it does," she said, "unless you repent your sins and join us."

"No, I don't think I can see my way to doing that."

"It will be a greater happiness than you can imagine," she said enticingly.

"No," I said. "Thank you just the same."

It was too cold to talk, and Miss Wiltsey and I walked silently down the road in the frozen starlight to her house, and we hurried in, breathless, to stand and shiver by the brazier. In the half hour that I had left before the town gates closed, she showed me her tiny dispensary, from which, with a few simple drugs and patent medicines, she tried to make her small indentation on the seething sickness and poverty of China. I thought of the millions of emaciated children with the scarlet cheeks and brilliant eyes of consumption, the syphilitic men in the bazaars, the worn women crouching in the huts, and listened to Miss Wiltsey saying, "I can't understand it, but they seem to have more faith in the magic and wicked, fake remedies of their own doctors—men with no qualifications. They only come to me when they can't afford the Chinese cures." And "I'm just terribly worried that we won't be able to get more supplies through from Shanghai."

I made some routine comment about how nice it was to have such a ready way to get to know the Chinese. Miss Wiltsey turned to me with some excitement. "Oh, if only they *would* let you get to know them, how much simpler my task would be! But the Chinese are very reserved. Do you know, this week, for the first time, one of my patients asked me to dinner at her house? If I can just get into their homes, it is so much easier to spread the Word."

"What was the dinner like?" I asked, with considerable curiosity.

"It's fixed for tomorrow," she said, "and I'm so upset. My good dress is terribly wrinkled from being packed so long. Let me show you." She hurried off, and returned with a dark-red velvet gown of a strange, old-fashioned pattern, with lace of a color that I think is called écru at the neck and wrists, and she also carried a thin blue pamphlet—the Gospel According to St. John. She pushed the book into my hand. "Certain passages are marked," she said. "Please read them carefully." Then she spread out the dress helplessly. "What do you do with velvet?" she asked.

"Steam it?" I said doubtfully.

When I was leaving, she walked into the courtyard with me, carrying the dress. I watched for a few moments while she spoke to the cook in his shack. With a look of absolute bafflement, he reached for a huge kettle steaming on the fire. I left her then, with a picture of that sad little scene in my mind—Miss Wiltsey, surrounded by clouds of steam; the billowing folds of the dress she would wear tomorrow for her first dinner party; the puzzled face of the Chinese cook.

At the Chinese inn outside the town walls, the innkeeper asked whether I had found the foreigner and had enjoyed my dinner. I said yes.

He said, "It is good to talk to your own kind in a foreign country." He smiled at me in a friendly way. Feeling suddenly at ease and comfortable, I smiled back and went to take my place on the large *k'ang* that I would share with two Chinese families.

As I took off my coat, I felt the blue pamphlet in the pocket. I thought of reading it, but the tiny oil lamp was too dim, and then, what would the Chinese think of reading in bed?

# FOUR

Our journey through Asia ended, of course, in India, where our party scattered. Faubion vanished into obscure south Indian villages and remote provinces searching for Indian dances. Now that his book on the Japanese theater was completed, he wanted to write one on Indian classical dancing and pursued it from Manipur, that magical state in the far northeast of India, tucked away in the corner of the Himalayas, to Cape Cormorin, the southernmost tip of the Indian peninsula. The others returned to their countries and jobs, while I, at first, stayed with my family in Bombay.

Once again it was a different India that now surrounded me. My father had returned from Washington and was now the Governor of the Indian Reserve Bank. My mother, still immersed in social and medical work, had now enlarged her interests to include one of India's most vital problems—population control. Conversation at meals was still one long series of discussions but now with different questions as their springboard. The old political arguments were, by now, largely settled by events: an independent, democratic India had to cope with a whole new set of problems. Could the country feed its people and would Prime Minister Nehru's GROW MORE FOOD campaign succeed? Other schemes should assist it. Would it be possible to establish family planning programs and clinics rapidly enough to take effect on the alarming swelling of population? Would the first five-year plan work? Were our economists good enough, experienced enough? Could we work out our dream of a mixed economy, partly private enterprise and partly state control? Could we, as a country and a democracy, survive if we didn't? Would the six hundred Indian princely states which had been incorporated into the Indian Union really accept democratic rule and constitutional monarchies? Or would there be subversion, unrest, rebellion? What about keeping law and order? What about Kashmir?

On and on the talk went until my head began to swim with the burst of new problems and new thinking in India. Betweentimes I was trying to write down my impressions of the Asian trip from an elaborate journal that I had kept. The excitement of my discoveries during the past two years, superficial as they were, proved so powerful that I decided to travel more widely in my own country, following up sights, aspects of life, ideas that had interested me in other Asian countries. I wanted to go to places I had never been before, to learn a little more about India purely for pleasure, to travel simply as a tourist, without a plan, just to see what I would find.

It was more than worth the trouble. I began to know some of the joys and amusements that India has to offer as well as the overpowering problems. Journeying slowly down the Malabar coast, taking small boats along inland waterways and lagoons, gazing at the ravishingly beautiful tropical countryside of luminously green rice fields and coconut groves stretched along scalloped white beaches, called to some small village by the thundering of drums in the middle of the night to see a dance-drama filled with gods and demons and heroic deeds, wandering through deserted palaces lost in the jungle, I decided that this was my favorite part of India. Later I traveled inland to the vast extraordinary ruins of Vijayanagar, once the capital of an empire, now a fantastic, carved, beautiful, scattered reminder of India's past glory and long history. I went on to the exquisite, sculptured jewels of temples in Mysore with their haunting record of India's heritage of art and music and dance, then south and west to Madras, the city where I was born, to find a different kind of Indian city life, a tough intellectualism, a religious orthodoxy, an exclusive, witty over-all personality, and the most impressive music I had ever heard in India. Here I was made aware on every side, by people, monuments and arts, of India's profound contribution to the world's philosophy and its basic great religions.

My excursions continued with visits to the great temples of Orissa, the celebrated caves of Ellora and Ajanta in Hyderabad, with stays in the elegant Rajasthan cities of the north, and all of them were interspersed with returns to Bombay and its curious, international, sophisticated, metropolitan life. There, a city poised between East and West was beginning to discover (or display) its own special identity. The contrast never failed to enthrall me.

We would wear our Indian saris to go to parties, but when we got there we would talk English because with Bombay's mixture of Gujeratis, Mahrattas, Tamils, Hindi-speaking people, English was apt to be our only common language. We would live in Western-style houses, but eat Indian food. We would work in air-conditioned offices, but be scornful of the British for being fussy about the heat. We were strongly nationalistic, but still managed to complain about all kinds of aspects of our new government. We would shock the orthodox by wearing the briefest shorts to sail across Bombay harbor to the great Elephanta caves, but delight ourselves with the magnificent Hindu carvings of gods and mythological scenes that we found inside. We were "modern" and defensive about it, and "traditional" and proud of it.

Several incidents remain in my mind from those days that are, to some degree, illustrative of the dual nature of life in Bombay. Once some friends of mine and I arranged a surprise party for the birthday of a middle-aged Indian prince of whom we were all very fond and who, we knew, loved entertaining and being entertained. This party happened to fall on a Monday, and when we telephoned him, as casually as possible, to ask him to come, he replied, equally casually, that he couldn't possibly manage it. Monday was his day for fasting and meditation, when he never saw anyone, never left the house, never answered the telephone. Didn't we know that? Please, would we forgive him for not having made this clear to us years ago. As I remember, we were disappointed but not astonished. It was easy for us to swallow in the same breath the idea of a day of retreat and a surprise party of a Western sort.

Another occasion, caught like a fly in amber in my memory, was when my sister and I, in our American car, on our way to the beach for an evening swim, passed a quarter of Bombay where a large number of Pathans (Muslims from the famous northwest frontier of what used to be India, is now Pakistan) lived. It was during the great Mohammedan festival of Ramzan, or Ramadan, and the stirring tribal dances with stamping feet and a hypnotic, pulsating rhythm formulated by drums and claps, danced only by men, was being performed. We stopped the car to see what the music and excitement were all about and, because we were Hindu, we were allowed to come into the enclosure and watch. Muslim women are traditionally forbidden to see these dances and the girls' roles are taken by adolescent boys dressed in flowing white skirts, plenty of hammered-silver jewelry and decorated headdresses. They whirl about with skirts and veils flying inside the circle of huge, bearded, stamping Pathans. It was a bewitching evening (we never did get to the beach) and even at the time I remember thinking that this was some kind of misty symbol of the new India—a religious Muslim ceremony in Bombay, Hindu girls permitted to stand (on the outskirts, admittedly) and watch only *because* they were not Muslim, a country, in short, dedicated to religious tolerance (in spite of the upheavals of partition), to the protection of minorities, to a civil and democratic government. I felt, that evening, very pleased to be even an insignificant part of it all.

A great part of my discoveries of India that year (not very original ones, goodness knows) were described in a long article I wrote for *Holiday* magazine and later reprinted as a book called *This Is India.* One of the Bombay interludes and some of the current Bombay atmosphere emerge in the following story.

## *The friendship of Albert Hall*

Everybody was drinking a great deal in Bombay winter before last. Prohibition had been set, appropriately enough, near April Fools' Day, so during the preceding four months all of us had been, as we said, "finishing up the stocks." Somebody had made the crack, which was quoted at every party we went to, that the government was taking the "pub" out of the republic, leaving us only a "relic." Before the city became a relic, we were all determined to empty our own and everyone else's cellars, and have nothing left to turn over to the government authorities on the sixth of April. On that date all surplus liquor could be confiscated, and unless one had a permit on medical grounds one could be arrested even for drinking it.

It was rather a Surrealistic time in Bombay. One went to a couple of parties every night during the week, and on weekends the parties began in the morning—beer or pink gins on the beach, beside swimming pools or tennis courts, in clubs, on sailboats in the harbor, and on picnics. After the Saturday races, people started drinking whiskeys or brandies or Tom Collinses while they were dressing for dinner. The drinking continued at somebody's cocktail party, at dances, and even in cars, driving home through the dim, deserted early-morning streets.

Normally, Bombay society is fairly formal. In the warm weather it is considered all right for the men to turn up at a party in bush jackets, although we Indian women usually wear saris, while the English and American women wear evening dresses. But that winter nobody seemed to care much. We went to dinners in slacks, and the foreign women's Paris and London gowns hung in their closets while they hurried off to parties in beach dresses or summer suits.

Another curious thing was that one received invitations from people one had scarcely met before. In Bombay, because supplies of foreign liquor arrived so irregularly, people used to buy as much as they could at a time. If you went to Europe for the holidays, you brought back a stock of wines. The desperate determination to finish it all had seized everyone, and so the parties were more than usually, as we used to say, "mixed"—meaning that Europeans, Americans, and Indians were all invited. Even in normal times Bombay, more than any other city, has a fairly free social exchange among the various nationalities living there, but our friendships with the foreigners were, until recently, rather remote. It was a short time, after all, since we had been on opposite sides of the political fence, and an even shorter time since approaching prohibition had brought us all together so frequently.

At the parties themselves, there was an atmosphere different from any other we had known in Bombay. Some of the foreign men whom I and my friends had never known well and had vaguely thought of for years as staid, rather dull businessmen would, around midnight, burst into song. More urging would produce from respectable English bankers imitations or half-remembered variety turns from the music halls of a London of twenty-five years ago. Women one had connected inescapably with fund-raising activities for St. George's Hospital, or with a good, brisk game of golf in heavy shoes, would suddenly do wild rumbas, or even, on occasion, sing operatic arias. There was a kind of young Englishwomen whom we used to call, among ourselves, *Splen*did Girls, who were always very proper, and even they would sometimes be seen, at these parties, flirting with somebody else's husband.

It all seemed curiously abandoned, and somehow embarrassing, because that kind of unself-consciousness is something that the English usually reserve for their own kind and rare occasions. I suppose it might have been pathetic, too, in a way, but we had never learned to feel the pathos of the colonial exile. To us, prohibition was something of a joke, a topic of endless conversation, a springboard for the inevitable criticism of the government, but not really too serious a change in our way of life or our activities.

It was through one of the unexpected invitations I've mentioned, at a fairly typical party, that I first met Albert Hall. And now, in retrospect, I find that in my mind those months in Bombay are indissolubly associated with him. It was after midnight, I suppose, because the usual floor show put on by the guests at the party had started. Someone was reciting "Flo-o-ora Macdonald, Flo-o-ora Macdonald," and I had heard it just too often at previous parties to be able to listen and laugh and applaud again. So I picked up the drink I had been holding for some time, with its melted ice and flattening soda, and wandered out onto the terrace for a cigarette in the chill night, away from the flushed whiskey faces.

I had been sitting in one of the low cane chairs only a few seconds when I heard a young English voice from the next chair say, "What *is* it about an Englishman that makes him want to sing a comic song —preferably in a funny hat—the minute he gets a little tight?"

I was impressed with the sobriety in the voice, and something that, to my surprise, sounded close to bitterness. "Well . . ." I said uncertainly.

"They make such *fools* of themselves."

A young man got up and stood staring through the big glass door into the room (where now someone was imitating a ballet dancer). In the light from the room, I could see his popping blue eyes shining in a kind of disbelief. He turned toward me suddenly. "We were introduced, but I don't suppose you remember. I'm William Hall." He paused. "They call me Albert, of course. Rather a bore, don't you think?"

"Yes," I said, giggling slightly. "It must be."

"A prep-school name. It's astonishing how they stick. I used to mind it."

I could imagine it very easily. He was exactly the kind of boy who would have been ragged at school—pale, with the fragile skin that colors easily and obviously, and thin, blond hair. And those rather demented-looking eyes couldn't have helped. The kind of boy, I thought, who probably wore extraordinary clothes at college and wrote denunciations of this and that for one of the college magazines. Albert, I could see, would be exactly the name they would pick for him. Albert Hall—that monstrous, fat wedding cake of a building would be the perfect term of scorn for the young Shelley.

"Isn't it a *farce?*" he was saying. "Here they are in *India*, and they might as well have never left Kensington."

"How long have *you* been here?" I asked, with some interest.

"Only a couple of months," he said. "Not yet 'pukka.'" He turned his attention to me for the first time and smiled.

"And you like it?" I asked.

"I couldn't say. I haven't been able to see anything of it yet. But I'm *going* to. I simply refuse to fall into this round of chota pegs and eternal counting of days until home leave. This is a country of history, of fantasy," he said with a touch of grandiloquence, "and I won't waste my time in a second-rate dream world." He stopped suddenly and asked, with some shyness, "Do you find that ridiculous?"

I assured him that I didn't, and inquired incidentally, to see whether my guess had been right, whether he had enjoyed his school.

"Yes," he said at once, then added, with a certain defiant honesty, "After I got on the cricket team, that is." He must have sensed my smile, because he told me seriously, "It meant a lot, you know, at school."

During that winter I saw Albert quite frequently, for a number of reasons. First of all, he had, in his own way, considerable charm. He couldn't have been much older than the young men from Oxford and Cambridge with whom I had gone out occasionally in London before the war, but he had a poise and a definiteness that I didn't remember in them. I wondered whether it was his experience with Arab troops in North Africa during the war that gave him his assurance (as well as his interest in Eastern people), or whether it was that young men these days seem somehow better able to order their lives, or whether it was simply that twelve years ago I was too concerned with my own problems of growing up to see other people clearly. In any case, Albert hadn't the nebulousness of those distant young men. Besides that, he had a rather appealing streak of naïveté in him, combined with a kind of honesty that I liked. And then I admired his defiance—and, inevitably, wondered how long it would last against the Bombay variety of cricket team.

But the thing that really started our friendship was the fact that my family's bearer's son went to work for Albert. For the first couple of months of his life in Bombay, Albert had been staying in what he called "a chummery, with three of the chaps from the office." "They'll be the ones," he had said cynically, "who in another ten years will sponsor me for membership in the Yacht Club, when we can all afford it." He had decided quite soon that he would never get to "know" India until he had a place of his own, where he could entertain Indian friends and also have quiet enough to pursue his study of Hindi. He had spent a few months at the University of London School of Oriental and African Studies, where he had started learning the language, but his firm had sent him to Bombay sooner than he expected.

Albert had searched around energetically for some time, and had finally managed to rent two rooms in the apartment of an Indian family. He had a separate entrance but no kitchen. A gas ring in his bathroom provided him with breakfast in the morning and tea on weekends, and the rest of the time he ate out or had food sent up from the neighborhood Irani shop.

He telephoned me one morning, soon after our first meeting, and asked how he should set about looking for a bearer. He said he didn't want someone who had worked for Englishmen before, because he expected to learn from his bearer about the country and practice his Hindi. Though he didn't say so, I think he wanted to show someone that his treatment of Indian servants was different from the usual foreigner's. Things like that are always, in India, arranged by somebody's knowing somebody else who knows of a servant. Accordingly, I told Albert that our bearer had a son named Ganesh, who had been trained in our house but had never had a full-time job outside. Would he like to hire someone with relatively little experience, and then only in an Indian house? Albert was delighted, and as soon as I had hung up I called in our bearer to tell him that I knew of a job for his son.

Ganesh was what we, in our family, used to call an "honest" boy —not because the question of stealing had ever, or would ever, come up (beyond, of course, the odd bits of food or coal that are almost an accepted part of a servant's right, and compensate in some measure for the low salary) but because he knew his work and did it conscientiously, and came from a family that we had employed for years and had reason to trust. He was about nineteen years old and good-looking in an unformed way. His most intense enjoyment came from classical Indian music, and sometimes, in the evenings, we would hear him singing softly in the servants' quarters, or see him in a far corner of the garden, teaching the gardener's children religious songs.

Ganesh's parents had arranged for him a betrothal to a suitable girl in his village, not far from Bombay, and as soon as he was adequately employed he would marry her. He had the dignity and the touch of arrogance typical of the men of his community—the Mahrattas, famous in Indian history for their independence and their great warriors. This meant that one couldn't correct him in public and, of course, couldn't give him orders concerning anything he already knew.

I told Albert all this, and advised him, as an example, that if he had only six glasses and had eight people coming for drinks, he should simply tell Ganesh the situation and leave it to his ingenuity to cope with it. He should not, above all, fine Ganesh for things he did wrong (as many foreigners did in India) but should give, as severely as necessary, a verbal correction—in private. A rupee might mean only ten cigarettes to Albert but to Ganesh it could easily mean having to postpone his wedding.

Albert, with his sense of fair play, made rather a point of wanting to give Ganesh Sundays off, and of outlining exactly how many hours he was expected to work, and on that, too, we had a consultation. Things like that work rather differently in India, I explained. If Ganesh wanted a few days off to attend to duties concerning his family's land in his village, or to take his place in any family ceremony, they must be given without question. On the other hand, if Albert had unexpected guests on Sunday, Ganesh would be perfectly willing to deal with them. His siesta should not be interrupted, but he could be asked occasionally to stay late at night for a party without offense. In India, the relationship between servant and employer is curiously flexible. While it has a certain intimacy, in the sense that an employer enters into his servant's life on levels that can range from medical care to settling family disputes, at the same time there are rigid barriers, which can't be crossed.

Things started very smoothly between Albert and Ganesh. I, naturally, got countless reports through the servants' grapevine, and even from Ganesh himself when he came to visit his mother and father in our compound. He liked the job; plans for his wedding were going ahead. Mr. Hall was a quiet man who read a great deal. His accent was atrocious, but he was trying hard to speak Hindi. He had few visitors. He had few complaints. He had many, many socks.

During the week I used to see Albert occasionally at parties, and he would say that Ganesh was exactly the kind of bearer he had wanted but that he found him reserved. Sometimes, on Saturdays, I would have tea with Albert instead of going to the races with my other friends. Early in the afternoon, Albert would have his Hindi lesson, and afterward I would join him and his munshi (teacher) for tea. Ganesh used to clatter gently in the bathroom and eventually produce cups of very strong, milky tea and some rather amateurish-looking sandwiches. The munshi, as an orthodox Brahmin, couldn't eat with a foreigner, so he didn't share the meal. He would settle back in his chair with his feet tucked up under him and his sandals placed neatly on the floor, rocking back and forth, discoursing with mild enthusiasm on obscure points of scholarship or the Sanskrit classics. They were pleasant afternoons: Albert frowning and trying to concentrate on the munshi's abstract, quiet voice, Ganesh humming distantly to himself in the other room, the clink of teacups, the breeze from the sea coming through the barred windows.

But more often I would use my family's car and chauffeur, to drive through the Saturday bustle of Bombay's streets, and Albert would say things like "It's magnificent! Why is the West so afraid of bright colors?" and "The *grace* of their walk! It must be something to do with not wearing shoes." He would stop before the most ordinary sights—women in a long procession, carrying baskets of sand on their heads to where some sort of construction was being done. He would tell me excitedly to look at the line of the back, the curve of the arm, the folds of the sari. In the car, he was always gazing out the window, watching and commenting.

Best of all he liked to watch the people on railway-station platforms. He admired the color of skin and of clothes extravagantly as we walked through the crowds or stared at the people patiently squatting near their bundles of bedding and their tin trunks, waiting for their train to come in. In the huge, echoing stations, the shouts of food vendors, the chanting of the little naked children, the cries from the men who owned the stands of painted wooden toys all delighted him. He asked eternally whether this costume signified any special part of India, whether that shade of brown skin placed a man as a Northerner or a Southerner, what the distinction was between various forms of turban, could you tell from a woman's jewelry what her caste was. I, too, was interested; there is nothing quite so flattering as being a guide, and few things as entertaining as seeing something you know well through sympathetic foreign eyes.

Once, at the station, we ran into Albert's boss. He was hurrying through the waiting room, a coolie trotting behind him, when he saw us. We pushed through the crowd toward him, because Albert said, "Better say hello to the old boy."

"Catching the Deccan Queen [the express to Poona]," Albert's boss said, and bowed formally, and with some surprise, in my direction.

Albert seemed to feel that an explanation was necessary, either of his own apparently aimless presence at the station or of the fact that he was there with me. "We just— We were just—" he said.

Fortunately, his boss broke in with "Got to rush." He put a hand briefly on Albert's shoulder and said, "You should get away some of these weekends. Do you good. Nothing like a breath of cool air in Poona."

As he turned away, Albert said, "Have a good time, sir," and looked at me with a suggestion of guilt.

That day, on our way home, another "incident," as I later classified such happenings in my mind, occurred. We were driving past an elaborate whitewashed arch, and Albert said, "What's that? Let's get out and see."

"It's the Mahalakshmi Temple," I said, detaining him. "Very dull. No decent sculpture–all modern cement."

But Albert insisted, and finally we went in. As a Hindu, I knew, of course, what was coming. As soon as we got beyond the first courtyard, the Brahmin priest rushed out from his prayers and waved us away. I tried feebly to argue with him and said something about here was a friend who had come thousands of miles to learn about India; surely we could let him *see*– The priest looked closely at me and interrupted, "Your family lives near here, and even your servants come here. They at least have a respect for their religion."

"Might as well go," I said to Albert. "I knew this would happen."

He looked disappointed, and for the first time I saw his defiance take a new direction.

A few days later Albert told me, with some enthusiasm, that Ganesh had asked him for permission to leave early one evening the following week to hear a very famous singer, who was coming to Bombay and would be performing somewhere in the suburbs. Albert had asked if he could go along. He had never been to an Indian concert and was especially looking forward to going with Ganesh, who seemed so keen on it. Ganesh had agreed to take him. Albert added, "I don't know if that is one of the recognized 'times off' or not."

I forgot about the concert entirely until I met Albert at somebody's house a week or so later. He said to me, "You know, I can't understand it. Do you remember that concert Ganesh and I were supposed to go to? Well, it happened two days ago, and he never took me, and he never asked for the evening off."

"Did he go himself?" I asked, knowing, of course, that he had, and wondering how to explain to Albert that Ganesh wouldn't want to take him, that privacies vary so enormously from country to country.

"When I asked him about it, he said it was already over. He *must* have been to it, because he said it was very good."

"He probably thought you were tired, or wouldn't want to sit on the floor for so long, or something," I said, looking for a way to change the subject.

"But he might at least have *asked* me."

"Oh, well." The last thing, I thought, that Ganesh would have wanted would be to share so intimate an experience with a foreigner. Doubtless he had put in a full day at Albert's and gone to the concert late. I said, "He probably has his own friends and had arranged to go with them."

"Yes," said Albert rather sadly. "I suppose so."

It took some weeks for me to notice the changes in Albert. He was losing some of his definiteness, for one thing. At first, it was only that he seemed to prefer staying in his own rooms for tea to driving about Bombay. I assumed that the novelty of the Indian streets and their people was beginning to wear off, or even that the old munshi's measured sentences were proving more exciting than the ordinary life of the city. Then, again, I noticed that he was watching Ganesh with closer attention than before. I would have thought that he was watching with a more critical eye if it hadn't been for the fact that there seemed to be a strange discomfort—too light to be called fear—in his manner. Everything else seemed the same. Ganesh still gave me his reserved greeting when I arrived, rather like a child acting out a formal part in a play and being careful not to smile. The munshi still swayed in his chair and wrinkled his forehead under its elaborate load of religious marks and ash.

On one of his frequent visits to our compound, Ganesh mentioned, in passing, that Mr. Hall was more irritable lately. He thought it was because the hot weather was coming on. Then he went on to talk about his wedding, which had been set for the end of April, partly because it was an auspicious time, according to the horoscopes of the pair, and partly because my family and I would be going away for the summer, and so his parents would be free to make all the necessary arrangements and ceremonies.

One Saturday I went to Albert's flat, to find that he had invited, as well, one of the *Splen*did Girls. She was not quite as clear-eyed and direct as some of them, but she still somehow gave the impression of having just come off a hockey field. One way and another, it was an uncomfortable afternoon. The munshi sat and smiled and made loud sucking noises with his teeth and seemed his usual calm self, but he didn't talk at all. Albert seemed ill at ease, and only the *Splen*did Girl chattered away, about happenings in Bombay, recent parties, a projected trip to Kashmir, the approaching heat, and, inevitably, prohibition. "*What* Bombay's going to be like I can't think," she said. "I suppose there must be some point to it, but I'm sure I can't see it. Can you?" She addressed herself politely to the munshi.

The old man smiled and didn't answer. Albert colored. He knew, of course, as well as I did that the munshi, like most of the conventional members of India's older generation, would be horrified at the idea of being expected to drink.

The *Splen*did Girl continued, "What are people going to *do?* What *will* the parties be like with one lemonade? It simply means that there will be an enormous black market."

It was all chatter I had heard before. I remembered discussing it with Albert. What, indeed, *would* they do without that synthetic sense of companionship? When they looked at the flamboyant Indian sunsets without a glass of whiskey, how *would* they still the urgent longing for gray evenings and the familiar intonations of a known language? How *would* they, at parties, keep from seeing in each other's faces the frustration, the emptiness, of their common life in exile? Would it be a disease, an epidemic, implacably affecting them all and forcing them into a solidarity of a new kind because the old was no longer possible?

"I know," she was saying, "there will be rations for all of *us*, but what's the use of a couple of bottles a month? And even that's bound to be cut down."

We all took a deep breath and relaxed somewhat when the munshi, rather earlier than was his custom, got up and left. Albert became more talkative, and said, almost apologetically, to the *Splen*did Girl, "He's really a very interesting chap, you know."

"Yes?" she said. "Yes, I dare say." And then came the expected remark, "Well, it's after sunset."

Ganesh produced a bottle of whiskey and some soda. He asked me in an undertone what proportions were used, because he had never had to prepare a drink for Albert or done "drinks-work" in our house; that had been handled by his father. The bottle of whiskey must have been bought specially for this occasion. When he left to fetch the glasses, Albert said tightly, "Why doesn't he ask *me?* Does he think I won't understand?"

Ganesh returned, and the drinks were poured. "Well, cheers," we all said, and waited for the ease and the friendliness that would come.

I left fairly soon after, and Albert said quickly, "We'll see you home."

I said, "Oh, no, please don't bother," but they insisted, and the two of them left me on my doorstep, saying that they would see me the following day at some party.

Early in March, the clear, brilliant winter weather of Bombay came abruptly to an end and the more sluggish days of warm weather slowed the pace of the city. The parties, however, continued, because by then the momentum was too great and the time before April was too short for them to ease off with the decline of the Bombay "season."

Once Albert telephoned to cancel a Saturday-afternoon date. He said he was going to the beach for the weekend with some colleagues from his office.

"How dreary for you," I said.

"Oh, well. One might as well keep up with them. It's expected of one. After all, I have to work with them every day, and—" he seemed very far away—"well, they aren't bad chaps."

"No, of course," I said, listening to his change of tone. "You sound strange."

"It's this damn heat, I suppose. I'm not used to it."

"And all this greasy food?" I supplied.

"Yes, I dare say." He sounded startled.

"We'll have tea another time," I said, finally, feeling a little ashamed of myself.

"Oh, yes," he said at once. "Yes, I hope so."

I hung up, vaguely depressed by the relief in his voice.

The next Saturday, however, Albert invited me to tea again.

When I arrived at his little flat, the old munshi was joking with him in his pedantic, inept way, about his lack of concentration on his studies. Ganesh had let me in with his careful formality. Albert jumped up to shake hands. He looked hot and rather distracted. The old man made his usual *namaskar*—the Indian greeting of folded hands. The curtains hung limp at the windows, and the room was filled with the saffron heat of the afternoon sun.

"Ganesh is going to get married," Albert said, almost immediately.

"Yes, I know. At the end of April."

"The life of man," said the munshi, "is divided into five parts—"

"He couldn't have picked a more inconvenient time!" Albert said tensely.

I couldn't quite understand what was wrong. "Well," I said slowly, "it's auspicious, and—"

"Yes, yes," Albert said, controlling himself. "He shall have the time off."

From where I was sitting I couldn't see the bathroom door, but apparently Albert could, because his eyes kept flicking toward it and away. The munshi was continuing his speech about the ages of man, and I could distantly hear the familiar humming and clatter from Ganesh.

It was hot in the flat, and I suppose Ganesh must have taken his shirt off in the stuffy bathroom while he was boiling the water, because suddenly Albert broke out with "Damn it, Ganesh, put your shirt on when you work here!"

There was only a couple of seconds' shock and embarrassment before the munshi picked up his sentence, now with his eyes fixed on the ceiling. I was staring hard at the munshi, but I was aware that Albert was blushing. The humming had stopped, and in a minute or two Ganesh brought out the tea things and with great deliberation served us.

I saw Albert a few times after that. Once or twice at the final, hectic parties in the last week of March. In one of those crowded rooms, he raised his drink to me from a far corner, and then frowned, in what looked like uneasy surprise, at the whiskey and put it down without sipping it. Possibly he wondered, as I did, at just what point things had started going astray. Then it was April, and in a few days prohibition had arrived, and somehow there just didn't seem to be any occasions at which we met. One of Bombay's stranger periods had ended in a jangle of hangovers and empty bottles, and we went back to the old pattern of moving in our own circle, seeing the people we had known for years, going to the houses of old friends. It was all, once again, familiar and ordered.

# FIVE

When my uncle, Sir Benegal Rau, was appointed Indian representative to the United Nations and the first Indian delegate on the Security Council, I found an excellent excuse to return to America. I had, by then, an incurable addiction to travel, and besides, I longed to see New York again, a city that had bewitched me from the moment I saw it on my first vacation from Wellesley.

The city was as stimulating and as continually electric as I remembered, though much of my time was spent on Long Island, where the United Nations was quartered until its Manhattan center was built. There I listened to countless sessions and debates, and eventually to the Security Council proceedings on the war in Korea. Between times I was making my first attempts to write for *The New Yorker* and in that way came to know Harold Ross, the distinguished editor of the magazine.

Like so many other writers, I learned more about clarity in prose from his celebrated marginal queries—"What mean?" "Why?" "Who that?"—than anyone else had been able to teach me. I can see him pacing across my uncle's living room, smoking incessantly, drinking nothing but plain water, assuring us, "I'm nothing but a circus manager. I can tell a good highwire act or a bad clown or a mediocre lion tamer. I can't do any of them myself." I can also remember the bewilderment of my uncle, who had been brought up in a quieter, more academic tradition. He had been expecting to meet a *literary* man.

The first time Ross came to dinner I was in a nervous panic at the thought of entertaining so great an editor. I had asked my uncle's Indian cook to produce the very best meal in his repertory. Accordingly, he shopped for spices in the Puerto Rican section of New York, found green ginger and fresh coriander in Chinatown, chilies, cuminseed and countless other ingredients in Harlem, so that everything, in the Indian way, would be freshly seasoned. Dried spices, he warned me, lose their flavor. He cooked a number of different kinds of curry. He covered the elegant pilau with paper-thin beaten silver as a proper salute to a grand occasion. (You eat the silver, though you don't taste it. It is supposed merely to present a festive appearance.) He concocted a number of Indian sweets, fried in butter, rich with nuts.

Ross could eat none of it because he was already suffering from the ulcers that later turned out to be the cancer that killed him. My uncle and I, deeply embarrassed, ate our way through our elaborate dinner while Ross ate poached eggs and a glass of milk and talked without stopping until the coffee cups were cleared away and we could forget our gaffe.

Afterward the cook said, "Americans have no manners."

"Mr. Ross *couldn't* eat your food," I explained. "Doctor's orders."

"He should have made a pretense," he said stubbornly. "Everyone would understand that."

"But he *couldn't*–"

"It is a question of dignity. One can't honor a guest with poached eggs."

"Oh, I'm sure he didn't take it as an insult."

"I am not speaking about *his* dignity, but about mine."

"Oh, well," I said, and gave up.

"Even an omelette is better," he announced scornfully.

Heady and exhilarating as my renewed acquaintance with America seemed to me, one thing in my private life took precedence over United Nations matters and the unfamiliar world of writing for American magazines. I had a date with Faubion that summer to meet in Paris to get married.

We had settled on France as our rendezvous for frivolous and sentimental reasons. The first time that Faubion and I had met socially, and consequently had come to know each other, was at the house of our dear friend Jean de Selancy who was, during our years in Tokyo, the military attaché to the French Ambassador. Jean had said, casually and only half joking, "My middle name really isn't Cupid, but I do think you two should get married. It would be so amusing for your friends." As a result, Faubion and I had regarded each other with considerable suspicion for a long time.

Jean had returned to France and married a remarkable woman called Sylvie de Bertier de Sauvigny, who had distinguished herself with the resistance movement during the war and been decorated by the United States Army for her extraordinary service. She had also been elected mayor—one of the few women mayors in France—of her home village of Manom in Lorraine. In France a mayor has the authority to perform a civil marriage ceremony, so it seemed to all of us both logical and pleasing that Sylvie should be the one to marry us and complete a rather bizarre pattern of events. We soon learned that this was a somewhat reckless attitude.

The situation was stated to me bluntly by a Paris official as "a Hindu girl wishes to marry a Protestant in a Catholic country when one is a citizen of India, one of America, neither one of France. My dear young lady, clearly you enjoy complications." The performance was, indeed, more complicated than we had foreseen. It required a certain minimum residence in France, several weeks of paper work which involved, it seemed to me, every agency from the Indian Embassy to the Quai d'Orsay, arguments with mystified officials, countless permits, all of which finally led to a brief ceremony in Sylvie's office in the tiny mairie of Manom the autumn of 1951. There was one chilling moment after the papers had all been signed when the assistant mayor handed me a small red booklet entitled *Livret de Famille*. "In this," he told me, "you will find space to record the names of your first twelve children. When this is filled, please return it to the mairie and we will issue you another."

Afterward we drank a lot of champagne in the local bistro because, as Sylvie explained, the local residents were intensely inquisitive about this very odd marriage and had been gossiping about it for weeks. Naturally they wanted a seemingly unplanned glimpse of the principals involved and it was only fair to satisfy their curiosity. "It is," she insisted, "a question of good form."

The bistro was crowded and many people stared at us politely but with knowing smiles and nods, others came over to our table and offered toasts for good health, happiness and a "fecund marriage," or accepted a glass of champagne with a cheerful word or two of greeting. It was a charming and touching evening, but I couldn't help wondering what my grandmother would have thought of such a wedding party.

Faubion and I spent our honeymoon in Spain, where I discovered that his wedding present to me was a rather original one. He had secretly learned Spanish, and only when we crossed the border did I realize that he could break into torrents of Spanish. Unlike Faubion, I am very bad at languages, so, to a large extent, I owed whatever I learned about Spain to his facility and the small amount of halting, embarrassed Spanish I managed to pick up from him.

Spain would not under other circumstances have been my first choice as a place to honeymoon. I still remembered from my school-days my strong feelings of sympathy for the Loyalist cause and disapproval of Franco's regime. Our trip would mark my first taste of life in a fascist country. However, I wanted very much to continue writing for *The New Yorker* and Harold Ross had suggested that a "Letter from Madrid" might be a feasible idea for both of us. Faubion, in turn, was writing a series of articles on Spanish dancing. The combination involved us in a rather unlikely series of encounters which modified my feelings about Spaniards and their country without actually changing my feelings about their government.

First of all, I hadn't been prepared for the look of Spain—dramatic, severe, exhausted, studded with improbable castles, forts, cathedrals, with children in rags running barefoot through the villages, with beggars, with women who preserved their modesty behind screens. I suddenly thought I might be back in Asia. Driving over the Pyrenees, planning to spend our first night in Spain in Guernica (immortalized by the Civil War and Picasso's immortalization of the Civil War), we crossed the Spanish border at a tiny mountain frontier post. The first thin layer of snow had already fallen and the country had taken on a really desolate air. A member of the Guardia Civil, in his dashing uniform and black patent leather hat, asked us for a ride to the next village. In the course of this short journey down the mountain we asked and answered the usual boring questions of strangers traveling together. But two things he said stayed in my mind. One was the reason why the famous Guardia Civil hat is flat at the back and juts out in front. "When we fight we will not give up until our backs are to the wall and even the extra inch that the shape of this hat gives us is important." The other was: "There is only one thing to remember about Spain: it is poor, *poor*, POOR!" I felt confirmed in my impression that I had left Europe as I knew it and entered some other territory.

Even in Madrid I couldn't get the idea out of my head. From time to time through a break in the buildings or from a high window I could see the arid sierras and the barren plateaus that surround the city. It is a view that brings a consciousness of the countryside—a rare thing in a capital city and a continual reminder that Spain must live largely on the products of a thin, impoverished soil and that Madrid is a deceptive city.

Like any other visitor, I was impressed by the amount of new building—huge new banks, government offices, scarcely finished avenues and boulevards where Madrid was expanding—and by the carefully tended parks and gardens. We wandered through "old" Madrid, enchanted with the narrow sixteenth-century streets and the handsome Plaza Mayor, more aware of the history and the charm than of the poverty and crowded rooms that it represented. In the places where foreigners were likely to stay there was no shortage of food or accommodations. I was delighted with the pattern of a Spanish day because it reminded me so much of India—the late lunch, the siesta, the long evenings of visiting, of sitting in front of a café sipping sherry and watching the world go by, of strolling past shops open until nine and ten o'clock, and at last, when the heat of the day is over, eating dinner at ten-thirty, or going to the theater at eleven, or night club at two in the morning. It was a life composed of both ease and glitter.

It took me a little longer to realize that, except for a small group of rich and showy Spaniards, most of the people had little part in either the ease or the glitter. I became conscious of this "other Madrid" first, perhaps, through the curious floating population of little boys, those canny, ruthless, tragic children who have learned a word or two of English and are always underfoot, volunteering the exchange rate of dollars on the black market, offering to find you a hotel or guard your car or sell you a package of smuggled American cigarettes, or simply begging for money. They slept in hallways, under bridges, anywhere, and if you asked them where they lived they would say Seville or Cordova, easily accepting the fact that they were hundreds of miles from home, living on their wits.

In a night club, once, a waiter putting down our coffees and cognacs asked with the natural curiosity of Spaniards where we came from and added that most of the customers were Americans.

"No Spaniards?" Faubion asked.

"Very few. It is too expensive. These two drinks will cost you three times what a man earns in a day." The bill was eighty pesetas—two dollars.

A number of incidents large and small served to show us aspects of the "other Madrid," and I recorded one of them as a sort of short story called "The Spy."

## *The spy*

The only time I have ever been spied on was one summer in Madrid. I had always before thought of spies as shadowy figures in trench coats standing in doorways or leaning easily against the bar in the very best hotels. But my spy had a style of his own. He was a youngish, pale-brown man with an air of rather desperate discomfort, and light eyes blinking anxiously behind pink-rimmed glasses. I could never quite determine why he gave an impression of such seediness when, actually, he was dressed with pathetic care. I always saw him in the same neatly pressed dark woolen suit, sad and out of place in the heat of a Madrid August. His white shirt, a little tight around the neck, was clean; his black shoes were beginning to crack at the creases across the toes, but they were highly polished. Yet he looked somehow dusty, as if the air of respectability for which he strove sat uneasily on him. Possibly this was because he always carried a somewhat messy package wrapped in newspaper. I met him a couple of days after I arrived in Madrid.

My only letter of introduction to anyone in the city was to an art critic, Señor de Paez, who spoke no English. I had telephoned and made an appointment with him, and, the day before we were due to meet, had called at one of the offices of the Spanish Tourist Bureau to ask if they could find me an interpreter to take along for the interview. The official there was most helpful, and asked the usual questions about how long I had been in Spain and what I was doing there. He looked up rather sharply at one of my answers. "So you are a writer, señorita?" he said. "For newspapers?"

"Well, not exactly—"

"Ah, you write romances." He nodded, with a touch of scorn.

"No, no," I said. "I write travel books about different countries."

He dropped the subject at once and told me that his cousin's brother-in-law was free these days and would gladly act as my interpreter. He would be at my hotel at ten the next morning, a Friday.

It was eleven o'clock on Friday morning before the hotel desk phoned to say a gentleman was waiting for me. (One of the things about my spy that I finally came to accept with a sort of resigned irritation was his consistent unpunctuality.) When I got downstairs, I saw his tidy, nervous figure standing by the desk. He had a newspaper parcel under one arm.

"Good morning," I said briskly. "We'd better get started. We're late."

"*Cómo?*" He blinked several times, and then introduced himself formally, and at length, in Spanish.

"You do speak English, don't you?" I asked, with the gloomy certainty that, of course, he didn't.

He spoke slowly, still in Spanish. "No," he said. "Pardon me." Then he added eagerly, "You are going to the house of Señor de Paez. I shall accompany you."

It was already too late to telephone the Tourist Bureau and demand explanations. There must, I thought, be some simple Spanish logic behind the whole thing. This man was an intermediary of some sort, an escort, perhaps. Perhaps the interpreter would be waiting at the other end.

In the taxi on the way there I worked out the Spanish for "Do you work for the Tourist Bureau?"

"No," the young man said, and smiled encouragingly.

After another pause, "Where *do* you work?" I insisted.

He made a long speech in Spanish, in which I caught the phrase "the Ministry of Industries."

We traveled the rest of the way practically in silence. I stared out the window at the tangle of traffic and the pretentious buildings around the Puerta del Sol, glaringly clean and with a sharp definition of outline in the morning sunlight. It was still too early for the sidewalk cafés to be crowded, but beyond the old palace there was a lot of activity where some of the many new buildings of the city were going up. My companion told me timidly, "Madrileños say of their city, 'Madrid is never finished.' " He had a trick, when he made a comment, of waiting to see if you would smile before permitting himself to laugh.

"The buildings were destroyed during the Civil War?" I asked.

He looked depressed. "The government is building many new houses."

When we got to Señor de Paez's house, I asked the taxi to wait for me. There was no interpreter there, and the interview without one could consist only of making another appointment. In my halting Spanish, I tried to explain to Señor de Paez what had happened. This would have been difficult enough anyhow, but it was made much worse by my escort, who kept interrupting with complicated explanations of his own, which I didn't understand and which seemed to puzzle Señor de Paez, too. In the end, Señor de Paez said to me, very slowly and clearly, that he was having a party the next evening, at which there would be a young man, a Señor Martin, who spoke some French, as I did; would I like to come? I accepted with relief, and got up to leave. The spy accompanied me to the door. I pointed to the taxi and asked if I could take him anywhere. He said, "No, it would not be polite for me to leave now."

With a faint hope of getting some clue to the muddle, I asked, "Please, how much money do I owe you? Or shall I pay at the Tourist Bureau?"

But when he shook his head very firmly and with apparent disapproval, I realized that it was useless to look for a coherent explanation, and repeated one of the most useful phrases from my Spanish book: "I much regret being a cause of trouble to you. Thank you very much."

"For nothing, for nothing," he said grandly, and closed the door.

I suppose that a more diligent traveler than I am would search for the reasons behind the mysterious little episodes that happen in foreign countries. I am apt to lump them all together in a useful and comprehensive category called the Language Barrier. The official at the Tourist Bureau couldn't, I assumed, have understood English as well as he seemed to. Possibly he had thought I was afraid to find my way about an unfamiliar city, and had, with typical Spanish gallantry, called on one of his friends to help me out.

It wasn't until the next evening at Señor de Paez's party that the explanation began to present itself.

I arrived at the party at eight o'clock. The apartment, which had seemed large and dim by daylight, looked a little more cheerful that evening, although the salon still had that stuffy propriety that only a great deal of dark-red plush can give. On the walls were big, heavily framed oil paintings, and from the center of the ceiling hung a single naked electric-light bulb, which filled the room with an incongruous glare.

As Señor de Paez took me around the room, introducing me to each guest, I had the feeling that someone was walking just behind me. After I had mumbled and smiled at the last guest, I turned to find my escort of the day before standing there rather edgily, with his hand out. I shook hands with him and said, "I didn't know you were a *friend* of Señor de Paez."

"No," he said. "You have enjoyed yourself today?"

"I have done nothing today."

"You have stayed in your room and typed." He wiggled his fingers in front of my face to make his meaning clear.

"Yes," I said, first surprised and then cross. I would have liked to walk away, but since I knew no one else at the party, I stood staring resentfully at him. It occurred to me for the first time and with incredulous excitement that he might be a spy. He tried out one of his timid smiles and, getting no response, quickly withdrew it and led me across the room to the young man who spoke French.

Señor Martin was thin and handsome and, like everyone else that I had met in Spain, had beautiful manners. The spy and I sat, one on each side of him, on stiff little chairs, part of the large formal circle of guests. Everybody was talking quietly with his neighbors, except one man—a gypsy, Señor Martin told me—who sat alone playing small, spidery tunes on a guitar. In one corner of the room, on a table, there were bottles of red wine and plates of sliced sausage, tomatoes, and bread. Occasionally, people got up to help themselves and then returned to their seats and their conversations. While Señor Martin and I were talking, the spy watched us most solicitously, jumping up to refill our glasses, and each time making himself a neat little sandwich, which he munched with a slightly furtive air.

Señor Martin and I talked about the guests, most of them artists, and progressed from there to Señor de Paez, his collection of pictures, and the beauties of the samples displayed in the salon. These questions and answers moved at a slow pace, because everything had to be translated for the spy, who leaned anxiously across us, throwing in comments like "Spain has produced the greatest artists in the world" or "The Catholic Church has been the inspiration and protector of all great art." During one of his brief absences at the buffet, I asked Señor Martin whether the spy was a friend of his, but he just looked infinitely preoccupied and continued to talk about art as if he hadn't heard me.

It must have been nearly an hour later, after many of the wine bottles had been emptied and placed under the table, and when people were talking with more animation and more laughter, that the guitarist started to play and sing with sudden passion and authority. The thin ladders of notes climbed up and up, trilled, and sank, and all the gaiety of the wine drifted away and a delicious sort of sadness took its place, a loneliness that engendered an urgent camaraderie. People longed to talk about themselves; they grew more earnest and drew their chairs into groups. The spy said hopefully, "It is beautiful, isn't it?" He took his glass and mine to the wine table.

The gypsy began another song:

> Antonio has died [Señor Martin translated],
> Let us all gather together and cry.
> He lives in my heart.
> All that knew him will sing,
> We will sing to the Virgin Macarena.

The guests all applauded and cheered. Señor Martin said, "Antonio was a great artist, a great friend."

"A real person?"

"Oh, yes. Everything I know about painting I learned from him."

"You, too, are an artist?"

"Yes," he said. "A modern. I am not a Surrealist, though. I admire more Regoyos and Sorolla."

I had never heard either name before and acknowledged apologetically that I knew nothing about modern Spanish art.

"Have you not been to our Museum of Modern Art?" He seemed shocked that I hadn't, and offered to take me there the next day.

The spy returned with our wineglasses and a little sandwich just at the end of this conversation. "You are going to a museum?" he asked.

"Yes," I said, with a despairing feeling of being trapped.

"I will be at your hotel tomorrow at ten."

"You really mustn't trouble yourself," I said, trying to be firm in a language that is implacably polite.

"It is no trouble."

"You have already been too kind."

"No," he said, with finality. "I must accompany you."

Eventually, when I rose to leave the party, the spy asked, "You return directly to the hotel?"

"Yes," I said coldly, certain by now that he must be a spy, "I shall eat dinner there and then go to my room."

"Thank you," he said, in a tiny voice and with complete understanding of my tone. I suddenly felt sorry for him. And then I felt secretly and rather guiltily pleased at being important enough to be spied on.

I shook hands with Señor de Paez and with each guest, in turn, and found my way to the cool, dark street. From the window above, the clear voice of the gypsy sang a lament to Maria Dolorosa, and gradually, as I walked away, it became confused with other guitars and other voices, from the little wineshops, and with the chatter and bright bursts of laughter from the cafés, the traffic on the big boulevard, the bustle and the footsteps of the people taking an evening walk on the wide pavements. The shops were lighted and busy, the restaurants were preparing for their first customers, music poured from the open doors of the movie houses. It was the hour when Madrid is at its liveliest.

On Sunday morning I stood at the window of my hotel room staring out across the roofs of Madrid, a rosy, choppy sea that stretches out in wild confusion. I waited for the spy until half past ten, and then decided that I had been given the perfect opportunity to shake him off. He didn't know which museum Señor Martin and I were going to. He would not be able to follow, and I might have a chance to talk to Señor Martin without a distracting buzz of translations. I set out with the exhilarating feeling of playing truant.

Señor Martin was waiting on the steps of the museum. He shook hands, asked if I had enjoyed yesterday's party, apologized for the fact that the museum was crowded, because there was no entrance fee on Sunday, and, in a haze of conventionalities, led me in. We looked at a number of pictures, which seemed, to my untutored eyes, quite mediocre, but I couldn't really concentrate, because I was beginning to feel somewhat ashamed of myself. I kept thinking about my poor spy standing in the hotel lobby, distressed and unbelieving, while the porter told him that there was no answer from my room. I gazed in a trance of boredom at huge, dramatic canvases of historical scenes, moments of heroism, battles, and victories.

Señor Martin was telling me in endless detail the life story of one of the painters when, with a kind of relief, I saw the spy hurrying down the gallery, waving his newspaper parcel at us.

"I waited at the wrong museum," he said reproachfully.

"I'm sorry," I said, "but you were late."

"Yes, yes," he admitted miserably. "It is all my fault." After waiting at the Prado for half an hour, he had remembered that Señor Martin was fond of modern art and had guessed that we might have gone to another museum. He was so delighted at having found me that he chatted along amiably and quite incomprehensibly during the rest of our tour through the galleries of nineteenth-century pictures, which occupied a surprisingly large part of the museum. "Modern" was apparently a flexible term in Spain.

It was when we reached the more recent work that my irritation began to rise again. I had asked Señor Martin why, in a museum devoted entirely to modern Spanish painters, there was only one early, and bad, Picasso. The spy replied promptly, "Spaniards do not like Picasso."

"They do not like Dali, either, or Miró?"

"No. You see that there are none here."

"But even if you don't like their pictures–" I began, and then gave up, because my Spanish isn't equal to arguments of that sort.

I turned to Señor Martin to repeat my question, but the spy was determined that I should hear *his* explanation.

"The Spanish do not like Surrealism. We like simple art with much emotion."

In exasperation I said, "I think with Picasso it is politics."

"No, no. It is simply taste."

After we left the museum, both Señor Martin and the spy accompanied me back to the hotel. "What are you doing this afternoon?" the spy asked.

"I study Spanish this afternoon."

"You have a teacher?"

"No," I said. "That is, yes. I mean I don't need one–I have a book."

"I shall return to the hotel–" he began.

"This will never do," I said, in English.

"Will do, will do," he repeated anxiously, in English. "The Spanish is not *all* indisciplinated."

I couldn't help laughing, and he took that as a good sign. "At four o'clock," he said, and bowed.

For the rest of the three weeks that I was in Madrid, I saw my spy nearly every day, and in the end his neat figure carrying the inevitable newspaper parcel came to be inextricably connected in my mind with the summer city. I suppose in those early days I should have found some way of dismissing him. Certainly his slogans and solemn reciting of things the foreigner was expected to think bored me, and even as a guide he was really quite useless, full of misinformation, always getting lost, and keeping me waiting. But I did nothing about it, at first because I was rather flattered by having a spy of my own, and later because I had developed a sort of exasperated concern for him. If he was ever more than his usual hour or so late, I used to fret and wonder whether his extraordinary lack of organization had got him into trouble of some kind.

On the whole, I found it much simpler to tell him my appointments for the day than to let him find out from telephone operators, commissionaires, or taxi drivers, or whatever his sources of information were, because I couldn't stand the suspense of the time between my arrival at, say, the Cathedral of San Isidro and the moment when I would see him puffing down the aisle toward me, bewildered and upset. Under his patriotic insistence that I see the sights of Madrid, I became a far more dutiful tourist than I had ever been before, and we would have the Spanish lessons that he patiently gave me every morning in palaces, museums, gardens, and churches, which were, at least, cooler than the grilling city outside.

Often, exhausted by this combination of a foreign language and concentrated doses of culture, I would invite him to have a drink or some lunch with me at the hotel. He never had a meal with me, but sometimes he would accept the drink. Sitting stiffly on the edge of a chair in the lounge, his newspaper package tucked away behind him, he was never entirely at his ease, and would usually make his little joke: "Shall I order whiskey?" I would always laugh politely to show that I knew whiskey was so fabulously expensive compared with other drinks that only the very rich and foreigners could afford it. We always ended by having sherry.

Although I had oppressively many opportunities to talk to my spy, I never discovered anything very much about his life. He was always ready to escort me on any excursion at any time of day; he seemed to have no life or friends of his own. I thought that "looking after" foreigners must be a very dreary kind of job, and I tried, by taking long siestas in the afternoon and going up to my room immediately after dinner, to give him a chance to see his family or have some time to himself.

I asked him once if he was married.

"Not yet," he said casually.

"Are you engaged?"

"Yes. I have been engaged for six years."

"When will you get married?"

"It is not yet the time."

On another occasion, when I was invited for cocktails with some Americans at the Ritz, I asked him to come along, too. With an air of considerable confusion, he said he couldn't.

"Oh, do come," I said. "You can practice English, and it is better than to ask the bartender what we say."

"It is not that I am not pleased," he said formally. "But I cannot go in these clothes."

"I like your suit very much," I said, hoping that I had not shamed him but knowing that I had.

"My other suit is not real," he said.

"You mean you have no other suit?"

"Yes, I have, but it is made of paper." He said this with forced lightness and waited to see if I would smile. When I did, he considered the joke established and laughed himself. I wondered if being seen with me—a foreigner—meant that he had to wear his best suit every day, instead of the one made of what I assumed must be ersatz material.

Apart from occasional conversations like that, my spy remained a withdrawn, rather dull, mystery.

It was shortly before I left Madrid that the glittering summer heat broke. One morning, when the spy and I were seeing yet another monument, and I was repeating my overworked phrases of appreciation—"How beautiful it is!" and "That is truly magnificent!"—the thunder that had been muttering about for a couple of hours crashed immediately overhead, making people start and smile at each other. The spy and I stood in the shelter of the doorway, at the head of a long flight of marble steps leading down to the street, and watched the traffic slow down and the people hurry away. In the rain, Madrid becomes suddenly a shabby city. The awnings in front of the shops and cafés become dingy and slack, chairs and tables are stacked in a damp, abandoned line close to the walls of restaurants, the chill dripping from the trees on the boulevard makes untidy puddles of mud.

The storm didn't last very long, and soon the spy and I started down the steps. It was then that the thing happened. I slipped on the wet marble and would have fallen if the spy hadn't twisted round and gripped my arm. In his surprise and abrupt movement, the newspaper parcel flew from his hand and went bounding gently down the steps, unwinding as it fell. The paper blew away near the bottom of the steps. The spy and I stood staring with a kind of paralyzed concentration at the bread roll that had been in the parcel, as it spun slowly across the pavement toward the dirty water rushing along the gutter. It didn't fall in. The spy made a slight noise, something like a sigh, and we both walked on down to the street.

He picked up the roll and looked at it vaguely for a moment. At last, he smiled at me in his timid way, wiped the moisture off the bread, and put it in his pocket. He said, in an ordinary sort of voice, "It is bread from the ration. I bring it for my lunch."

"Only bread?" I asked, because those were the first words that occurred to me.

"In a *colmado*, I can buy a glass of wine and perhaps some sausage with it."

I didn't say anything. He continued rather wearily with his explanation, as though I were a particularly obtuse child. "Bread on the ration is four pesetas a kilo," he said. "But the ration is not sufficient. In this part of town, to buy extra bread–"

"Black-market bread?"

"Why not? It is ten pesetas a kilo. In the part of town where I live, it is eight pesetas, so I bring the ration bread and my mother and sister eat the other."

"Look," I said, filled with a confused wish to do something–cover my embarrassment, probably–"I'm poor, too. Let us eat lunch together."

"Poor?" he said, with a bitterness that startled me. "You are a foreigner."

"I can still be poor."

"With many clothes? Living in a hotel? Smoking American cigarettes?"

"But I don't drink whiskey," I interrupted, with an attempt at flippancy.

He smiled politely. "Will you do me the honor of having a glass of wine with me?" he said.

This was the first time he had ever invited me anywhere, and he took me not to one of the tourist restaurants that he had so often recommended but to a small, dark cave in one of the city's narrow side alleys. There we sat on a wooden bench and sipped sour red wine out of thick glasses. The place was cool and smelled of a musty damp. A few workmen in overalls sat at one table, exchanging shouted remarks with the bartender.

I didn't know how to return to the noncommittal conversations we used to have. I might have known that the inescapable courtesy of the Spaniard would rise to such an occasion. "Do not be sorry," the spy said encouragingly. "Spain is a poor country. It has always been so."

"I understand," I said, "but a government servant–" I wanted to say, "shouldn't have to scrimp over two pesetas for bread," but I didn't know either the words or that construction in Spanish, even if I had had the courage to say it.

He put in quickly, "I am more lucky than most. My job at the Ministry gives me eight hundred a month, and sometimes in my vacation month the cousin of my sister-in-law recommends me for a job like this." He had never before referred to his spying job. I waited for him to elaborate, but he only said, "Besides, we are a very small family."

"How many are you?"

"My sister and our mother."

"What does your sister do?"

"She cannot find work." He added irrelevantly, "None of us smoke."

I said, "What?"

"She sells our cigarette ration."

"On the black market?"

He seemed amused at my insistence. "Like everybody," he answered.

"But when," I asked, trying to work out his finances in my head, "will you get married?"

"At the moment, it is enough to live," he said easily. Then, with a sort of exhausted patience, "My brother is married and has children. He works in a furnace"–this took a certain amount of explanation, a little pantomime of how a fire is stoked, and the mask over the stoker's face–"and he is sick. He works fourteen hours a day and earns six hundred pesetas a month. His wife must take care of the children. It is not enough to live, but what can they do? How will they continue? They never"–he searched for something I would understand–"for instance, go to the cinema. He has not even taken the tram in to the Puerta del Sol once in the last year." He shrugged and said with no feeling in his voice, almost lightly, "You think everything in Madrid is beautiful. I could show you a Madrid that only Spaniards see."

"Why are you not angry?" I asked. "Why aren't all Spaniards angry?"

He repeated my question, not understanding it.

"I speak badly. Pardon me," I said, trying to find words to convey the idea of resentment. "Why do you not take money—steal it?"

At this the spy began to laugh. "It is easy to say steal a million pesetas from the bank, but where will I get the fifty céntimos for the tram fare?"

When the spy took me back to the hotel, I said, "I am going to a bullfight this afternoon. Tomorrow I would like very much to see the Madrid that only Spaniards see."

He looked at me in an entirely absent way and repeated his usual formula: "I shall be at your hotel tomorrow at ten."

I never saw my spy again. He telephoned the next day to say he was ill, and he sounded both ill and apologetic. He promised to call again, but he never did. I wondered whether it was embarrassment at the bread-roll incident or the fear, perhaps, that he had betrayed himself into the hands of a foreigner that kept him away. More likely, it was simply that whoever made such decisions had come to the conclusion that my activities in Madrid were too innocuous to deserve my spy's full-time attention. In any case, I was leaving Madrid a day or two later. I wanted to write him a note of thanks before I went, but I remembered then that I had never known his address.

From our window, early on those Madrid mornings, I used to watch the men and women from the country drive their donkey carts, loaded with vegetables, in to the markets. There was a great clatter and shouting, and the donkeys brayed with a wild hysterical sound. Later the housewives came to shop. They bought very carefully, examining each vegetable and haggling a long time over the price. All this, after my experience with my spy, was no longer a quaint storybook picture. It raised a question to which I never really got an answer: How did the Spanish people survive? Certainly they worked thirteen or fourteen hours a day in spite of union regulations, but that didn't bring in enough to feed them adequately. Admittedly everybody was a small-time black marketeer, but the commodity that was really being black-marketed was the individual's ability to do without. "Does nobody take action against the black market?" I asked an acquaintance.

"Who should take action?"

"Well, the police, the officials?"

"But the police are Spanish too. They must do the same thing to live."

Under conditions like these it seemed to me extraordinary that people could see the advantages of the situation. "The Spanish are wonderful people—anything can be settled for five hundred pesetas," somebody told me. Another recounted this little incident: "I was late getting started for an appointment, and the taxi I took turned up a one-way street the wrong way. The policeman stopped us and began to make a scene. I gave him a few pesetas and said, 'Perhaps this will make it all right.' He said, 'Perhaps you are not unreasonable. In another two hours the regulations change for the evening anyway.' I got to my appointment on time."

Although an easygoing attitude toward graft and black marketing seemed to be shared by both residents and foreigners in Madrid (at a time when you couldn't, by law, eat white bread in Madrid, every restaurant served it and every bakery sold it), it didn't mean that one heard no criticism of the government or of General Franco. In fact it showed me a side of the Spanish character for which I was unprepared. While I had expected some characteristics of Spaniards, such as their courtesy—if you stop a stranger on the street to ask the way, he may well abandon his own errand to escort you to your destination—still I knew little of their pervasive sense of humor mixed engagingly with an offhand irreverence for their government. Faubion's work and my curiosity took us among a giddy assortment of dancers, musicians, writers, and members of the Falangist party. From them we heard countless little cracks or stories about life in Fascist Spain. "The Russians only *think* they can invade us," someone remarked, "—they don't know Spanish trains."

A popular joke concerned a schoolboy who is asked the winner of various famous battles—Lepanto, Waterloo, etc.—in each case he answers "Franco." At last the teacher says, "You have answered everything wrong and I shall have to fail you." The child replies, "Fail me if you like, but all I can say is you must be a Red."

My favorite anti-Franco joke was a parody on a very popular song of the time, "María Cristina." The song is about a henpecked husband and his description of his wife. The original words ran, "*María Cristina me quiere gobernar, Y yo le sigo, le sigo la cor-*

*riente*" ("Maria Cristina wants to rule me, And I follow the line of least resistance"). The song goes on to recount the various orders she gives. "She tells me to go to the market, and I do. She tells me to climb to the attic, and I do. She tells me to go down to the river, and I do. She tells me to take a bath in the river—take a bath in the river? *No, no, no, no, María Cristina, que no, que no!*" The parody ran: "*Francisco Franco no sabe gobernar, Y sus ministros le siguen la corriente*" ("Francisco Franco doesn't know how to rule, And his ministers follow the line of least resistance"). "They say the price of potatoes will go up, and it does. They say the price of lentils will go up, and it does. They say that salaries will go up—salaries? *No, no, no, no, Francisco Franco, que no, que no!*" These undercover words had become so well known that when the tune was played in a public place people would glance at each other and smile.

However, there were soberer and harsher attacks against Franco, too. These generally came from the older intellectuals we met who remembered the pre-Civil War days of greater intellectual liberty. A poet contrasting the two regimes said to me, "All Spain speaks in whispers now. We have lost our courage. We used to be a country of great explorers, but now we are afraid to take a trip to Barcelona." But even the Leftists were afraid that the deposing of Franco would mean another civil war, and the memories and scars of the last one were still raw and terrifying. Spaniards would often remind us that a million people were killed in it, which meant, in a country of only twenty-eight million, that scarcely a family escaped without a loss. One young journalist described to us almost lightly the times when, as a child, he used to scrounge through the dustbins of Barcelona collecting potato peelings for the family supper. Altogether the stories gave me a chastening lesson in idealism, the realities, and the urge to survive somehow, anyhow. And the indestructible right to gaiety. Spain, not quite of the West, not yet of the East, marked for me, I thought, an important step in a kind of education about the world, an illustration of the vital if banal fact that we deal only in shades of gray, not in black and white.

# SIX

The following year Faubion and I returned to India, where, in the correct Indian way, I could await the birth of my first child under the elaborate, sometimes maddening, sometimes funny, always solicitous care of my family. One of the joys of wearing a sari is that one needs no maternity clothes. A sari, which is only six straight yards of material, can, by its very nature, fit anyone, be draped tightly or loosely. And it never goes out of style. Accommodatingly it clothes you as you swell with pregnancy without requiring you to buy an entirely new and special wardrobe.

There are other advantages to having a child in India. Relatives are always around to help with the knitting of tiny garments, collecting a layette, making you feel important—and, inevitably, more than ready with advice. Some of it had a certain wild imaginative scope. An old and charming widowed aunt of mine came to make an extended stay in my parents' house. She coddled, advised and scolded me in a truly enchanting way. I mustn't drink black coffee, it would make the color of my child's skin unappealingly dark. "If the child is a girl she will, of course, want to live in India. If she is too dark she will have trouble finding a suitable husband. A dark skin may be fashionable in city circles—your sister never listens to me when I warn her about sun bathing—but most men, especially in the north of India, prefer a pale skin and a delicate complexion."

Then, again, I mustn't drive a car or work the sewing machine because either activity was certain to bring on a miscarriage. I must drink quantities of buttermilk, rub myself with coconut oil, and sleep on the floor. Most of all, I should be proud of my growing girth and wrap my sari to display the fact that I was soon to become a mother. "I remind you," she said, "because you have lived so much in the West and there, I understand, they try to pretend they are not women."

An American college friend of mine who had just had her first child sent me a copy of a book called *Natural Childbirth*. My aunt was with me when I opened the package. I showed her the title. In alarm she asked, "In America do they have children some *other* way?"

Absorbed as I was in these details, there was still time to look at the changing India around me. A couple of family encounters brought the situation vividly into focus. Faubion and I had, of course, to pay a visit to my only surviving grandparent, my father's father. Although the family was scattered all over India and a large part of the outside world, still it was only courteous to present a new son-in-law to the head of the family. Accordingly, Faubion and I traveled to south India, where my grandfather, by then eighty-eight years old, lived in retirement and meditation.

As we drove up to his house we saw his thin figure in a starched white muslin loincloth and white shirt, bent over his cane, standing on his veranda waiting to receive us. He was a frail, courtly old man with impeccable manners and great precision of speech. He was, at this time, nearly deaf, but he wore a hearing aid which had been ordered for him by one of his sons and of which he was usually rather suspicious. On this occasion, however, he overcame his dislike of gadgets because he wanted to hear the sound of Faubion's voice. At the top of the veranda steps he shook Faubion's hand and said, very formally, "How do you do, Mr. Bowers. Welcome to your home." From then on he called Faubion "son."

In the deep tranquillity of his drawing room we were served a simple tea. In the Indian tradition, at his time of life, one is beyond fancy living, beyond the luxuries and pleasures of one's senses. It is a time for thought and austerity, not for a comfortable life of leisure and hobbies and security and now-I-can-do-all-the-things-I've-always-wanted. On the rare occasions that my grandfather made a journey, he would never travel first class on the trains, but always third class, squeezed in among the laborers and street sweepers and peasants, surrounded by their baskets of vegetables, their chickens and goats and squalling children, a gentle, absent old man, his hands resting on the cane between his knees, a look of utter serenity on his face. His hearing aid, if he wore it at all, would be switched off.

That afternoon, in the shadowed room, his quiet, careful voice asked Faubion questions about his family and about America. (I couldn't help remembering my grandmother's attitude when I had come to visit her on my first return from Wellesley, bursting with eagerness to tell her all about my American experiences. She had simply pretended that America didn't exist. In a deflating voice she had said only, "They tell me you have been away from your home for some time. You must resume your education now that you are back." I knew, of course, that she had disapproved of the whole venture. "You are making it impossible for the child to find a husband," she had told my mother severely.) Faubion tried, as best he could, to describe his not untypical American family, who rarely saw each other and who, absorbed in their own lives and activities, did not miss too keenly the concern, demands, and comforts of a large family unit.

My grandfather nodded at intervals, though much of what Faubion told him of his own life and of our plans for our life together must have seemed like the most improbable fantasy to him. At last, with a twinkle in my direction, he said, "It is a good thing that one gypsy married another gypsy. Which Indian husband would put up with this child's whims?"

Our visit must have marked for him, as it did for me, the end of an era. My sister and I were the only children among all his sons. With my marriage the family name died, but even for the sake of preserving the name for a few years longer he wouldn't have wanted me to remain unmarried—he couldn't have imagined any decent or satisfactory future for a woman except at the side of her husband, dignified in her home, the mother of children. Any other aspirations would be "whims." Even if the price was, startlingly, an American grandson-in-law, it was worth knowing that I was "settled."

Toward the end of teatime he came to the most important part of ours, or any, marriage. "When are you going to have a child?" (Not "if" or "do you want," just "when.")

He was delighted when I told him I was pregnant. A wide smile on his haggard face, he said, "I hope I shall live to see my great-grandson." It never occurred to him that I might have a daughter and graciously, in the ceremonial way, he wished me a hundred sons. To our sorrow he died before my son was born.

We stayed for a couple of days with him, eating his vegetarian food, keeping his strict hours—rise at 5 A.M., sleep by 9 P.M.—cherishing the hour or two a day in which he had the strength to see us. The rest of the time he lay on the wooden planks of his bed with his thoughts and his books, a withered twig of a man inside his immaculate clothes, waiting for death. When I went to say good-by to him, and held his hand, light as the claw of a bird, he used the childhood diminutive of my name that he had given me, "Santhu, Santhu, don't let your son lose India."

"Of course not," I replied briskly. "I'll bring him down to see you."

"Yes," he whispered, "yes. Bring him to see me."

Our return to Bombay could hardly have provided a stronger contrast to the twilit days in my grandfather's house, a different world really. My father's youngest brother, the irrepressible, exuberant, bewitching Shiva Rao, was visiting us. India was preparing for its first free elections, and Shiva Rao, after a long and varied career in the forming of India's first labor unions, its early independence movements, its increasingly important foreign affairs, and its representation at the United Nations, was now running for election to Parliament from the family's home state on the southwest coast of India.

He had just returned from a campaign tour, and although he was dashing in and out of the house to political meetings and conferences, he managed to find time to regale us with stories of his electioneering adventures. Because India's election machinery was being tested for the first time, the country had been divided up into sections which voted at different times, and the full count for the whole nation was not completed for some months. Shiva Rao's constituency had completed its poll, although the results were not yet in, and he was still full of the serious and the absurd aspects of the campaign. The election procedure was much more entertaining in the villages than in the towns. Along with the political discussions and promises, the rural audience got a good measure of dancing, cockfights and other amusements. At nine-thirty in the evening, drums would sound out from a village to announce to every community within ten miles that an all-night performance of old dramas from Hindu mythology (the Kathakali dances, for which the south is famous) would soon begin. The families would arrive on foot or by bullock cart with their children, some food, and a mat to sit or sleep on. Tea stalls would be set up, and in the intermission men would sell betel nuts or handmade cigarettes. As soon as a large enough crowd had collected, Shiva Rao would make his appeal.

Cockfights, he told us, weren't always such a success in this regard. "Have you ever heard a hundred cocks all together at one time?" he asked. "The competition they put up is much too fierce for a politician. I prefer Communist heckling any day."

Water-buffalo races turned out to be more suitable. In these, three or four teams compete, each consisting of two yoked buffaloes dragging a plank behind them. A small boy stands on the plank, somewhat in the manner of a surf rider, and guides the buffaloes as they race across a paddy field about nine inches deep in water. The fact that the boys come out unrecognizable under a thick coating of mud provides the amusement, and heavy betting provides the excitement. The important thing from the candidate's point of view, Shiva Rao said, was that buffaloes are very quiet creatures and offer no competition to a speaker.

More seriously he told us about a friend of his who had stood for election in a rural district where there were a large number of Muslims. His campaigning was complicated by the fact that if he couldn't provide screened areas for the Muslim women to sit out of sight of the men, then the women would not turn up at all. He expected virtually no vote from the women, who would, in any case, support their husbands' choice. On the morning of polling day he woke early, while it was still dark. From his window he saw a long procession of lights winding down to where the polling booths were. He went along to see what was happening and found that the lights were being carried by Muslim women who wanted to get to the polls before it was light enough for their faces to be seen. There were so many of them, however, that only a small proportion could cast their ballots before it became light. The ones who missed out didn't leave, but squatted patiently in a queue.

Those who were to poor to own a *burka* (a garment rather like a tent which envelops a woman from head to foot) hid themselves behind improvised screens of bed sheets. Some were asked why they didn't go home now that the sun was up. One replied that, quite frankly, it was fun to get out of the house for a change. Another said, "But today is a very important day. Today we are going to choose the *panchayat* for the whole of India." The *panchayat*, a long-established form of village government in India, is composed of five elected elders of a village, who administer their unit and settle disputes; in the old days, though, women were not permitted to help in the choosing of the *panchayat*.

Another aspect of the campaigns concerned the untouchables. One candidate told me that at pre-election meetings held by his party, the untouchables wouldn't mix with the rest of the crowd but stood by themselves, in deference to the old prejudice against them. On polling day, however, there could be no such distinction; there were no special booths for untouchables, and inevitably they got mixed in with the other voters in the queues. The hopeful straw in the wind was that at *post*election meetings the untouchables no longer stood aside but sat among the rest of the voters.

In Bombay city the election was more prosaic than Shiva Rao's highly-colored experiences, but still it provided its moments of amusement and interest. I remember reading a report about an earnest group of Bombay Hindus who felt that they needed divine guidance before they cast their ballots, so they placed a flower on one of the right hands of a four-armed image of a Hindu god and another on one of the left hands. Then they sat and prayed until one of the flowers dropped, indicating whether they should vote for the Right or the Left. The story didn't announce what the divine preference turned out to be.

Like millions of my fellow countrymen, I would be voting for the first time in my life in the largest free elections ever held in the world. Understandably, I followed with fascination the whole procedure as it progressed in Bombay. Because most of India's electorate is illiterate, the machinery devised for holding the elections was slightly, but not much, more complicated than polling systems elsewhere. Each ballot box in the 1,450 booths in the city carried, in addition to the name of a candidate, the emblem of the party he represented or, if he was standing as an independent, whatever emblem he had chosen for himself. The Congress party, which led the country to independence in the days of the British raj and at the time used Gandhi's spinning wheel as its emblem, changed under Pandit Nehru's leadership to a pair of yoked bullocks, to signify united action and to appeal to the huge majority of agricultural laborers in India's population. The Socialists used a banyan tree as a symbol of spreading growth and protection. Communists used the familiar sickle but replaced the hammer with three stalks of grain. One young candidate running on an antiprohibition ticket (Bombay had been dry for two years) used a whiskey bottle as his symbol and "Vote for the Bottle" as his slogan. (He didn't get elected.)

Everywhere in the city there were political rallies, speeches, cars with loudspeakers cruising through the streets, posters and slogans painted on walls and banners. Election day itself was very exciting. I walked down to our local polling booth and found that I was part of a long procession, laughing and chatting with strangers, singing, exchanging last-minute reports about how the polling was going elsewhere. The women were all dressed in their best clothes with jewelry and flowers, children danced along behind them unwilling to be left out of a national celebration. Many of them carried garlands to decorate the ballot boxes of their favorite candidates. (They weren't allowed to leave the garlands.) As we entered the booths each of us was stamped on the back of the hand with indelible ink, which would not wash off for two days, thus ensuring that we couldn't vote twice. And when we left it was with a really heady feeling that we had contributed at least one tiny gesture to the first democratic government of our country.

During those months in Bombay I couldn't help making frequent and rather banal comparisons between the India of my grandparents and the city around me. It hardly seemed possible that in the generation between my childhood and the India of 1952 so much could have been so tumultuously overthrown and centuries have been bypassed. At dinner one night with the dowager maharani of one of India's largest states, an old friend of the family but a woman whom I found both admirable and terrifying, many of my thoughts were crystallized. "Can you imagine," she asked, "an

India without princes? I still keep my title, but it is meaningless What have we come to? Where are our states? We wander about like the Jews. To me it is all a dream. I can't yet believe it. I wish I hadn't lived to see it."

I murmured timidly that possibly one might see it as progress and felt silly when she turned her sharp old eyes on me and said "What do *you* young people know about progress? It is *we* who understand the responsibility of privilege. You think there is some virtue in the *common* man. I am eighty, and I know that the common man only wants our privilege without our responsibility."

I hadn't the nerve to argue with her. What could she—or my grandmother—make of an India in which tradition was becoming a stumbling block, a sense of caste was becoming disgraceful, and an untouchable could claim the same rights as a Brahmin? Thirty five years earlier my mother had been ostracized by the orthodox members of her community because she had insisted on going to college and, worse, had insisted on teaching after she graduated Only six years earlier I had been considered at best eccentric, a worst immodest, for taking up an ordinary paying job on a magazine Yet now, all around us in Bombay, girls of "good family" were working in government offices, business houses, in the All-India Radio, on newspapers, even in movies. Many were independent o family support, many insisted on choosing their own husbands instead of leaving this delicate matter to their parents, many insisted on homes of their own, gradually weakening still further the disintegrating fabric of the Indian family system. In the old days woman would not have thought it proper to ask her husband about politics. Now it would be cheek for a husband to ask his wif how she had voted if she didn't volunteer the information. And al this had come about in one generation.

The princes, I often had need to remind myself, in spite of thei flamboyant methods of expressing themselves, were probably no the group with the most legitimate grievances. Bombay's hug number of white-collar workers, underpaid and overworked, cam in for few of the privileges of independence and of the new regim in India. They were the people, always seen but seldom noticed, wh linked the obvious extremes of very rich and very poor in the city

Another aspect of life in Bombay that interested and impresse ıe was the sudden new flowering of Indian arts. A friend of mine ad once remarked to me, "It took us three thousand years to evelop our arts and a hundred and fifty years of British rule to orget them." Apparently the Indian memory was not so weak. very day we heard about a new painter, an experimental writer, vigorous and popular young dancer. Evidently Indian independ- nce was pushing back horizons in every direction, and one had he sense of a freshet of national energy suddenly released. India vas clearly going to be an exciting country to live in for the next ew years.

That summer, on my aunt's advice that hot weather was debilitat- ıg for a pregnant woman, Faubion and I spent three months in ashmir. There we lived on a houseboat moored to the bank of he Jhelum River which runs as a main thoroughfare through the eart of the city. It was a wonderful, lazy time of thinking over ur Bombay impressions, of speculating about the future of the ountry, but mostly of enjoying ourselves in the beautiful valley hat had been the homeland of my mother's ancestors. We took *bikaras*, a variety of small gondola, to shop for flowers and fruit, o swim among the lotuses of the lovely lakes, to look at the mustard ields brilliant with yellow flowers, or the splashes of wild purple ris on the riverbanks. We used to walk in the evenings in the nagical Mogul gardens of Shalimar and Nishat Bagh and watch he sunset mirrored in ornamental ponds, tinting the pleasure avilions with rose and gold. We rode small mountain ponies into he high country to catch a glimpse of the menacing beauty of Nanga Parbat, one of the highest peaks of the Himalayas.

At the same time, as a constant reminder of India's muddled resent and uncertain destiny, there were the acrimonious, end- ess discussions with friends, at parties, with chance acquaintances n a coffeehouse, about the "Kashmir problem." Everywhere one oticed the presence of United Nations observers, talking in low oices at the hotels, setting out on tours to the remote frontier areas, valking deep in talk with local politicians through the gardens. We listened to the Muslim arguments, the Indian replies, the ex- hange of abuse on the radio programs, and met the harried officials f the government trying to make sense of the situation, to carry n normally and present a constructive approach to a sour stalemate. I remembered a favorite remark of my grandmother's: "No child is born without blood."

We returned to Bombay and there, in the autumn, my son was born. We had, of course, to have his horoscope read—my old aunt would have been horrified at the neglect of such a simple precaution against possible disaster. We were also instructed about auspicious names for the child. He was born on the anniversary of the last day of the famous (in southeast Asia) mythological battle of the good King Rama against the forces of evil which is recorded in the Hindu epic, the *Ramayana*. Consequently, his name must incorporate some form of the word for "victory" to show that he was on the winning side, the forces of good.

We chose the simplest of the possibilities for his name, Jai, and gave him Peter as a middle name in case he turned out to be incurably American and embarrassed by an unfamiliar name. As it happened, it was only in Russia, years later, that he decided to be Peter (or rather Pyotr) for a few months. This was partly because he was delighted to be so surrounded by references to his middle name—Petrograd, St. Petersburg, Peter the Great, Peterhof, the Peter and Paul Fortress—and was convinced for a short, intoxicating time that all of Leningrad belonged to him, partly because he got very bored trying to explain his odd first name to puzzled Russians.

When Jai was three months old we had to make a decision that in one way and another has plagued us ever since. Faubion and I were supposed to go to East Africa to write articles for various American magazines. Should we take Jai along on what would clearly be a long and strenuous trip in the middle of Kenya's Mau Mau uprising? Both Faubion's family and mine, from opposite ends of the world, argued hotly in favor of leaving Jai safely with doting grandparents. We decided, with many misgivings, that since our life was composed mainly of travel and writing our child had better learn to fit into a nomadic existence.

Our child, we thought, should learn to adjust to his parents and their way of life rather than adjust, more fashionably, to a "group." He has traveled with us on all our extensive journeys ever since and so far we have had no cause to regret it; still the situation has occasioned innumerable outraged arguments with friends, relatives, educators, stray busybodies about our cavalier attitude toward his "security." But this gratuitous outside concern has been virtually our only problem and we, on the whole, have been far more conscious of the rewards of having him with us and enjoying his growing awareness of a very big world. So far he has been to school in New York, London, Moscow, Bombay, and again New York. So far he has liked them all.

# SEVEN

In December of 1952 we sailed off to Mombasa on the Kenya coast, carrying Jai in a basket and wondering whether we were being absurdly irresponsible. For months we traveled through Kenya, Tanganyika, Uganda, Zanzibar, visiting strange tribal areas, going to *ngomas* (local dances) in distant jungle villages, touring through game preserves, meeting both the British rulers and the African leaders, or any African we could persuade into conversation. Uganda was my favorite state for atmosphere and living, Tanganyika for scenery, Zanzibar for exoticism and history, but for politics, excitement and a sense of the future of Africa, Kenya was the most controversial and interesting of the unique amalgam of states, trust territories, and protectorates that make up East Africa.

Consequently, we spent most of our time in Kenya and I have seldom lived in a more astonishing and contradictory atmosphere. The simplest things of our daily life became unpredictable and adventurous. It was not an unfamiliar situation to the people of Nairobi, the capital of Kenya. They like to think of their city as a frontier town, and certainly it has the look of a half-built, growing center—new concrete buildings in the heart of town, but government departments still housed in temporary barracks. Roads stop in the middle of nothing. Within ten minutes you can be out of town in a game reserve where giraffes canter casually among the thorn trees and there isn't a sign of human activity all the way to the horizon.

We soon learned that Nairobi had in fact been started only fifty years before on the site of a waterhole to which the nomadic Masai tribesmen led their cattle from time to time, and that when the first railway was carried to the interior of Kenya the idea of building a town there was considered so farfetched that the railway was known as the Lunatic Line. However, as news spread of the enormous possibilities of the land, of the wonderful climate, the magnificent countryside, the cheap and easy living, more immigrant Englishmen arrived to become "white settlers." Indians came as traders and merchants. Africans of the district became farm laborers, took menial jobs in the homesteads, or retreated to their tribal reserves. By the time I saw Nairobi it was a flourishing and established town even though it hadn't lost its pioneering air. And all the white population seemed to carry guns. "In the old days," an English friend told me, "one never walked unarmed or alone in Nairobi at night because of the lions on the streets. Now one doesn't because you can't take chances with Mau Mau."

Mau Mau, that secret society of African terrorists, and the threat it held over Kenya life were to haunt us all the time we were there. Our first experience of this was when we were invited to dinner by some acquaintances in the English residential section of Nairobi. There the houses are set back from the road, surrounded by gardens, along wide, shady avenues. We had arrived by taxi and, since it was some distance from our hotel, had asked the taxi to call for us again at eleven o'clock. Kenya maintains an anachronistically formal social life. If you are asked to dress for dinner it usually means that the men should wear white ties–it is assumed that you would wear a dinner jacket and black tie in any case, even for a dinner at home alone with your wife. Our first dinner out was, then, an "informal" one, the men were in dinner jackets, the women in long, but not "evening," dresses.

When it was time for us to leave, our host said politely to Faubion, "You're armed, of course?"

I thought for a second that he was joking, but clearly he wasn't because from the pockets of well-cut English dinner jackets and trousers revolvers were produced and from the jeweled evening bags of the women, from among the lace handkerchiefs and lipsticks, smaller guns appeared and were most generously offered to us as protection during our taxi trip. At the time, I think, our fellow guests understood neither our amusement nor our incredulity. Within a few days we no longer thought of life in Nairobi as a Surrealist dream—we had become so used to the muddle of moods and people and attitudes that the city so casually provided and so entirely took for granted.

Within the New Stanley Hotel, for instance, the European *jeunesse dorée* (known in Kenya as the Pink Gin Set) met for lunch in the Grill Room. In the dark-paneled bar would be the farmers in riding clothes who had just come in from upcountry or Boers with beards drinking beer. Between the bowls of peanuts, among the drinks and swizzle sticks and ashtrays, the customers slapped down their guns. Like us, they too had become accustomed to the cautions that the local papers, magazines, special pamphlets, and word of mouth issued daily. Never, the white settler was warned, move an inch without your gun—even from your bedroom to the bathroom, or when you step into the hall to answer the telephone, or when you walk across to the liquor cabinet to make yourself a drink. Your gun should always be within reach of your hand, "always loaded and cocked with the safety catch off," one list of instructions read, "not buttoned up in a holster, not on the mantelpiece, not in your handbag or under a cushion; but always, always, always within inches of your hand—on your lap, on the arm of your chair, on the edge of the bath, on the table beside you. The criterion should be: can you shoot within one second?"

Meanwhile, outside the hotel, standing in the brilliant crystal sunlight of Kenya, on one of the city's busiest street corners there might be a group of Masai tribesmen, barefoot, carrying their spears, dressed only in a dusty blanket slung over one shoulder and with their bodies and hair rubbed with red ocher. Possibly they were in town to sightsee or perhaps to shop. A group of Indian school children might wheel past on their bicycles on their way home for lunch. Veiled Muslim women of Arab descent might be peering at the things displayed in the shop windows—cloth from India, canned goods from England, dresses from South Africa.

These three main population groups—the European, the Asian, and the African—lived in the same city with a high degree of mutual exclusiveness, or, as a friend of mine described it, as a racial pousse-café, each element necessary to the whole, each retaining its separate identity, and, in the opinion at least of most Europeans and some Indians, a disastrous and unpalatable failure when the various elements mix. Three things were shared by all of them—anger, bewilderment, and a sense of danger.

Faubion and I, partly because we were strangers and transients, and partly because our different antecedents made us rather hard to classify in the Kenya social pattern, moved with a fair degree of freedom among the three groups. In Nairobi we listened to some of the more diehard of the white settlers speaking nostalgically of the Good Old Days when there was no trouble from the Africans, when they were "nature's gentlemen" uninterested in political or economic advancement. "Why, after all we have done for them," they would ask plaintively, "why aren't they grateful?" Upcountry, in the extraordinary and dramatic chasm of the Rift Valley which cuts through the middle of the White Highlands, one of the most eminent of the white settlers still maintained the full ritual of a formal dinner, but with certain unusual trimmings. As the guests were seated, each man present was assigned a door or window to cover. Each sat with his side to the table and ate and conversed as best he could with half his attention fixed on possible movement outside the house. As the servant entered with the soup he was covered. While he served and until he left the room the gun was kept trained on him and the door locked behind him because in many of the Mau Mau attacks the terrorists entered through the kitchen, intimidated the servants, and used the houseboys as shields to get to the front of the house and attack the white settler and his family.

Other settlers were even more careful than that. They changed their meal hours every day so that there would not be a routine on which a possible enemy could count. They cooked and served their own evening meal. They cleared all shrubbery from around their homesteads to make vigilance and shooting easier. Sometimes they would come to Nairobi for the weekend—not to enjoy a taste of city life and amusements but simply for a couple of nights of uninterrupted sleep in a hotel. Those who had obliging friends in Nairobi or on the coast sent their children away from the farms. A friend of mine, who used to make the long tedious trip by bus into the city every week to see her one-year-old daughter, had tried at first to keep her child upcountry. "But it simply became too exhausting. If I went out to the garden for a few minutes for some flowers, I had to pick her up and take her along too. We used to put her to sleep in the living room and then carry her crib into the dining room with us when we went in for dinner. She didn't even get any fresh air because it was much easier to watch her indoors than out, and at night all the bedroom windows are kept tightly closed."

It was in Nairobi that Jai was asked to his first children's party, and under the circumstances it seemed to me a remarkable affair. The little girls looked delicious in their party dresses–miniature bubble baths of frilled tulle and lace–which had been specially flown out from Europe for the occasion. The boys were in velvet shorts and ruffled Lord Fauntleroy shirts. Starched English nannies enlivened the afternoon (for me) by calling out in typical nanny voices, "Lady Caroline, Lady Caroline! We don't sit on the grass, dear, in our new frock!" or "Eat what's on your plate *first*, Henry, before you help yourself to more."

Predictably enough, tea consisted of cucumber sandwiches and scones and honey, birthday cake and bonbons and fresh lemonade. Afterward the older children played musical chairs and twos-and-threes, while I sat with Jai (dressed in diapers and a T shirt) on my lap, chatting politely to the other mothers and watching with fascination the children at their games, like an illustration from a Victorian novel, and the fathers, hands on guns, stationed among the rosebushes and formal flower beds, a reminder of modern Africa.

We saw, as well, members of the Indian community of Kenya, and listened to their worried speculations about what would become of their businesses and their lives. They, too, lived in special residential areas the other side of "Grogan's Swamp," a rather slummy neglected strip of the city owned by one of the most conservative of the white settlers and leased extremely profitably to Indians and Africans. The Indians still had their own clubs, restaurants, schools and hospitals–but not by choice. They seemed to be torn by resentment of the social barriers erected against them by the British and a rather guilty awareness that they erected comparable barriers against the Africans in their social life.

Meeting the Africans, who, of course, suffered the severest form of segregation, was a continually exasperating embarrassment. If, for instance, we wanted to talk to the top African leaders, or to members of the Legislative Council, or to ordinary friends of no exalted position, the same tedious arrangements had to be made. We couldn't invite them to hotels, restaurants or clubs. They, understandably, were shy about asking us to their shabby and overcrowded homes. There was one restaurant that allowed a multiracial clientele. It was called the Blue Room, though many of our African friends rather bitterly changed its name to the Blue Moon because of its rarity. Most of our meetings with them took place there, and even then, we discovered, you were not allowed to offer an African any drink stronger than beer.

African social life had been considerably hampered by the banning of all public meetings of Africans in the White Highlands. This had, as was intended, cut out all political meetings, but it also suppressed the huge and popular *ngomas*—communal dances which were the chief African amusement on a Saturday night. Besides this, Africans were not allowed on the streets after dark. If for any reason they had to be out at night they needed a pass, signed by a European, proving that they were on legitimate business.

These ever-present irritations were deeply wounding to the Africans and the effect on the educated ones was both corrosive and dangerous. Years before, my mother had once remarked to me that social insults would probably break up the British Empire as surely as political injustice. Certainly the situation in Kenya seemed to be proving her right. Much of the malaise of the colony was summed up in the words, the personality, and the activities of East Africa's most formidable leader, Jomo Kenyatta. He had been arrested and was to be tried for being the chief of the Mau Mau movement. In attending and writing about that trial I think I learned more about the grievances and aspirations of the emerging countries of Africa, and the worries and convictions of the colonial rulers, than any other single event could have taught me. Here, then, were some of its aspects that seemed to me to have the most significant bearing on the tangled problems of race relations and colonial government.

# *The trial of Jomo Kenyatta*

The trial of Jomo Kenyatta, the only African to emerge as anything approaching a national leader in British East Africa, began with a certain degree of local interest in an obscure village in a wilderness on December 3, 1952. It ended four months later in a flurry of world-wide publicity, in the wake of a massacre, with the conviction and seven-year sentence of Kenyatta on charges of leading and managing the secret society of African terrorists known as Mau Mau.

To the people who were following with fascination the progress of the trial—the foreign journalists, the white settlers in Africa, the Labour members of Parliament in England, the representatives of the Colonial Office both in Britain and in Kenya, and of course the Africans—the outcome was never in very much doubt. But the issues held such enormous interest and importance for Kenyans, whatever their race, that the circulation of the chief newspaper reporting the trial in Swahili (the closest thing to a vernacular lingua franca for Africans) more than doubled during those weeks; and as the tension grew through the months of the equatorial summer and autumn, both the weather and the royal family were superseded in the Englishman's small talk by details of the Kenyatta trial.

Perhaps to an outside observer, like me, the Kenyatta trial seemed an extraordinary, bizarre, and ominous affair, exposing as it did many elements of magic, witchcraft, Christian fervor, atrocities, politics, and, even more horrifying, the chasm of misunderstanding, fantasy, and ignorance between the races.

On October 21, 1952, Jomo Kenyatta was arrested in Nairobi and detained under the emergency regulations that had come into force to deal with the disturbed conditions in the colony as a result of Mau Mau activity. Specifically, Kenyatta was charged with "management of an unlawful society, Mau Mau, which is dangerous to the good government of the Colony." With him were charged five other Africans, all members of the Kenya African Union.

These six men were charged with conspiracy "by use of physical force or by threat or intimidation, to compel persons in Kenya to take an oath, or engagement in the nature of an oath, purporting to bind those taking it to act, or not to act, in any particular way." To the layman these charges were inclined to seem vague—which was not altogether surprising since Mau Mau itself was so ill-defined. The one clear point was that they referred to Mau Mau procedure and organization. This conspiracy, the government claimed, was intended to promote disaffection and discontent in Kenya, and to cause friction between the races.

The Europeans in the colony put it more simply and more catchily—if less accurately. To them Mau Mau was an anti-European movement designed to kick the British out of Kenya by terrorism, murder of human beings, slaughter of livestock, and possibly, in the end, a scorched-earth policy. They called it "the African Stern Gang" or, sometimes, a "Ku Klux Klan in reverse."

The felonious activities for which the six men were arrested were supposed to have taken place between January 1, 1950, and the date of Jomo Kenyatta's detention on October 21, 1952. Actually, the secret society called Mau Mau had been known as a functioning if elusive organization since 1942. For ten years the authorities saw no reason to worry about Mau Mau. Sir Philip Mitchell, Governor of Kenya until 1952, declared about three months before Kenyatta's arrest, "You will even see it reported that East Africa is seething with African unrest—of all inexplicable nonsense!"

Relatively little was at first known about Mau Mau beyond the fact that it was confined to the Kikuyu tribe, one of the most advanced of East Africa's 220 tribes; that its members seemed to be mostly in the Rift Valley, the vast geological fault that runs like a monstrous trench through the plateaus of Kenya; and that its membership, enrolled by oath, was confined to men. Even after the murders and massacres attributed to Mau Mau, after the extensive publicity it received, after the committees, officials, policemen, soldiers, and journalists had all inquired into it, Mau Mau still retained most of its original mystery.

The purposes of Mau Mau remained almost as obscure as the

meaning of the name. It had come to be pretty generally accepted (except by the more diehard of the white settlers) that one of the reasons for the rise of Mau Mau was the Kikuyu land hunger. The huge productive plateau straddling the equator in the middle of Kenya is known as the White Highlands, because here the Englishmen who arrived around the turn of the century to establish Kenya as a colony ruled that no Africans or Asians might own land, and that the Highlands remain white in the racial sense.

In the past fifty years the population of the Kikuyu tribe has grown enormously, largely because the white man, in a way, brought his own destruction with him. Epidemics and tribal wars, which had previously kept the population pressures at a perilous equilibrium, were extensively controlled by the newly arrived foreigners. The land set aside for the Kikuyu tribal reserves could no longer contain them. Even on the land that they had they were forbidden to grow the better-paying crops such as coffee, sisal, and pyrethrum (a variety of marguerite from which is extracted an essential component of most insecticides).

Finally, as Dr. L. S. B. Leakey, the most distinguished authority on the Kikuyu and their customs, claimed, it is firmly established in Kikuyu tradition that the White Highlands were leased, not sold, by the tribe to the foreigners. Now the Kikuyu wanted them back. Mau Mau was supposed to force land concessions from the British.

To the average white settler who had bought his farm in good faith with all the right legal documents, developed the land far beyond its previous state, invested his money, and made his home in the Highlands, this whole argument seemed, naturally, to be the outrageous nonsense of Socialists or malcontents.

Other versions of the purpose of Mau Mau were that it was a strong and sudden return to magic and the old beliefs in the power of tribal chiefs and witch doctors because missionaries had broken down the security of the African in the rigid structure of his tribe and the compulsive fears and confidence in his religion of magic and terror without providing an alternative society that was close enough or comprehensible enough to the African, and without substituting a religion that he could understand. Or that Mau Mau was only a sort of gangsterism, an extensive protection racket. Or that it was a genuine nationalistic movement designed to get self-government for Kenya Africans, and that its terrorist aspects were an unfortunate by-product that grew up—against the wishes of the leaders—among the impatient elements who felt that there was no chance of receiving a just settlement from the British by peaceful means.

When Jomo Kenyatta was tried, there was a good deal of evidence to back up every one of these conflicting theories. For each there was also a good deal of discrediting proof. Altogether it was rather difficult for the outsider to make out precisely what—in the broad sense—Kenyatta was accused of.

Defenders of the African cause were quick to claim that Kenyatta's arrest was simply an excuse to ban the Kenya African Union, the first organized and politically aware group of East Africans to flourish and gain support for their work. The other extreme felt that unless Mau Mau leaders were dealt with firmly Africans would lose respect for British sovereignty and government.

Only this much at least was certain, out of all the conflicting theories and explanations: that Mau Mau contained elements of blind superstition, intimidation, and political aspiration accompanied by savagery, brigandage, and murder of the most horrifying sort. Because of these the Europeans' anger against Kenyatta from the time of his arrest rose sharply.

When Kenyatta was first detained it would have been possible under the emergency regulations for the British authorities simply to exile or intern him without any trial at all. During the more explosive moments of the trial, and as the list of European murders mounted to a total of eight in those weeks, a good many of the people involved wished that the authorities had done just that, for the Kenyatta trial quickly grew into much more than the exile of a troublemaker.

Kenyatta was arrested in Nairobi, but because the police felt that there was danger of public uprisings and trouble in the capital if the trial were held there, he was taken up to the Northern Province. This is a vast desolate frontier region of Kenya where the tribes are supposed to be particularly primitive. It is a "restricted area," where nobody is allowed in or out without a police pass. It was to this area that troublemakers, Communists, and various political and criminal prisoners were exiled or held in detention. And it was in Kapenguria, a tiny village there, that the trial of Jomo Kenyatta was held.

The point at which world attention suddenly focused on Kenyatta was when every European lawyer in Kenya refused to handle his defense. To do so would have meant professional ruin. However, D. N. Pritt announced that he would take the case and become the chief counsel for the defense of Kenyatta and his five colleagues. Pritt is a lawyer of considerable distinction, a queen's counsel, a Labour M.P. for fifteen years, a man who made his reputation on political trials and who is perhaps best known in the United States for his successful defense of Gerhart Eisler when he jumped ship in England.

Pritt flew to Kenya and plunged at once into the tangle of misunderstandings and the great gap between cultures that would characterize the trial. He was met by an enthusiastic crowd of Africans, many of whom, it turned out, had heard his title "queen's counsel" and assumed that Elizabeth II had so taken Kenyatta's cause to heart that she was sending her personal lawyer to defend him. The next few days, however, made it clear that Pritt brought no such overwhelming authority.

Pritt's very first act resulted in an antagonism that quickly grew to fury among the white settlers as the trial progressed. He appeared before the Kenya Supreme Court to declare with angry bluntness that the indictments against his clients were "the vaguest allegations of conspiracy I have ever seen in forty-three years' experience" and to demand that the venue of the trial be changed to Nairobi, where he would have access to libraries, essential documents, and witnesses.

Pritt's fireworks made the Kenyatta trial news for most of the world and such a *cause célèbre* in Asia and Africa that several lawyers from India and West Africa joined the defense team. This, in turn, raised a number of complications. It became clear that the trial was no longer a private Kenya affair. Inevitably the position of all Africans was going to be discussed. Probably the presence of the British in Kenya, even in all East Africa, would be considered. A number of vaguely discreditable and definitely disturbing facts about life in Kenya were going to get an uncomfortably public airing.

The various defense lawyers ran immediately into one of the bitterest issues between the races. They met it first in the matter of living quarters. All of them except Pritt were, in the Kenya sense, colored. They could not therefore stay in hotels, in clubs, or in wayside inns. They couldn't eat their meals in European restaurants, or travel first class in trains, or get a drink in a bar. Eventually they all crowded into the home of an obliging Indian businessman.

Kapenguria itself is too small a village to have any public accommodation. All the people involved in the trial lived twenty-four miles away in the nearest town, Kitale. There the one hotel and one residential club were exclusively for Europeans and the color bar (or the "culture bar," a genteel phrase some of the Europeans insist on using) excluded all the defense team except Pritt.

The Kenya Supreme Court turned down Pritt's request for a change of venue, and in an atmosphere of growing tension and hard feelings the trial opened on December 3, 1952. The setting itself added uncomfortably to the drama of the occasion. Kapenguria has no courtroom, so a little red schoolhouse, normally used for government-sponsored classes in agriculture, was requisitioned for the purpose, and the only large classroom was arranged as a court. The immediate grounds of the schoolhouse were surrounded by barbed-wire fences and enclosures to which Jomo and his five fellow prisoners retired for their luncheon recess. The spectators from the nearby farms and counsel, as if at a picnic, sat on the grass munching sandwiches and bananas and drinking coffee or warm Coca-Cola.

The surrounding area and the roads leading to Kapenguria were patrolled by armored cars and by special details of police. Occasionally, driving to the trial, we would see groups of men from the wild and primitive Suk tribe that lives in the restricted area. They would be standing at the roadside, watching enthralled as the daily procession of cars (more than would normally pass that way in a month), each with its accompanying fog of pinkish dust, swept by to Kapenguria. We strangers in turn stared at the Suk, naked except for the nodding ostrich feathers in their headdresses and their beads or bracelets made of copper wire stolen from the electric lines across the country. A newspaperman told me of seeing a Suk girl wearing only what was apparently her most cherished household possession, an aluminum teakettle, on her head. Sometimes the mutual scrutiny became embarrassing, and the Suk, as is their habit when they are shy, would cover their faces with their hands. In a few seconds the cars would be gone.

Inside the cheerful, humdrum little room the antagonisms, the loyalties, the tensions, and the rancor were so vital as to change the quality of the air. About fifty spectators could be seated comfortably in the room at the scratched school desks with the scribbled figures of old calculations on them, the carved initials, the doodles. In front sat the prosecutor, A. G. Somerhough, large, round-faced, balding, with the cultivated Englishman's sense of humor and sarcasm, a popular man in Kenya for his distinguished war record, his work on the trial of the war criminals in Germany, and, more recently, for the ability he had displayed as the second-in-command to the Attorney General of the colony. Both he and his blond, handsome assistant wore the conventional formal black coats and striped trousers—startling and incongruous in the equatorial sunlight.

Next to them at the defense tables the lawyers were more informally dressed in tweeds and lounge suits. In front of them and to their right was the witness box. At the end of the room was the low dais where R. S. Thacker, the magistrate, sat in his robes and wig with his back to a blackboard and under a colored print of the young and smiling face of the Queen. To the left of the audience, on a long narrow bench set against the wall, sat the six prisoners, looking unexpectedly short and shabby. They were guarded by two tall askaris in their uniforms of navy-blue sweaters, khaki shorts, and red Moslem fezzes, observed by several English CID men both inside the room and from the veranda. Through the windows, across the barbed wire and the patrol cars, we could see the tall silver eucalyptus trees, the blue air of the high country, and the incredibly beautiful foothills of Mount Eglon.

Naturally most interest centered on Kenyatta himself. He is a stocky man with an ugly, powerful face. As the magazines and newspapers were soon to prove, he can be photographed to look either like a frog or like one of the more impressive and saintly biblical prophets. He has a short, sparse beard and a big, curving mouth which shows uneven yellow teeth when he smiles. His nose is broad and his hairline receding. It is his eyes that transform his face, his admirers claim, into the dedicated countenance of a righteous leader. They have been described variously as hypnotic, flashing, brilliant, mesmeric, cunning, and blank. An Englishman once described him as "part mountebank, part Hampstead intellectual," but all the same he was just about the only African whose name was known throughout East Africa and who had devoted friends and followers among the most educated and the most backward of the Africans. Perhaps his most famous asset is a formidable gift of oratory. When he spoke in public he drew audiences of thirty to fifty thousand.

In 1946 Kenyatta returned to Kenya after seventeen years in Europe. To all black Africans educated abroad the return home is a disheartening experience. In Europe they have been treated as equals, if not actually lionized by the people they have met and worked with. At home they are again thrown back to the irritations and insults of the color bar and the more concrete grievances of lower pay and lesser jobs and virtually no possibility of economic advancement, all countenanced by law and jurisprudence.

Kenyatta set himself the extensive job of founding African schools independent of the foreign missions—to this, ostensibly, he gave all his time that was not taken by the semipolitical activities of the Kenya African Union until his arrest.

Sitting among the spectators in the court, I found that almost every day there was some new excitement, usually of a melodramatic sort. The prosecution's case was entirely concerned with Mau Mau and fell into three broad sections: the first was intended to show that Kenyatta had taken and administered the Mau Mau oath; the second that on the occasions when he had denounced Mau Mau he was insincere and that his real policy, along with the policy of the organization of which he was president (the Kenya African Union), was anti-European and pro-Mau Mau; and the last that he had allowed himself to be idolized, with his name blasphemously substituted for Jesus Christ's in hymns; and that these actions were consistent only with his role as manager of Mau Mau.

The first few prosecution witnesses—all of them Africans—set the mood for mystery, magic, and barbaric rites. They were the ones who claimed to have seen Kenyatta take the Mau Mau oath himself and administer it to others. All begged Thacker to withhold their names from the press because they were afraid of reprisals. They were all kept in a specially guarded encampment, for it was not considered safe for them to live in their villages. To a question of whether these witnesses needed such elaborate protection because they were committing perjury, Somerhough replied acidly and with considerable effect, "It isn't a question of witnesses committing perjury but of committing suicide."

Among them the witnesses established what became the classic description of the ceremony of the Mau Mau oath taking: the walk through the banana-leaf arch, the eating of the sheep's meat, the touching of the mucus and liquid from the sheep's eye to the lips, the payment of sixty-two shillings and fifty cents. One of them explained that the ritual had taken place in his village and he had been forced into participation against his will. His flat, rather surly account was curiously evocative of the evening in a hut three years earlier.

"I saw a lamp inside burning low," he testified. "It was practically out. I felt my hands seized by a man and I was told by him: 'Take off your boots and if you have any money get rid of it.' " The man was joined by Kenyatta. "He said, 'You have got to go in. . . .' As they pushed me in they tried to calm me down, saying, 'It is nothing bad.' I was taken back into the house where I had been told to take off my boots. There were two rooms in it and a lot of people were present. There was a lot of murmuring. I saw an arch of banana leaves and other things. Jomo Kenyatta took hold of me and passed me with him through the arch.

"We stood side by side on the far side of the arch. I heard a murmuring of voices saying, 'Eat this meat . . . Eat this meat . . . If you sell our country or our people, may this meat destroy you.'

"Because I was angry I did not bite it, but it was rubbed hard against my lips. I was told again, 'Eat this meat. If you ever sell our land to the Europeans, you will die.'

"Again I was told, 'Eat this meat and you will pay sixty-two shillings and fifty cents. Unless you do, this meat will hate you and cause you to die. . . . If you ever disclose the secrets to any person not belonging to these secrets, may you be hated by this meat.' "

Throughout this ceremony, the witness said, Kenyatta was beside him and "was having done to him what was being done to me."

It must have occurred to a good many people who saw the trial or read about it that this whole question of oath taking and the government stand on it could create considerable confusion in the minds of the average uneducated Kikuyu tribesmen. Were the British for it or against it? Clearly the government considered the articles of the Mau Mau oath described by the witnesses wicked and worthy of punishment, though, to reverse the situation, an Englishman commits himself to many of the same things. An Englishman, for instance, cannot sell land in the White Highlands to anyone of another race; he too would be considered a traitor were he to "sell his country or his people"; and presumably he too lives under the threat both of punishment and of social ostracism.

Besides the commandments to which a Kikuyu was sworn under the Mau Mau oath, the manner of his swearing apparently aroused considerable disgust, deepening to utter revulsion, among the Europeans. Yet, fantastically enough, even more drastic ceremonies were condoned or initiated by the government authorities. In a ritual that undertook to release Kikuyu from their Mau Mau promises, which was officially called a "cleansing ceremony" but which became more popularly known as a "de-oathing," the authorities were looking for a ceremony so powerful that it would undo even the terrifying Mau Mau oath.

The procedure was, accordingly, intensified. Instead of simply touching the mucus of the sheep's eye to the lips, in the de-oathing one had to eat the eye, the theory being that a stronger witchcraft would destroy the weaker magic. This routine so upset members of Parliament in England, who deplored the using of barbarism to defeat barbarism, that the more extreme forms of the de-oathing had to be suppressed. However, the ritual of de-oathing continued in a milder way.

One such ceremony that I saw was officially sponsored in a part of the Kikuyu tribal reserve, where there was supposed to be an extremely high incidence of Mau Mau influence and membership. It was conducted by a fully qualified witch doctor wearing his regalia of ostrich plumes and scarlet jacket over rather patched and worn clothes. He was decorated with safety pins and carried the traditional quiver full of arrows. He performed the de-oathing ceremony with one of the magic *ithikari*–sacred stones which have seven holes in them to represent the seven orifices of the body. The man who was being cleansed placed the end of a sliver of bamboo in each hole. Holding the ends of the seven sticks, he repeated the oath of loyalty to the British government. The oath followed very closely the pattern of the Mau Mau's. It must have been puzzling for the ordinary Kikuyu to decide just where foreigners stood on the question of witchcraft.

Soon after the opening of the trial an African acquaintance of mine pointed out a news item in a magazine. It described a Mau Mau "court" which was discovered while it was in session by some of the members of the Kenya African Rifles, a regiment that had been called up to help maintain law and order. Thirteen Kikuyu members of the "court" were arrested, and among their confiscated paraphernalia were a rhinoceros whip and a white furry cap worn by the judge. "Look," said the African, "here in the Nyeri district it is a white cap and a whip. In Kapenguria it is a wig and a gavel. One is magic and one is British justice. Who should tell the African the difference?"

Another source of confusion for many people was in the fact that all the prisoners and many of the early witnesses who were in the box for having taken an oath were immediately put on oath again. To those of them who had accepted Christianity, possibly there was no doubt of which was the higher oath. To others, who had felt betrayed by Christianity and had specifically renounced its conventional form before they ever came to trial, the issue was less lucid. What in such cases constituted perjury? Which oath or loyalty should a Kikuyu abide by? What, in the end, is the power of an oath beyond the willingness to be bound by it or the threat of what will happen to you if you aren't? In most of Kenya there isn't even a social stigma attached to going to jail—it is popularly known as "visiting King George's Hoteli." The work is light, and there are the advantages of fairly good food and secure shelter.

To a stranger like me in Kenya the puzzling point is, which of all the laws that seem to surround the African does he consider binding? I asked this of an African friend of mine and received the answer, "The law with the biggest stick behind it." This in turn left me—as possibly a good many Africans are left—with a tricky question of judgment. Who has the bigger stick? Mau Mau or the British government? Missionaries or witch doctors? One's neighbor in an African village or the European on a big farm or in a distant town?

These objections may well seem specious to the Englishman accustomed to the truism that a court does not administer justice, it administers the law. To the African without the great tradition of British justice to comfort him, I imagine that this seems at best arbitrary and at worst complete chaos. In either case it is certainly open to the political interpretation that the British, having established themselves in Kenya and wishing to preserve their position there, have enacted laws to protect that position and enforce them to ensure that it remains protected.

The Mau Mau, in any case, were apparently following a similar pattern. By whatever means they established their power, once it was established they also enacted their laws and enforced them. Their actions too were deeply motivated by political exigencies, however inchoate. Early in the trial the whole question of the political significance of Mau Mau and the involvement of the Kenya African Union came to the surface when Prosecutor Somerhough put into the witness box three deviationists, officials of one of the branch offices of the Kenya African Union, who testified that Jomo Kenyatta had appeared to speak at a public meeting in their part of the country. They asked him why in his speech he had not openly denounced Mau Mau. Kenyatta, they said, had evaded the question, and eventually they were forced to close their branch of K.A.U.—presumably for being unwilling to support pro-Mau Mau policies.

Here was the direct implication that East Africa's only large, serious, well-organized, and actively functioning native political organization was not only deeply sympathetic with the aims of Mau Mau (whatever they might be) but was actually the main channel for the spreading of subversive propaganda and a front for its wilder methods. Kenyatta himself, of course, made the flat assertion from the witness box: "I say that K.A.U. has no connection with Mau Mau."

It might occur to the observer that there is something deeply unhealthy about a situation in which all the African politicians of stature are concerned with Mau Mau and, further, that the solution has to be more fundamental and more searching than simply the imprisonment of such political leaders. The Europeans could answer with justification that no political rapprochement was possible until Mau Mau and its leaders were destroyed, that Mau Mau itself was the clearest indication of the African's political immaturity and the continuing need for British government in Kenya.

The Kenya Independent Schools—Kenyatta's special baby and one of the chief branches of activity of the K.A.U.—also came heavily under attack. These schools were designed to meet the African's enormous enthusiasm for education, which needed more outlets than the missions or the government could provide. (The European and Indian schools were not open to Africans.)

Now it was suggested that these schools too were used as channels for propaganda, that many of the hymns that were soon to become famous in the emerging testimony were first taught and sung to the school children. These hymns substituted the name "Jomo" for "Jesus" and "white people" or "the British" for "the wicked"; they spoke of Kenyatta as "the Savior." All this was blasphemous—that is, if you happened to be a Christian. The hymnbooks that were produced over and over again in evidence contained passages like "The hearts that are brave were made brave by Jomo" and, more ominously, "The judgment will be delivered by Jomo." When Somerhough read from one of the hymns an extract that ran, "The love of Jomo Kenyatta is very great, he gave himself to become an agitator for our land," the prisoner interrupted fiercely and banged his fist on the edge of the witness box. "You are after my blood, my friend," he said. "I am not an agitator. The word means a fighter with words and demands." Somerhough represented a large part of Kenya's European opinion when he replied, "There is not much difference."

One of the early witnesses, a girl who had overheard a Mau Mau ceremony, established the connection between the atheistic sentiments of the hymns and Mau Mau. Among the fragments of conversation that she had overheard at the ceremony were "I know there is no God" and "Jesus Christ they talk about is an Englishman." Her uneasy comment in the witness box was: "To my mind Jesus Christ is the son of God and right to the end of the meeting I had no joy in my heart because of this."

Sitting in that classroom, looking out at the sunlit hills, at the farms which are ordered and productive only because some Englishman has fought the forest, cleared the land, set up his homestead, and adopted Kenya as his country, it was easy to understand the bitterness the settler now felt at the suggestion that he was a wicked imperialist exploiting the native and should now go home.

Kenya, these Englishmen had always thought, was different. It wasn't a colony in the usual sense of the word. The men who followed Lord Delamere to Kenya considered themselves genuine pioneers. They made farms out of the wilderness; they made a nation out of scattered, warring tribes; they created a country in which they planned to live and which they hoped to bequeath to their children. Apart from their loyalty to the Crown, they considered themselves entirely separate from the Englishmen in other parts of the Empire who performed their tour of duty—even if it lasted twenty-five years—but then returned to England. Those people were colonists. Here, in Kenya, they were settlers.

Without them, they felt, the young Masai warriors, their bodies smeared with red ocher, living off fresh milk and cow blood drunk from a reed inserted in the vein, would still be raiding the Kikuyu villages, stealing the women and cattle and slaughtering the men. Without the settlers, East African agriculture would still be a primitive scratching of the soil, for they were the ones who had made Kenya a smiling and a lavish country. There would be no written language, no schools, hospitals, or roads. No central government ever existed before them, no public services, no towns, no police force.

"It may sound patronizing," an English friend told me, "to people who haven't lived here, but we *are* better for the Africans than the Africans are for each other."

But my friend, like nearly all the Englishmen I met in Kenya, lacked only the quality that is chronically lacking in whatever one means by the English character—an understanding and compassion for the other person's sensitivities. Much that is confusing in Kenya life, so many misunderstandings, such deep and genuine bafflement between the races, such a hopelessness of explaining or accepting purposes and motivations, were crystallized during the trial of Kenyatta. The trial was punctuated by a series of these extraordinary moments.

On one occasion Pritt lost his temper with an African witness and asked rhetorically, "Do you always think everyone who doesn't agree with you is Mau Mau? Do you think I am Mau Mau?"

"I don't know," the witness replied seriously. "You come from Europe."

The prosecution called Kenyatta himself as the last witness on its list. He was questioned for ten days. During this long, frustrating examination, when Somerhough tried to establish that he had never openly denounced Mau Mau, the accused replied that he had. "The curse," Somerhough said, "was not a strong one and it had a double meaning."

Kenyatta replied that as far as he was concerned there was no longer or stronger curse.

Somerhough said he understood that the earth was one of the most sacred things on which a Kikuyu could take a curse.

Kenyatta looked puzzled and pointed out that the fifty thousand people he had been addressing at the time could not put a single piece of earth to their lips and, further, that the earth oath was an oath to deny or accept something, not a curse. The strong curse, the one that he had used, had been handed down among the Kikuyu for countless generations.

Somerhough, at the end of his patience, asked, "That is the strongest thing you could have done? Translated in *Baraza* [the official Swahili paper] as 'Let Mau Mau go and be hanged'?"

"The translation has not the same meaning as the Kikuyu words to the Kikuyu people," Kenyatta answered, making perhaps a larger generalization than he realized about the state of affairs in Kenya.

Again, after denouncing Mau Mau in a public speech, Kenyatta was supposed to have said, "Now let us all take a pinch of snuff." Again, in a fog of semantics and half-understood psychology, there was a fruitless exchange about whether or not Kenyatta had made such a comment and, if he had, whether it meant the same to the Kikuyu tribesman as "Take all this with a pinch of salt" would mean to an Englishman.

Certainly the whole world of curses and their ritual was foreign to the foreigners there. It was rather more surprising that even the language was foreign to Kenyans. But most frightening of all was the chasm between the two minds, the two races, and the two worlds.

Yet again, in questioning Kenyatta about an inflammatory anti-British speech he had made, Somerhough asked him, "Did you say the English had relieved you of the slavery of the Arabs and then ask who purchased the slaves from the Arabs?"

"Yes, I did."

"Did you say that before the English relieved you of Arab slavery they themselves used to carry away slaves in a ship called *Jesus?*"

In effect, Kenyatta answered that he had.

"Do you know [Somerhough was getting angrier] when the English abolished the slave trade in East Africa?"

"Whether they did or did not, did not prevent me relating a historical account of the slave trade. . . . Even if they abolished Arab slavery, we were put into worse slavery. Our land was taken away and we were put to forced labor."

Somerhough protested: "This is not an answer; it is a speech."

"The wages given to our people were so low that we lived in a sort of serfdom." The intensity of Kenyatta's voice rose. "Formerly a man could walk and feel like a man. All that was changed and we were subjected to the color bar and all kinds of humiliations. . . . If slavery was abolished, a new kind of slavery was introduced. When you have taken somebody's land . . ." He stumbled over his words. "Leaving him . . ." His voice broke off. "I can't go on."

"Go on," Somerhough said with infinite sarcasm, "I am hanging on your lips."

Briskly Kenyatta recovered his composure. "I hope you do not fall," he said in a cool voice. "If you had to change places with an African and live like him for a week—or even two days—I bet you would not stay there. You think they are happy but they are not."

Meanwhile tensions built alarmingly among the Englishmen themselves and continually exploded in quarrels in the courtroom and in the jeers and anger of the spectators. In the little Kapenguria courtroom the trial had become an abortive and unsatisfactory political battle in which few points were made but everybody's bitterness deepened. The rift between the races grew wider. The testimony at the trial seemed to be clarifying no issues and demolishing no barriers. Near the end of his days on the stand Kenyatta said, "The disease of the heart cannot be cut out with a knife."

After the long succession of witnesses and the special drama of Kenyatta in the box, after all the turbulent questions that had been raised, Pritt's defense seemed short and relatively flat. It consisted mostly of contradictions of what the prosecution witnesses had claimed. Witnesses who were supposed to have been at oath-taking ceremonies described earlier in the trial appeared to testify that Kenyatta had not been present. For the one prosecution witness who testified that he had been present to see Kenyatta administer the Mau Mau oath, Pritt produced ten to say he was lying. To refute the prosecution witness who had connected Kenyatta with the Mau Mau initiation ceremony Pritt produced eight men with contradictory evidence.

One woman whom Pritt called to the box was obviously rattled by the whole procedure. She claimed that the statement she had made for the prosecution had been extracted by threats and force. A police officer, she said, had threatened to take her up in a plane and drop her out.

Why, if the statement was false, had she allowed her thumbprint to be put to it? (But that she should feel that a thumbprint should have any authority was open to question.) Well, her hand had been held by force. To her, clearly it all seemed quite reasonable. "I wanted to be released and go away," she said. "I wanted to be returned to the place where I lived." But most of the spectators must have sympathized with Thacker when he said it was a very peculiar position. "I cannot follow the African mind, I'm afraid," he added sadly.

"The question," an English lawyer who had practiced for some years in Kenya remarked to me, "should be, 'Does the African mind follow Thacker?' In court," he continued, "as you watch these solemn black faces listening to English questions, translations, interpretations, the whole elaborate business of English court procedure, what on earth do you suppose they make of it?"

I asked him what was the biggest stumbling block in legal forms to most of the Africans. "The laws of evidence, I think," he answered. "Especially what is hearsay and what isn't. You ask a man how he knows something, and he says, 'The chief told me—how else would I know?' You tell him, 'But in that case you don't *know,* you *heard.*' He doesn't understand at all and says, 'But I just explained, I know because the chief told me.' Of course," he added, "when you reach philosophic concepts like 'a reasonable doubt' you're really lost." Most Africans, he assured me, think in terms of testing innocence by ordeal.

How, I asked him, would they react to the Kenyatta trial? Surely they didn't see it as an elaborate ordeal to test him.

"The purpose of a trial like this wouldn't, in their minds, be to establish guilt or innocence. Everyone would know that Kenyatta was Mau Mau. To them the only remaining thing is to settle how much he has to pay—how many goats or cattle."

However it may have appeared to the Africans, the Europeans for the most part didn't seem too surprised by all the shifts and contradictions of testimony. Such, apparently, was only to be expected from Africans and only added another sort of mistiness to an already obscure situation.

Pritt, in his final address to the court, which he read in a monotone at breath-taking speed, used the general obscurity to claim that there was never a real case against his clients at all. In fact, he said, the prosecution had never really decided just what the charges against Kenyatta were. He flung a series of questions calculated to disturb almost anyone in Kenya. If Kenyatta was charged with managing Mau Mau, then the prosecution's job should be to show just what it was that he was managing. Why, and in what fashion? In what office? With what policy or with what documents? Was he the sole manager? Was he just one of a number of members of the management? And, of course, at the heart of all these questions was a problem of very long standing: What was Mau Mau?

Not only, Pritt continued, were the charges "vague and woolly," but the evidence produced by the prosecution was designed to show that Kenyatta was sympathetic to Mau Mau, that he had not denounced it forcibly enough, that he was anti-European, or even, to push it to its furthest limits, that he had taken the Mau Mau oath. Of course, Pritt said, the defense claimed that most of this was untrue, but even if it were true, "the charge is not of being friendly to Mau Mau or of lacking in zeal in discouraging Mau Mau. The charge is of managing Mau Mau."

As to the political aspects of the case, Pritt insisted that Kenyatta had never said or written anything in contradiction of the published statements of the moderate and constitutional policy of the Kenya African Union. Obviously, he indicated, the answer was that the government did not wish these Africans to carry on propaganda of the sort demanding "more land for the Africans," as this would tend to be embarrassing to the British.

One by one Pritt checked off the points made against his client in the prosecution's case: the points about the oath taking which he felt had been refuted by the testimony of his witnesses, then the evidence of the three deviationist K.A.U. officials, who, he said, were "almost as obsessed with Mau Mau as a Washington politician is with Communism." These men had demanded that Kenyatta denounce Mau Mau, which he had done; the rest of their evidence could not be credited.

On the various occasions that Kenyatta had spoken in public against Mau Mau there was no evidence that he was not sincere. And as for the various songbooks, hymnbooks, and exercise books that had contained verses in praise of Kenyatta, well, the accused could not be held responsible for anything that anybody thought fit to write about him, and the fact that some of the documents were found in his house certainly did not prove either that they were his property or that he had any connection with them.

That, said Pritt, was the whole of the case against Kenyatta in this "very important political prosecution." Clearly, he concluded, Kenyatta and the other five accused should be acquitted.

Somerhough, immediately on beginning his final address, protested that Kenyatta's trial and prosecution were certainly not "political"; however, "it would be a fair retort to say that the court had heard a political defense."

But it was when Somerhough began to reply to Pritt's "Where?" "Why?" and "How?" that the true and very broad political aspects of the case emerged. The answer to "Where is Mau Mau?" was simple, said the prosecution counsel. Mau Mau was in Kenya. This was, of course, altogether too simple for some of the observers of the trial to swallow without any mental chewing. It stated a fact without either answering the question or accepting its real, and to Kenyans extremely important, meaning.

The answer to "Why?" was slightly more complicated. "If the Crown were asked why it has suggested that these people should have managed and controlled Mau Mau, the answer would be 'the lust for power.' It must be that, and can't really be anything else."

(Of course it could be something else. It could be several other things ranging from nationalist fervor to gangsterism.) "It has increased their prestige and increased their hold on the people so that they could exercise more power."

Possibly unintentionally, Somerhough by this statement made it clear that this was, after all, a political trial. Possibly unintentionally, he had suggested that the danger of Kenyatta and the other five accused lay in their increased prestige. If participation in Mau Mau had given them greater standing with their own people, then the political strength and use of such an organization became obvious, and Mau Mau appeared as much more than the amorphous and inexplicable thing that Somerhough himself later described as a "purely barbaric movement accompanied by circumstances of revolting savagery."

The answer to "How?" was, again, Somerhough continued, fairly simple. Mau Mau was run largely by propaganda. Africans were told that they had been robbed of their land. They were encouraged to drive out the Europeans, and in the hymnbooks designed to spread the propaganda there were "fantastic allegations about slavery and that sort of thing." But the real damage was done to the "simple African," who was being taught to feel he had grievances.

Immediately after this, Somerhough tacitly accepted the political and emotional power of those grievances—imaginary or otherwise—in his comment that if you can find people "to follow their leaders and do as they are told, obey the orders of the leaders and to come when they are called, then you are building up an army of persons who are bound to you by a strong sanction. This sanction appears to have reached a strength which it is very difficult for a European to comprehend." To the foreigner the striking point was that it was a sanction that for the Kikuyu, at least, superseded both their previous emotional ties of loyalty or affection to the Europeans and their political ties to the government.

Kenyatta, Somerhough concluded from his replies to Pritt's queries, was the only man with the "personality and the education" to manage an organization of the scope of Mau Mau.

Later in his speech Somerhough came to the heart of the tangled situation in Kenya that had made the trial such an extraordinarily bewildering series of cross-purposes and muddles, and in a way diagnosed the sickness of most of Africa. "We maintain that Mau Mau can only flourish in an atmosphere of hatred between the races. It is no good telling Africans to drive out Europeans or to tell Europeans to do likewise if they like each other. Neither party will listen to you. The only soil in which Mau Mau could flourish would be in soil poisoned by racial hatred."

Among the Africans of various shades of political opinion to whom I talked in Kenya, certainly none would have disagreed with Somerhough. They might, however, have wondered where the poisoning of the soil had begun. In colonization or in Kikuyu land hunger? In economic grievances or in anti-European propaganda? In the color bar or in Mau Mau?

During the month that Thacker spent considering the evidence and the cases of the defense and the prosecution, Kenyatta's case remained in the news and in the horrified conversation of Kenyans.

A news item before the verdict concerned Pritt's departure from Kenya with the honors given him by the Nairobi Africans—a stool, a robe of colobus monkey skins, and a fly whisk—the traditional equipment of an African tribal elder.

Most of the Europeans of Kenya seemed to feel that Pritt had only contributed to the worsening of the situation; that he had so played up the race war and political angles of the trial that he had really done the Africans a disservice and made it much harder for them to deal in a friendly and equitable way with the Europeans in the future. But I think an African I talked to about this spoke for many of his countrymen when he said, "It is very wonderful for us to see an Englishman fight so bravely on the side of an African."

Eventually, protected by soldiers and Sten guns, Thacker gave his verdict in the Kapenguria schoolroom. For Kenyatta and the other five accused, the sentence was seven years' hard labor—the maximum he had the authority to impose, though even that, he said in the course of his speech, was "quite inadequate" for what Kenyatta had done.

Kenyatta replied that he and his colleagues were not guilty and did not accept the magistrate's ruling. In his opinion the purpose of the trial was simply to strangle the K.A.U., "the only African political organization which fights for the rights of African people." "I am not," he said, "asking for mercy, but that justice might be done and that injustice against the African people should be righted."

Thacker, apparently despairing of any solution for Kenya's problems, said, "I am sorry to say I don't believe you."

Early in the trial Pritt had said, casually, "It is more important to fight this case than to win it." In retrospect it seems that the fighting of that case may well have marked the beginning of perhaps one of the most inflammatory chapters in history—the political and emotional self-assertion of the Africans in the eastern, central, and southern countries of their immense continent.

# EIGHT

From Africa we returned to New York, where we spent a year writing and preparing for yet another journey. This time, we decided, there was to be no time limit. We were going to travel very slowly through Asia, visiting countries we had been to before and as many as possible of the ones we had missed because of wars, revolutions or considerations of time and convenience. We would take Jai with us and also his nurse, to give us real freedom of movement. Faubion was to write articles for *The New Yorker*, I was to write articles for *Holiday*. Faubion was also gathering material for a book about Asian dance and drama.

For the first time we were traveling through an Asia that, after hundreds of years, was free of colonial rule and foreign domination, either benevolent or exploiting. One very small fact kept coming to our attention in the course of our journey: the last time we had been in Asia the street signs, most of the advertisements, the names of railway stations and government offices, had all been in European languages—English, French, Dutch, Portuguese. Only Thailand had retained both its independence from colonial rule and its script and language as a means of public communication. Now, only five years later, the signs were in Vietnamese, Cambodian, Indonesian, Burmese—whatever the local language happened to be. It seemed strange that this change alone could represent one of the most sweeping revolutions in history. Certain small pockets of foreign rule, of course, remained—the British in Borneo, the Dutch in New Guinea, the Portuguese in Timor, Macao or Goa—but, broadly speaking, these were insignificant exceptions in an Asia newly expanding into a sense of national and continental identity.

From years before, when I had been living with my father in Tokyo, I remembered a chastening conversation that I had had with a Japanese friend. It was the day of Gandhi's death and from seven in the morning I had done nothing but cope with reporters, with people who had come to call, with condolence messages which poured into the embassy. There had been no time to eat or rest and I was exhausted by evening when my friend Kumiko came in. She expressed her regrets, and said, formally, that Gandhi would be a great loss to the Japanese too. Inexcusably, I had replied, "Really? His first principle, you may remember, was nonviolence."

Deeply hurt, Kumiko had answered, "It is a principle that we, as Buddhists, understand very well. Another of his great principles was freedom for Asia." Then, with a burst of frankness remarkable in a Japanese woman, she had added, "You, at last, have your freedom in your country and you are the first nation in Asia to do that. But the rest of us? Are we not in chains? The Dutch, the French, the British rule Asia. In China the Americans try to build up their idea of a 'good government' with billions of dollars. And now we, the last to be subjugated, are a conquered nation too." She asked me to consider the independence movements that had started in Asia since the war, in Indo-China, Indonesia, Malaya, Burma. "It was only possible for them—weak countries—to fight their conquerors *after* they had seen the white man beaten. Beaten by Asians, working for Asians—that was when their prestige vanished and the subject peoples had morale enough to revolt. After the war," she finished quietly, "the 'democracies' returned those nations to their foreign rulers. Like all wars, it ends in mysteries . . ."

However false Kumiko's reasoning may have been, there was no doubting a certain core of truth in her speech. The wartime defeats of the colonial powers in Asia had beyond question precipitated the postwar demands for independence. The return of colonial governments had to a great extent sparked the revolutions that then seemed the only way for Asian nations to win their freedom. Now we would have a glimpse—a superficial glimpse, admittedly—of what all those years of struggle and bitterness had brought to Asia.

Our travels started in Japan, where the Occupation had ended. Tokyo not only was rebuilt but had become the biggest city in the world—and one of the most attractive. Not that it was particularly fetching to look at, but it carried the dynamic air of a Big Town, unmistakable when you meet it, impossible to describe satisfactorily. We rented a charming Japanese house in Tokyo, taught Jai to sleep on the floor and eat with chopsticks, and then began to reacquaint ourselves with a place that both Faubion and I had always loved even though he had first known it under the stringencies and suspicions of the prewar totalitarian regime and I had seen it only when it was bruised and battered by war and ruled by foreigners.

Standing one evening on the Sukiyabashi, a bridge in the center of town, I watched thousands of people stream past in kimonos and wooden sandals or in Western clothes. Some turned toward subway entrances, some to a movie house or a restaurant, some paused at shop windows. I listened to the streetcars racketing toward the Imperial Palace, gazed at the shoeshine girls and the sidewalk vendors of toys, food, newspapers. I looked up to the moving lights of the *Asahi* building, flashing the day's news in Japanese characters, or down at the scummy water of the canal and the slow Japanese barges moving under the bridge. I realized that I was standing at the heart of a city as noisily individual as any in the world and that for the first time I was seeing its exuberant character released—an extraordinary mixture of cultures, ages and continents, each contributing to the Tokyo atmosphere, all fused and modified by the special personality of the city, of a city that remains the most exciting one I know.

Once we went to a bar with some friends for a late drink. As usual, the men at the next table stared at us inquisitively, and then one of them reached across with his bottle of sake, filled our cups, invited us to drink and, as usual, asked us where we came from. When we made the same inquiry he replied, surprised, "Tokyo, of course Tokyo."

One of us explained the silly question by adding that there were so many country people in Tokyo these days that one couldn't always be sure.

The man laughed. "You can always tell the Tokyo man," he said, "he will be the only one enjoying himself."

After only a few days in the city we decided that if that was the definition we were certainly Tokyo people. Tokyo isn't a city in which to sightsee. On the whole, it is quite ugly but it has the most vigorous, gay and expansive life. For sightseeing we went to Kyoto and spent some weeks wandering through its incredibly beautiful gardens, palaces, temples, and the flawless alleys in the old part of town. But even if Kyoto people with their unassailable snobbishness referred to Tokyo as "only a branch office of New York," I was delighted to return to the gaudy, bustling air of the capital.

For the most part our life in Tokyo consisted of seeing friends, walking about the city streets, and going to the theater. I still can't imagine a pleasanter way of spending my time. Faubion was, of course, ecstatic to be back among his beloved kabuki actors and most of our social life and entertainment centered on the vast, newly built kabuki-za in downtown Tokyo. Of the four great acting giants that Faubion had known before the war and I had met during the Occupation, three were dead. Only Kichiemon, thin, old, almost continually ill, was left to dominate the great kabuki stage. Meanwhile the younger actors who had been our closest friends during the Occupation had risen to become stars, lived on the lavish scale that a leading Japanese actor expects to maintain, surrounded by servants and attendants, served elaborate meals, dressed and decorated their houses with incomparable elegance. Some of their sons whom we had known as babies were now old enough to begin their training for the stage to take over the famous acting family names of their fathers and grandfathers. It all made a very cheerful contrast to the pinched and shabby life they had known immediately after the war.

Through them and through Faubion, in our long walks through the city, I came to know some of the stories that give Tokyo an extra dimension of romance and history for its citizens. The Sumida River, for instance, winds through the heart of Tokyo as it does through countless legends and tales of loves and battles. It is spanned by a number of celebrated bridges, among them the Ryogoku. Here a samurai of the seventeenth century, as violent in his jealousy as he was in his love for the beautiful courtesan Takao, took her for a boat ride. As they moved slowly downstream admiring the famous cherry trees on the riverbanks, watching the bright pink petals drift down to the water, Takao sang to him. But while she sang, the samurai became convinced that in her heart she addressed the love songs to some other man. Desperate with love and anger, he killed her. In the convention of the samurai, he cut off her head with his sword and threw it in the river. Tokyo girls will tell you that Takao's ghost haunts the Sumida. In the spring twilight sometimes they wait on the bridge, thinking of love and tragedy and listening for the faint beautiful voice that is supposed to drift down the river when the cherry trees are in blossom.

In the same spirit, Tokyo men pause at the street corner known as Naka-no-Cho. Nowadays it is an entirely ordinary-looking spot, but once it was the gateway to Yoshiwara, the most glamorous section of the city, the playground of Tokyo's seventeenth-century café society. The district was fenced in and, with the exception of the palace grounds, was the only area where men were forbidden to draw their swords, for here the passionate and quick-tempered Tokyo men came for the luxurious life and here countless quarrels and feuds began in the great inns, the drinking houses, the gambling halls.

In Yoshiwara too the most celebrated geishas lived in astonishing splendor. Fortunes were lost in extravagant efforts to win their favor. Renowned for their elegance, their wit, their artistic talents, they chose their patrons with a highhandedness that plunged the poorer, less handsome men into despair. Famous beauties paraded along the narrow streets of Yoshiwara on lacquered slippers that raised them six inches above the dust of the roads. With a true Tokyo sense of display they wore several layers of embroidered outer coats to prove their wealth, and they always walked with two attendants, one ahead so that the courtesan could rest her hand on his shoulder to steady herself on the pebbles of the street, and one beside her, to shade her with an umbrella.

One of the Tokyo stories began with the arrival of a farmer in the city. His first wish, of course, was to spend the evening in Yoshiwara. He dressed himself for the occasion, stepped through the famous gate, and walked into the sparkling atmosphere of the pleasure district. There he saw, sauntering down the street, a courtesan of such unimaginable beauty and grace that he knew she was the woman in all the world that he wanted, on whom he would lavish without a thought the money he had accumulated after years of hard work. When this scene is played on the kabuki stage (as so many of Tokyo's stories are) all the humiliation and sadness of the countryman, the unsophisticated, is concentrated in the moment when the great courtesan pauses in the middle of the street, turns to look at the staring farmer, and breaks into helpless laughter.

Like our actor friends, I soon found that I too paused for a moment whenever I passed Naka-no-Cho, peopling the streets with the phantoms of dead samurai, or lost courtesans, remembering some of the splendid Tokyo stories, before I turned back to the tangled traffic, the hustling, lively atmosphere of modern Tokyo. Out of it all was emerging Japan's own blend of Western influence and a sense of the country's history and standards, the legacy of the Occupation tempering traditional values.

There were, of course, some disappointments in the rest of our tour through Asia. We were unable to go to Korea because military permits were necessary. Even sadder, we couldn't return to China, now under a Communist government, because Faubion, as an American, couldn't get a visa, while I, as an Indian citizen, could enter China but after such a visit would probably be unable to get a visa to return to the United States. Reluctantly we gave up the project and tried to comfort ourselves with the idea that Okinawa, still under American military government, was (with difficulty) accessible. And anyway the British crown colony of Hong Kong would give us at least a glimpse of China.

Jai had his second birthday in Hong Kong and was given a rather unusual birthday treat. He was taken to the Chinese opera, where he was madly excited by the crashing of cymbals and the banging of drums, the stylized fights and gaudy costumes. But, like many of the Chinese children there, he fell asleep abruptly in the middle of the performance while his elders sat on to see how the splendid mixture of singing and mime, of princesses, generals, comedians and acrobats, of tragedy and farce, would come out in the end.

Our journeying also produced some unexpected pleasures. On our tour through Vietnam, Laos and Cambodia we discovered to our great joy that Jean de Selancy, from whose house we had been married, was ending his two-year tour of duty with the French Army in Indo-China. The war between France and the Indo-Chinese was over, United Nations teams were supervising the retreat of France from its former colony and the establishment of the new independent government, guerrillas from the forests and mountains were returning to their villages, refugees were flooding into the capital from the north complicating further an already tangled situation.

We went to stay with Jean in his battalion headquarters in Cambodia, and with him watched the sad-happy ending of an era in Asia. Jean drove us the two hundred miles over a dusty, bumpy road and we seemed to be the only car going north. Across the road, the long, slow-moving line of army lorries, jeeps, tanks, staff cars headed for Saigon, and as we passed them we caught glimpses of turbanned Moroccans, or Foreign Legionnaires, or Zouaves in their giddy uniforms yelling, "Vive les coloniales!" The flooded rice fields or the herds of water buffaloes tended by small boys would have provided a placid, typical view of the countryside had it not been for the fact that one nearly always saw somewhere in the landscape a road or village sign pitted with bullet holes, or an overturned burnt-out truck, or a strip of forest cleared against ambushes.

Jean had arranged for us to stay in the house of a rubber planter, long since returned to France. Set in the shade of giant acacia trees, surrounded by the dark-green ranks of rubber trees, the house itself was big and cool, with stone floors, high ceilings, deep verandas covered with bougainvillea. It was easy, there, to imagine the old, luxurious colonial days, dozens of servants, cool drinks on the veranda in the evening, with the hand-cranked gramophone playing dated French jazz. A Somerset Maugham kind of life.

The contrast came when we joined Jean for our meals in the officers' mess. There we learned the army slang for red wine (*pousse au crime*), listened for the grim little jokes that the juniormost officer would make as he read the menu aloud to the table. Once he wished us all *bon appétit* and begged the senior officers to eat till they burst "because that is the only way we will ever be promoted in the French Army now." Every day there would be fewer officers at the table because every mail brought a new batch of transfer orders. Almost every afternoon or evening there were small parties of celebration or farewell after the French had handed over to their Cambodian counterparts. At night at dinner there would be modest, formal presents offered to Jean as battalion commander from the new Cambodian officers—usually glassy-looking dogmeat sausages, or the special rice cakes of the district, or buffalo steaks—clearly the food in the officers' mess was going to change a great deal very soon.

Afterward we would go back to the great, empty, echoing house of the vanished planter.

The French tricolor was lowered for the last time, and in its place was raised the exotic national flag of Cambodia—a golden elephant on a red ground. We saw it fluttering against the bright tropical sky as we drove back to Saigon with Jean. The rule of the last major European power in a major Asian country was over.

Our travels took us on to the Philippines, which Faubion had known only under wartime conditions and which I didn't know at all. There too we tried to see as much as we could of the different sorts of life that make up the intricate pattern of the islands: the glitter and charm of city life in Manila, the special organization of remote mountain villages in central Luzon, where the Igorot and Ifugao, among the earliest settlers, had been until a few years before practicing head-hunters, the slow-paced, old-fashioned, eminently graceful plantation life of the sugar estates in the Visayas. However, the most shamelessly storybook experience of all was our visit to the Sulu Islands in the far south of the Philippines, scattered across the ocean between Borneo and Mindanao. A thousand years ago the Sulus were the fiercely guarded hideout of the notorious Malay pirates who terrorized the shipping of all the southern seas, while fabulous stories of wealth and beauty drew adventurers to the islands from all over Asia. Even now the slim racy boats of the islanders raise their big square sails striped with yellow, gray and black, and sail off on smuggling trips, skimming expertly through the tricky currents and treacherous sandbanks of the Sulu Sea. In the old days they used to return with silks and ivory, slaves and gold. Now they bring in English whiskey and gin, American cigarettes, French perfume, Indonesian pearls and sarongs. On land, in their capital, Jolo, they strut through the streets and markets in their flashy trousers—intense green, purple, pink, flame—but most of their life is spent on the sea.

Once we went on a pearl-diving expedition with the sea gypsies and watched them sitting and chatting casually in their narrow canoes, apparently paying no attention to their surroundings, until suddenly, in the middle of a sentence, one of them would slide off the boat, vanish underwater for what seemed an impossibly long time, and then reappear with the huge gray disk of an oyster in his hands. Quickly he would pry it open with a sliver of bamboo, knead the flesh with his hands, and if there was no pearl, would save the shell to be sold for buttons and ornaments and the meat for oyster stew. Afterward we were served a truly memorable meal—Jolo rice with shark meat, dried stingray, oyster stew, the liver of a fish called pogot dressed with lime juice and chilies, and a plate of what looked like dented ping-pong balls and turned out to be turtle eggs. In the tepid starlit evenings dancers might come to entertain us, clattering their wooden sandals and flirting discreetly as they sang intimate descriptions of the joys of beauty and the pleasures of love. Isolated, arrogant, ruthless if they are crossed, the Sulu Islanders continue to lead their strange amphibious life with a rigid independence from the way the rest of the world may go.

Yet another special pleasure of our journey was a return visit to Bali. Five years earlier I had lived for several months on Bali and had been so bewitched by the place and the people that I had solemnly planned to spend the rest of my life there. I remember that when I had to leave (I had run out of money and my family was worrying about me) I was very sad, and talking one evening to the little boy who lived in the neighboring compound, I had said mournfully, "Can you tell fortunes? Tell me if I shall ever come back to Bali." He had examined the palm of my hand very gravely, and then had traced with a grubby brown finger the four main lines that in most people's hands form the letter M. "Do you know what this M stands for?"

"No. What?"

"It stands for *Manusia Musti Mati*" (Mankind Must Die). "That's all the fortune anyone needs to know. Yelling with laughter at his joke he had dashed away to join the other children. Somehow his casualness and his refusal to be sentimental had cheered me up considerably.

Like most foreigners who have fallen in love with Bali, I was afraid that the island would have "changed," that its magic would have dissipated and its people lost their attraction. Like most returning visitors, I found that Bali *had* changed (it would be a pretty dull civilization if it remained static), but the magic and the attraction were as strong as ever because Bali seems always to change within its own rules, transforming outside influences to fit its own pattern of life, blending it all with some special vitality and integrity of its own. It would have been easy to stay on and on in Bali, going to the magnificent dances and concerts at night, walking through the terraced rice fields of an afternoon to visit a painter or sculptor, or sitting about in one of the pavilions of the village where I had lived, gossiping with old friends and new acquaintances. This time, when we had to leave, I was determined that there would be no tearful regrets—the Balinese would only think it silly. But when I went to say good-by to my host, I couldn't help adding, "I shall miss you all very much, and—" waving a hand at the frivolous palm-thatched pavilions with their painted pillars, the courtyards lined with fighting cocks in cages, the endless stream of people meandering by intent on some errand but always willing to stop and chat—"and I shall miss all this too—all Bali, in fact."

"Of course," my host replied calmly.

We moved on to other islands in Indonesia, the mountains and forests and lakes of Sumatra, the ravishing countryside of Java, the Celebes, all struggling to build some sort of coherent regime from the chaos left by the bitter revolution against the Dutch. Our journey took us on to Thailand, to the fantasy of Bangkok's palaces and temples and the modern city life that bubbled around them, to the jade-green hills of Burma's Shan states and the emerging form of an independent Burma that one saw in the cities of Rangoon and Mandalay, to the driving commercial ferment of Singapore, to the pleasant, accommodating pace of Ceylon's beautiful coastal towns and the splendor of its ancient ruined cities in the central mountains.

At last, as usual, we ended our tour in India, where we settled down for some months to catch up with my family and to do our writing. Out of this long and, to us, absorbing journey, Faubion wrote a book called *Theatre in the East*, and I wrote *View to the Southeast*. However, a couple of incidents from the trip were not recorded in *View to the Southeast*, and like other experiences included in this book, they represent occasions that moved, impressed, instructed or interested me.

# *Makassar robbery*

The Grand Hotel in Makassar has that air of drab pretension that is almost as inescapable a part of the conventional picture of the tropics as stengahs, beachcombers, and monsoon rains. Makassar is, of course, the capital of the Indonesian island of Sulawesi—or Celebes, as it was called by the Dutch. I had been spending some time in Bali, and, still having a week before I was to meet my husband in Java, I thought it might be pleasant to see a little more of Indonesia. I arrived in Makassar in the middle of a morning thunderstorm, went in a pedicab through the flooded streets from the ship to the hotel, and noticed at once, with a comfortable sense of recognition, the Eurasian clerk at the desk, the red-faced European in a corner of the lobby drinking gin at nine o'clock, and a couple of rather shady-looking types in Muslim caps talking in low, serious voices over small cups of coffee. Of course, much of the old grandeur is gone. The Grand Hotel, where the menus are still typed in Dutch, doesn't expect its guests to dress for dinner any longer. In the lounge, the locked piano and the dusty band platform are an apologetic reminder of distant dance nights, of blonde girls in sleeveless dresses strolling through the tall glass doors to the terrace and the cool night and the indeterminate rustling in the dark garden. The bar, with its large beams stained a deep brown, its wooden bar stools, and its fretwork pictures that screen the wall lights, still makes a halfhearted attempt at intimacy. But I saw people in the bar only once—a Chinese family, who ordered orange crush for the children and tea for the adults.

The public rooms make up one wing of the hotel. The other wing, which contains the bedrooms, runs parallel to it and is connected to it by two whitewashed arcades that now have greenish patches of mildew under their eaves and little cushions of moss between the tiles of their floors. A long veranda runs the length of the bedroom wing and all the rooms open on it. On the veranda, in front of each bedroom, wooden screens form a sort of living room. Long-term residents have given some of these living rooms a touch of hominess, strangely contradicted by their lack of privacy. The one next to mine, for instance, had cushioned chairs, reading lamps, a coffee table with a lace cloth on it, and a radio. My own had two rattan chairs, a table, and a desk.

My bedroom itself was very dark, and the damp had outlined fantastic maps on the walls. The bed and a small table were enclosed in a metal screen, a protection against mosquitoes, and you got in through a little door in the screen. Seedy and depressing as the room looked by the light of the foggy overhead bulb, it was equipped with all kinds of senseless gentilities. You could, for instance, draw a curtain around your mosquito screen, like a covering on a parrot cage, to ensure privacy while you slept, or you could drop your cigarette ashes in a miniature dog bowl guarded by a small metal dog. On the backs of the chairs were dreadful bits of embroidered cloth to save the upholstery from hair oil. For some reason, the sight of antimacassars made me feel very glum.

Only the garden, inside the hollow square formed by the hotel wings and arcades, retained a look of luxury. Great banks of pink oleanders grew there, along with an extravagant flowering of cannas and zinnias, two frangipani trees in heady blossom, and a trellis covered with purple morning-glories.

When I had been shown to my room I left my luggage there and went to see what I could find to do in Makassar for a five-day holiday. I had a disappointing morning. I hired a pedicab at the hotel and asked the driver, in a mixture of Malay and English, to take me to see the sights.

"Sights?" he repeated, looking baffled.

"Well, whatever there is to see."

"There is nothing to see."

"There must be *something*," I said. "Old buildings? The market? Anything."

He pointed across the street to a high, lichened wall. "Fort Rotterdam?" he asked doubtfully.

"Good. We will drive through Fort Rotterdam," I said.

"It is forbidden to enter. The soldiers are there."

"Indonesian soldiers?" I asked.

"Yes. There is discontent in Sulawesi. They are meant to keep peace."

"But they make difficulties for you?"

"We are half dead from the soldiers," the driver said. "There is no trouble in Makassar. Upcountry, there is discontent. Yet we get the soldiers, and upcountry they are free."

So we drove along the road by the bay and briefly visited the market, moist and half empty because of the intermittent rain. Piles of fruit—mangosteens, smelly durians, big green pomelos—lay about partly sheltered by banana leaves. Women crouched under umbrellas. Here and there, the owner of a restaurant stall stood over his charcoal stove grilling bits of meat on bamboo skewers. Eventually, we went soggily back to the Grand Hotel, and there, unexpectedly, my pedicab driver said, "If you like, this evening I can take you to the Sirène. It is the best thing to see in Makassar."

I had no idea what the Sirène was, but at least it sounded romantic. "Let us go now," I said.

"Not until six," he replied firmly.

Mystified, but expectant, I spent the remainder of the day in the lobby of the hotel, reading detective stories and gazing out of the doors at the passers-by—men in bright sarongs, women with white gauze shawls over their heads, neat government clerks in Western clothes. At six, the pedicab driver appeared, and a little later he set me down, with a satisfied flourish, at the door of the Sirène. It was a movie theater, showing an old Indian film.

I was, of course, disappointed, and the driver couldn't understand why. "This is what people like to see," he kept repeating. When I insisted that I didn't want to see the film, he sulkily took me back to the Grand Hotel, and I went to bed.

Even with the bedroom door opened wide, the air inside the mosquito screen was stuffy and smelled of damp. I didn't sleep well. I thought the stuffiness was to blame, or the hard wooden bed, or simply the depressing prospect of four more days in Makassar. Rustlings and footsteps mixed with my dreams, and I woke before daylight. As soon as I got up and went out through the door in the mosquito screen, I found why at least part of the night had been troubled. I had been robbed.

Clothes from my suitcase were scattered about the floor. A basket of fruit that I had bought at the market had vanished. About a hundred rupiah (nine dollars) that I had left in a jacket pocket was gone. I rushed back to the table by the bed and looked anxiously through my handbag; passport, traveler's checks, tickets were all safe. Apparently, the thief hadn't come inside the screen.

It was now seven o'clock, and the room boy appeared with tea. He looked with astonishment around the disordered room. "There has been a thief," I announced proudly. "Money has been taken."

I waited for sympathetic noises, commiseration, or at least a regretful shaking of the head.

"You should lock your door," the boy said casually, and slapped the tea tray on the table.

Rather nettled, I asked, "Is there no night watchman in the hotel?"

"There is a night watchman."

"Then it should be his job to watch at night," I said.

"He is here at night," the room boy said patiently. "He has to be here, since his job is to be night watchman."

"But he doesn't see thieves when they enter the hotel?"

"No, he doesn't see," said the boy. "He sleeps at night."

I went to see the manager of the hotel. He listened to me with the dignified concern of an undertaker. "This is very bad," he said in Dutch-accented English. "You have been robbed? Is it true?"

"Yes," I said irritably. "I can't think why the night watchman didn't see the thief. He must have walked in perfectly openly through the veranda door."

"The night watchman sleeps," said the manager.

"So I heard. Why don't you fire him?"

"I cannot do that," the manager said, alarmed. "I must pay him four months' wages for firing. And what is the use? *All* night watchmen sleep at night."

I couldn't think of any answer to that.

"Was much things taken?" the manager asked.

"About a hundred rupiah," I told him. "The rest of my money was in my bag by the bed. The thief didn't come inside the screen."

The manager laughed genially. "It is a timid thief, I think," he said. He assured me that he would call the police.

Later that morning I was asked to come to his office and talk to the police inspector, who proved to be a cheery, good-looking young man, delighted at the opportunity to practice his English. At first he was very correct. He seated himself behind a table and, in an impressive official manner, asked for details of the burglary. "Actually, I can tell you very little," I said. "Someone walked into my room last night and took some money from my pocket."

"Only money?" he asked, and when I nodded, he said sadly, "Ah, in that case it is hopeless. The Chinese family in the next room have good chance. From them, a camera is taken." I must have looked startled, because he explained kindly, "A camera is something to search for, but money is hopeless. You know, probably, the man which took these things?"

"No," I said, now thoroughly puzzled; and I added loftily, "I arrived only yesterday. I am not yet acquainted with the criminals of Makassar."

The policeman bounced anxiously in his chair. "You are not yet acquainted? In Sulawesi, we peoples are very friendly."

"Really?"

"In Sulawesi, it is a custom, peoples come from abroad we must welcome them," he went on. "They enter my house, I must offer them food and to drink. This is the Muslim way."

Becoming interested, I said, "We have the same custom in my country, India."

"But you are not Muslim?" he asked.

"No. I'm Hindu."

"Ah, we have the better chance than *your* men!" He laughed loudly at the little joke he was about to make. "We can marry four wives!"

A room boy had come in a few minutes before, and was standing listening. "What does she say?" he asked in Malay.

The conversation and the joke were translated for him by the policeman. The boy shook his head. "To keep four women in one house, a man must be brave like a tiger," he said.

"Or clever like a snake," I suggested. (I didn't know the Malay for "tactful.")

"Or, best of all," the policeman said, slapping the table and trying to suppress his laughter, "best of all, blind like a bat, which sees nothing in the day and at night goes out of the house altogether!"

At this sally there was an appreciative murmur from behind me, and I turned to find that a couple of strange men had come in by a door I had not noticed before. I wondered confusedly if they had come to see the manager about something. One of them asked, with a slight air of offering a correction, "But is it not true that the Hindus too may have more than one wife? In Bali, which is Hindu, it is done."

"Yes, sometimes, but nowadays it is discouraged," I answered.

"And you?" the stranger asked. "Your husband has probably another wife?"

They all looked at me eagerly. "No," I said. "He is American."

"*American!*" they all said with interest, and smiled at each other.

The man behind me who had not yet spoken remarked wistfully, "I, too, would like to marry an American."

His companion nudged him indulgently and explained, "An American film was here last month. Ever since, his dreams have been of Doris Day."

At that moment a waiter came in, unbidden, bringing cups of sweet, black Indonesian coffee for all of us. Imperceptibly, the atmosphere in the room had changed, and now we were all part of a social gathering of which, somehow, I was the hostess.

"You have quickly learned our manners," the policeman said joyfully as he sipped his coffee.

"It is a pleasant custom," I said, feeling guilty about taking credit for the appearance of the coffee but afraid to abdicate my role as hostess in case someone else should have to pay for it. I supposed that the manager must, thoughtfully, have sent the coffee, assuming that I would want it served.

"You came here only yesterday!" one of the newcomers announced with pleasure, and when I nodded, he asked, "What are you doing here?"

"Well, at the moment I'm reporting a burglary," I said.

The policeman took out a ball-point pen and a notebook, and asked me, with a brief return to his official manner, where I could be reached in the next few weeks. I gave him my address in Java, to which I would be returning for another month.

"Bogor?" the room boy interrupted, catching the name of the town. "My wife's family come from Sunda. Their music is very good."

"And their women are the most beautiful in Indonesia," one of the men behind me added.

"And their countryside is the loveliest I have ever seen," I contributed.

"We also have beautiful rice fields," the policeman said. "Have you seen? No? You will do me the honor, perhaps, to take tea this afternoon with myself and my wife—my *only* wife." We all laughed. "And then we will drive to Sungguminasa."

"Thank you. That is most kind," I said.

"Do not miss the palace of the Raja of Goa," said the man who admired Doris Day.

"Or the brick factory on the way," his friend added.

Nothing more was said about investigating the robbery, and we spent most of the rest of the morning chatting about ourselves, about travel, and about the beauties of the island of Sulawesi, which, I was told, to Indonesian eyes is shaped like an orchid.

The expedition that afternoon was delightful. The policeman's wife, silent and smiling, sat beside me on the back seat of a pony cart while the policeman, splendid in a fuchsia sarong, sat next to the driver. To the accompaniment of the bells that bedecked the pony, we drove through Makassar, past the houses of friends of the policeman, who called out greetings to them, explaining who I was and where we were going. We jingled along between bright-green rice fields, past charming painted wooden houses, each with a frivolously decorated bird cage hanging from its eaves. We watched a football game in Sungguminasa and drove by the sprawling wooden palace there, returning at last to Makassar just after dark.

The policeman and his wife and I met often in the days that followed—to sip coffee at tiny stalls, to watch some Chinese rehearse a dragon dance in preparation for the coming New Year celebrations, or simply to stand on the sea wall in the flaming evening and stare at the square-sailed boats that came gliding in between the islands of Makassar Bay. Nobody mentioned the burglary again. I didn't think of it myself until my boat was moving away from the Makassar wharf and I was gazing regretfully at the pink and turquoise sarongs of the people lounging against the warehouses—and then I felt glad that the thief would never be caught.

## *The laughing Dutchman and the devil dancers*

Supernatural affairs absorbed me deeply during the three months I lived in the small walled town of Galle, on the south coast of Ceylon. I had gone to Ceylon with my three-year-old son largely to escape the steamy monsoon season of Bombay in a midsummer holiday at the beach. Ceylon, of course, is hot, too, but its rains are more equitably divided through the year, and even though Galle is only a couple of degrees north of the equator there is always a fresh wind off the sea. Galle has a climate that suits me particularly well—a climate for cotton dresses and bare feet, for long afternoon siestas, for idling about, for wandering down the beach after dark and finding that the nighttime sea is warmer than the air above it. It was only a day or two after I had moved into the New Oriental Hotel (" 'New'!" the manager used to say to me. "That always makes me laugh. It's the oldest hotel in Ceylon—dates from Dutch colonial days") that I discovered that this was also a climate for the pleasing chill of magic. It all started after dinner one night, when my room boy brought me a carafe of water to put beside my bed and remarked, "Madam mustn't be disturbed if she hears music. It's only the dance party."

I thanked him for his solicitude and watched him walk barefoot down the wide corridor that led from my open door to the staircase. He had surprised me with his message about a dance, for the hotel seemed too sleepy and unfashionable to bother with such entertainment, and so did the twenty-odd people whom I had already learned to recognize as the residents—the two retired civil servants who no longer had the money to live in style in Europe, the Singhalese couple with their numerous children who were spending the school holiday in Galle, the elderly British women with their bird's-nesty hair and their sketch pads, the three young men on a shooting trip, and the rest. I climbed into bed and turned out the light. Lying in the wide bed, on a hard, cool mattress, I looked around my room. The dim light from my windows doubled and flattened the huge black beams across the ceiling, and at that hour the whitewashed walls had none of the clean reassurance of daylight. Reed blinds rattled at the windows of the corridor outside, and the broad teak planks of my floor settled down for the night with occasional creaks and rustles. Somewhere on the floor below a door slammed. But I couldn't hear a sound from the dance downstairs, and rather sleepily I decided that they really knew how to build houses in *those* days.

The next morning, on my way to the beach, I stopped at the hotel desk to ask for letters. The manager was there, busily typing something at his office table, and since I had already acquired that bemused, expansive mood that comes over one on a beach holiday, I congratulated him on the peace and charm of his hotel. "Do you know," I said, "I didn't even hear a murmur of last night's dance. I think that's really astonishing in a town as quiet as Galle."

He looked up, smiling in a slightly irritated way. "The boys have been talking again," he said.

"All he said–" I began.

"We never have dances here," the manager told me patiently. "Unless, of course, someone wants to hire the lounge for a wedding and a party afterward."

"But he–"

"I know, I know," the manager interrupted. "He told you to pay no attention to the music. It's an old story, and so far no one has ever been worried by it."

"Oh, I wasn't *worried*."

"You see, this is a very old building–one of the oldest in Galle–so naturally stories grow up." He rested his arms on the top of the typewriter and continued to smile pleasantly. "It used to be a private house. That must have been more than a hundred and fifty years ago, when the Dutch still ruled Ceylon. The lady who used to live here was– Well, she must have had money, because it's a big house for a single woman, and we know that she used to entertain a great deal. Her husband died here, but she stayed on–didn't want to return to Holland, and who can blame her? And she continued to give her parties. Very gay they were, as you can imagine—silks and satins, and the young officers in dress uniform. Why, the reception room covered all of this ground floor. Well, I dare say the other ladies in the colony didn't entirely approve—I mean, being next door to the Dutch church, and all—and I wouldn't be surprised if the stories about her started then."

"I see," I said, quite entranced by the picture of beautiful, splendidly dressed women sweeping down the curving teak stairs, of a string orchestra, and spruce young men in blue and gold. "What happened to her?"

"Well, nothing much. She grew old, and the parties became quieter, and in the end she too died here. She must have been lonely at the end, because it turned out that she had no one to leave the house to. It went, with the rest of her property, to distant relatives in Holland. They never came out here, I'm told. They must have thought of her as something of a black sheep. They sold the house without ever seeing it. The army bought it and turned it into officers' quarters." He crinkled his eyes and added, in a mildly naughty tone, "Rather appropriate, don't you think? I mean since she had . . . *entertained* so many of them before."

I went off to the beach, still pleased by the idea of her daring dance parties, and determined to listen on future nights for the ghostly sounds of those remote strings, the chatter and laughter of distant Dutch voices, the whisper of brocades down the wide corridors.

Most afternoons, after my child woke up from his siesta, I used to take him for a walk on the ramparts and fortifications. These old walls, overgrown with short, springy grass, are now disintegrating slowly toward the sea. The ancient, crumbling turrets, left over from the sixteenth century, when the Portuguese, before the Dutch, ruled Ceylon, are lined with moss and goats skip among their crenellations. My son used to run after the goats, and I used to run after my son. Warm and out of breath, we would usually end up at the lighthouse, which is built on top of the ramparts and overlooks both the eastern bay of Galle and the immense expanse of ocean to the south. Very often on these early evenings we would meet a Mr. da Souza and his five-year-old son soberly playing cricket together on the clear stretch of grass near the lighthouse. My child would immediately abandon the goats in favor of the cricket ball, and, rather to my surprise, young Francis da Souza was very patient with him, in spite of their two-year age difference, and would allow him to swipe wildly at the air with the bat while he bowled slow, easy balls to him. Mr. da Souza and I sat on the lighthouse steps and watched the children as we exchanged polite, impersonal comments about our surroundings. He was a native of Galle, a short, dark Singhalese with heavily oiled hair and even, small features. He spoke a strongly accented, rather careful English, and his remarks to me were always gently instructive, displaying a fondness for factual detail and a schoolmarmish mind softened by the usual courtesy of his people. Once, as we gazed at the huge breakers crashing below us against the fortress walls, he said, "It is extraordinary, is it not, that these waves come rolling up to us all the way from Antarctica."

"Really? Isn't there any land south of Ceylon?"

"There is no land *directly* south," he corrected. "No land at all."

Gradually, by oblique questions or direct assumptions ("Francis, I suppose, goes to an English school? He plays cricket so well," or "Someone like you, Mr. da Souza, who understands the workings of the government administration . . ."), I learned that Mr. da Souza was a minor official in the Government Accounts Department, stationed in Galle. His wife had died a couple of years before. Francis was his only child. His sister kept house for him. They lived in one of the new, cheaply built houses in the sprawling development of New Galle, a community that had expanded along the edge of the bay outside the fat gray walls of the old city. I also learned that he was a Catholic and that his family had been Catholic for generations. ("You see," he said to me once, with a smile, "the Portuguese colonists were successful in at least one of their aims.") However, in spite of all this general information I acquired about him, Mr. da Souza did not, in truth, interest me very much until we began talking about devils and magic.

After three weeks, our informal rendezvous at the lighthouse had become such a daily habit that I was surprised one evening when Mr. da Souza and his son failed to appear. Several days then went by without a sign of them. I wondered if Francis was sick. Or perhaps Mr. da Souza had leave and the family had gone away for a holiday, although I couldn't imagine why anyone would leave such a perfect holiday place as Galle. Eventually, after an absence of about a week, he did reappear at the lighthouse, and while neither he nor I mentioned the interruption of his normal routine, I could see that something had happened, for he was restless and preoccupied. On the day of his return he was too distracted even to watch the children playing cricket, or to remark, as he often had, on how odd a nearby Buddhist temple looked amid the surrounding eighteenth-century European architecture, or to speculate about what life might have been like in this enclosed fortress before the great walls had become no more than a charming addition to the atmosphere of the town. He couldn't talk and didn't want to listen, and an uneasy, unfamiliar silence fell between us. Suddenly he sprang up from the lighthouse steps and said commandingly, "Come. I will show you some of the sights of Galle."

Obediently I got up, although I had seen the sights of Galle many times. It is a small town; it takes only about twenty minutes to walk the length of the point on which it is built, from the great Indian Ocean on the south to the huge gate that leads to the inland fields, jungles, and mountains, or to walk from the docks of the Galle harbor to the crumbling ramparts on the turbulent western bay. However, Mr. da Souza clearly wanted to walk, so we set off down the road from the lighthouse toward the beautiful square that used to be the center of town, trailed by the children, who kept dropping the cricket ball in the gutter and waving the bat dangerously. Throughout the walk Mr. da Souza made comments about the buildings or streets that we passed, but the usual gently informative joy in the town and its history was absent from his voice. "Scarcely changed in two hundred years," he said abruptly, waving a hand toward the slender arcades around the square, where previously he would have peopled them with the bustling, elegant foreign life of the colonial days. When we passed a crowded alley of open-fronted shops where men sat on the floor polishing a cloudy glitter into piles of moonstones, or sorting opals, or working tortoise shell into elaborate hairpins, Mr. da Souza said nothing at all. Still puzzled by his unhappy silence, I tried to amuse myself by mentally reciting the foreign names for Ceylon that Mr. da Souza had taught me—the heady residue of ancient history: Taprobane, Tenerisim, Ilanare, Serendib.

We turned in to the wider street that sweeps downhill between the Governor's house and the old bell tower and stopped at last before the eastern gate. It is always an impressive moment when you see a sunlit scene through the tunnel-like darkness of an archway. We stood staring at the harbor and the shining bay framed by the deep and lovely gate cut in the outer walls of Galle, and I said conventionally, "It's magical, isn't it?"

Mr. da Souza turned to me alertly. "Magical?" he repeated. Then, in a different tone, he said, "Yes, there is too much magic here."

"Mr. da Souza," I said, unable to disguise my curiosity any longer, "you are obviously worried about something. Do come up to the hotel and have a drink with me and tell me about it." He looked at me coldly for a second, and I was afraid that I had offended him, so I quickly added, "Or don't tell me about it, if you prefer."

"Thank you very much," Mr. da Souza said formally. "I would like to have a drink with you."

At the hotel, waiters brought a table and chairs out onto the lawn for us, and we sat with our backs to the sunset, under an enormous rain tree, gazing out to the darkening bay below us. The children played and chattered with the group of vendors that always hung about the hotel steps, examining models of outrigger fishing boats and prodding at tissue-paper packets of star sapphires and water sapphires. Mr. da Souza ordered beer and sipped it in silence.

"Something happened a week ago," he said at last, "and I am very troubled. We are good Catholics, you understand, and that makes it yet more difficult. I will tell you about it." But then he stopped and said nothing at all for a while. "My sister is not imaginative," he announced suddenly. "She will make a good wife to somebody one day. She's a sensible housekeeper and she has taken good care of the child and me. She used to laugh a great deal. That's it." He looked straight at me to give his words emphasis. "I'm sure that's it. She should never have laughed at him."

"At Francis?" I asked uncertainly.

"No, no." He waved a hand in an impatient gesture. "At that man—that Dutchman. A week ago—last Tuesday—she was returning from church, from the vesper service, and on the walk back to our house she passed an old building. It is used as a godown now—a rather dilapidated little warehouse, actually—but it dates from Dutch times, I can assure you of that. At first I thought she was mistaken when she told me what she had seen. It was twilight, you understand, and she could easily have been mistaken, and it seemed so unlikely that she should see him when she was returning from church and was filled with goodness." He shook his head sadly. "The man was standing on top of the wall of the godown and he was dressed in the manner of the colonial Dutch—tight breeches, short jacket, buckled shoes, and all that. But she didn't recognize the clothes. She takes no interest in history. She thought he just looked funny stand-there in those strange clothes, and she laughed at him. I told her, when she described him to me, that she should not have laughed. It was impolite, whoever he was."

I said, "Do you mean that you think the man was a ghost?"

"Can there be any doubt?"

"Well, in that tricky light . . ."

"Ah, I too hoped it was only a question of the light. But that night the man came to our house. He must have followed her."

"Came to your *house?* Did you see him?"

"I couldn't see him, but she could. Suddenly she stared at one corner of the ceiling and screamed. 'He is there!' she said. 'He is looking at me and laughing!' As you can well believe, I was very distressed. I tried to tell her she was imagining things, but she wouldn't listen to me and ran into her bedroom. But the Dutchman appeared again, in a corner of the bedroom ceiling. He appeared always, you see, at the same height as when she had first seen him, on the wall of the godown. I have never seen anyone in a true frenzy before, but that was my sister's state. She ran out to the veranda, but there he was again, floating above the veranda railing. She began to throw herself about in terror, shouting and crying. Her hair came down and she tore her sari. She was in such a condition that she would not have felt it if you had jabbed a pin into her. She found a stick somewhere and tried to strike the ghost. She made so much noise that the neighbors came over to see what was happening. They tried to help me calm her, but she wouldn't listen to us, or couldn't hear us. It was terrible. At last she fell exhausted to the floor, and ever since then she has been incapable of coherent speech. She either lies quite stiffly on her bed, without moving, or leaps up and screams and pleads with the laughing Dutchman in the corner of her ceiling. Poor Francis now has no clean shirts to wear. The neighbors have been very kind and have come in to cook the meals. But the house has not been cleaned. The chickens have been fed only when someone has remembered. And even Francis' pet dog has run away." He paused and looked into his empty beer glass. "What to do?" he said, in soft despair. "What to do?"

"Perhaps you should take your sister to a psychiatrist," I suggested after a moment. "If you know of a good one somewhere in Ceylon."

"That is what they would do in India?" he inquired sharply.

"Well, not in India so much. I was thinking more of America."

"You have lived for long in America?"

"A few years, yes."

"Yes." He nodded with a sort of gloomy resignation. "There too they believe in magic."

"It's not really considered magic," I said carefully. "I mean it's supposed to be a science."

"That is what the devil dancers tell me, also." He caught my look of astonishment, and added, "That theirs too is a science. Like psychiatry, you understand. They cure such–ills. I believe some of these men are wise, for they have seen many afflicted people." Suddenly he burst out, "But I am a good Catholic! How can I have dealings with magic?"

"You couldn't bring yourself to try psychiatry–to accept it as medical treatment?" I asked.

"Or a devil dance," he insisted. "If I accept one, why not the other?"

"Surely they're a bit different."

But he shook his head. "All magic. You try to cure what you cannot see. Where is the soul? I ask of you. Has it blood? Flesh? Cells? How can I believe in medical treatments for the troubles of the soul? I must think. I must *think*."

"Do let me know if I can help," I said rather stupidly.

"You are already too kind."

"I could look after Francis in the afternoons."

"I could not trouble you."

For the next few days I didn't see Mr. da Souza, and though I often thought about him and wondered whether he had solved his problem, I didn't have quite the nerve to telephone him at his office. On Sunday morning, however, while I was standing on the veranda trying to decide whether there was time to get to the beach and back before it rained, Mr. da Souza, with Francis beside him, drove up to the hotel steps in a small horse cart. He walked slowly toward me while my son rushed out to talk to the horse and to Francis and the driver.

"Good morning," Mr. da Souza said abruptly, and then he was silent for several moments, watching the congregation file into the Dutch church next door. At last he said, "Will you come to a village with me? It isn't far."

Before I could ask him where we were going and why, he had turned away and was striding back to the cart. I followed him, thinking that he would probably explain once we got started. The children sat in front, next to the driver, while we sat with our backs to them, watching the receding road. Mr. da Souza said nothing at all as we rattled down the short, steep hill to the inland gate of Galle, passed the large circular green outside the old city, where the Galle boys usually played football of an afternoon, and turned into the road that follows the curve of the eastern bay and leads to New Galle. By that time, intimidated by his silence, I couldn't bring myself to ask any questions. Then, as we drove past the Catholic church in New Galle and heard the bell ringing and saw the last stragglers hurrying up the path, he nodded toward the building and remarked bitterly, "You will see what I have come to!"

We must have driven three or four miles before we left the main road, turning first into a narrow side road and then into a lane. Finally, we went bumping and jingling between the palms of a coconut grove, to stop quite suddenly at a sort of village. A few small, square houses, with whitewashed walls and coconut-frond thatches, stood around a clearing of beaten earth. We climbed down from the horse cart and stood about rather helplessly. There seemed to be nobody around except two boys, who were crouching on one side of the clearing and playing some elaborate game with sticks and stones. They looked up from this absorbing ritual when the driver yelled at them, and then fled behind the biggest of the houses. "This is the devil dancers' village," Mr. da Souza told me. "I hope you do not mind that I brought you."

"Not at all, not at all," I said, inadequately.

Within a few moments the door of the biggest house opened and an old man in a red-and-green checked sarong and a white shirt came toward us. He was tall, and looked taller still because he stood very straight and walked with the easy confidence of a much younger man. He was smiling pleasantly, but I thought I detected under his affable manner a thoughtful, analytical expression. I noticed that his hair was dressed in the old-fashioned way–scraped up into a bun high on the back of his head, and held in place by a semicircular tortoise-shell comb. There must have been some tiny brilliants embedded in the tortoise shell, for as he moved the sunlight flashed on the comb, giving it the authority of a crown. His gestures were old-fashioned too. He ignored Mr. da Souza's outstretched hand, with a look too fleeting to be called contempt, and, instead, brought his own hands together, palm to palm, in the traditional Singhalese greeting. The alert, considering eyes took in my beach clothes and Mr. da Souza's Western suit. The old man spoke a few words to Mr. da Souza in Singhalese and then snapped his fingers and said something sharply to the two boys behind him. They immediately scuttled into the house and came struggling out again with three rickety wooden chairs, which they placed some distance apart in the middle of the clearing. Mr. da Souza indicated where I should sit, and took the chair next to me, and then the old man sat down facing us.

The courtesies in Singhalese continued, and since I couldn't understand what the two men were saying, I watched the boys getting coconuts for us. One of them hitched up his sarong and, with a neat economy of movement, shinned up a palm bole, produced a knife from the cloth at his waist and cut down three coconuts. The other stood underneath, caught the coconuts, stripped off the outer fiber, sliced off the top of the inner casing, and brought one to each of us. I sat there and sipped the thin, sweetish liquid, keeping an eye on Francis and my son and half listening to Mr. da Souza, who seemed to be conducting complicated negotiations with the old chief of the devil dancers. I found that I was enjoying the warm, moist morning and the pleasing cadences of a language I didn't understand, but I did wonder occasionally why Mr. da Souza had brought me along on this expedition.

He talked away earnestly, with frequent emphatic movements of his hands. The old man nodded from time to time, or interrupted with a few words, and quite often glanced at me with polite amusement. Once he said, in halting English, "Tourist, is it?" and I smiled and nodded.

Mr. da Souza said to me, "I hope you won't mind . . ."

"Of course not," I assured him. "After all, I *am* a tourist."

Later, the old man turned to me again, and said, "Seventy rupees. All right?"

I looked nervously at the two men and began to wish that I spoke Singhalese. "Seventy rupees for what?" I asked sternly.

But before the old man could reply, Mr. da Souza burst into another torrent of Singhalese. He was answered heatedly. He retorted with scorn. Just as they seemed about to reach the point of real anger, the old man spread out his hands and said sadly to me, "All right. Fifty rupees."

"What *for?*" I insisted.

"For we do you the dance."

"You do the dance for *me?*"

Mr. da Souzi seemed most upset. "Naturally, I will handle the payment," he said.

"I see," I said, not seeing at all.

"I had to tell him that you were a tourist who wanted to see one of Ceylon's celebrated devil dances," he continued rapidly and in a low voice. "I was not able to ask for myself. Do you mind?"

"Well . . . no." I understood at last why my presence had been necessary for this visit. Since Mr. da Souza was known in Galle as a good Catholic, it would certainly have been embarrassing for him to have the devil dancers for himself. A favor to a visiting tourist, however, was quite another matter.

In the horse cart, on the way back to the hotel, Mr. da Souza asked again, anxiously, "You're sure you do not mind that I arranged it in this way?"

"On the contrary," I said, feeling by this time rather excited about the whole thing. "I'm looking forward to the dances. I believe in magic, you know."

"I know you do. I knew it when you recommended psychiatry for my sister."

I started to protest again over his confusion of the two, but Mr. de Souza went on talking quite cheerfully.

"The old man made some trouble to begin with. He said that it was not proper to do the dances unless there was a patient, an illness to be cured. So I told him that my sister chanced to be ill, and we could therefore hold the dances most suitably at my house and manage to satisfy your interest at the same time."

"It all worked out very neatly, didn't it?" I said, with a touch of annoyance at the way he had used me.

"Yes, didn't it?" He smiled at me disarmingly.

I couldn't help asking, "But what made you decide on a devil dance after all?"

"By now," he said thoughtfully, "Francis and I have learned to take care of ourselves, and I have arranged for a servant to look after the house. But with my sister things have become more serious. Yesterday she found an egg."

"An *egg?*"

"Oh, naturally we have eggs in the proper places for eggs—in the kitchen or in the henhouse—but this egg she found in her bedroom. Or so she said, at least."

"Yes, that does seem unusual."

"I do not entirely understand the meaning, but it is certainly a sign of some kind. The old man was very interested in that egg when I told him about it."

Word of our arrangements for the devil dance seemed to spread instantly about Galle. A couple of the room boys in the hotel assured me they would come to watch. The manager said, "I hear you're having a devil dance. I haven't a doubt you'll find it interesting, but—a word to the wise—you won't swallow all the stories they tell you about it, will you?"

"Oh, of course not," I said, heartily but without real conviction. I had certainly "swallowed" Mr. da Souza's original story, and now, since he felt happier about devil dancing than about psychiatry, and since the cost was so much less, I had decided that it was very sensible of him to try the best available therapy. Some teen-age boys at the beach with whom we often went swimming had told me that the devil dancers Mr. da Souza had chosen were the most reputable troupe in the area.

On the day of the event, I watched the soft-clouded sky anxiously, hoping that the rain would either hold off entirely or expend itself before nighttime. At half past eight that evening the two room boys and my son and I all climbed into a horse cart and clattered excitedly off to New Galle and the house of Mr. da Souza.

It turned out to be a conventional square, whitewashed house, set back from a side road and with a small garden in front. Mr. da Souza was waiting at the gate. He fussed about us as we dismounted, and he insisted upon paying the horse-cart driver. Smiling, exhilarated, talkative, he seemed entirely different in the Singhalese sarong and shirt that he was wearing in place of his customary white drill trousers and white cotton shirt.

He and his neighbors must have been busy all day erecting the bamboo pavilion that now covered most of the garden space. A strong, thick bamboo trunk was set like a pillar at each corner of the pavilion to hold up a lacy arrangement of palm leaves, which served as a roof. I guessed that the neighborhood children had been sent to pick the flowers that were tucked here and there in the ceiling. There were more flowers—hibiscus, marigolds, and poinsettias—tied to the pillars, which were also wrapped with vines and leaves, making each pillar into a bizarre tree. At one end of the pavilion was an altar—a high table with round bamboo legs and a slatted bamboo top. The altar was covered with little hills of saffron-colored flowers and pretty, leafy decorations, and around its edge were streamers of palm strips, hanging down almost to the ground, like an odd sort of tablecloth. From each end of the altar a rather crumpled muslin curtain was stretched to a pillar of the pavilion. The three other sides of the pavilion were open to the garden, to the inquisitive stares of passers-by on the road, and to the veranda of Mr. da Souza's house. Immediately in front of the veranda someone had placed a low bed—really just a wooden platform—covered with a white sheet. Two glary kerosene lanterns illuminated the fragile shelter. Already a considerable crowd of friends, neighbors, and uninvited townspeople was standing about watching, and rows of barefoot children sat on the ground along the edges of what proved to be the dance area.

Mr. da Souza and I sat in straight chairs set near the bed, and Francis and my son settled down on the ground with the other children. Mr. da Souza told me that the dancers and musicians had arrived but that nothing could begin until the preliminary religious ceremonies had been completed. The headman from the dancers' village and another old man were standing in front of the altar, intoning prayers and mantras, some in Singhalese and some in what I guessed to be Sanskrit. Various people—several of the dancers and several neighbors—were piling offerings of coconuts and fruit and rice on the altar, and from time to time one of the old men would sprinkle these with water. At the other end of the pavilion the musicians were unconcernedly spreading a mat on the ground, arranging the drums, and taking their places. A group of singers were already seated nearby.

Then there was a stir behind us, and I turned to see two women helping Mr. da Souza's sister down the veranda steps. She was dressed in a white sari, her hair neatly bound up in a knot at the back of her head. She seemed calm, but she walked stiffly and showed no particular interest in the proceedings. She lay down on the bed, closed her eyes, and turned her face toward the house. This did not seem to be a gesture of defiance but more one of weariness. She had the blank, uncomprehending look of someone badly shocked, but what impressed me most of all was that she appeared only to want to be left alone. When the two women turned her so that she was facing the pavilion, she did not resist, but she seemed not to be a part of all the fuss and ceremonial excitement around her.

It was now about ten o'clock. The chanting ended and the headman came over to say something in Singhalese to Mr. da Souza. By that time only Mr. da Souza and I were keeping up the pretense that the dance was being held to satisfy my tourist curiosity, but I still felt entitled by this fictitious position to demand explanations, so the rest of the evening was punctuated with my questions—"What are they doing?" "What did he say?" "*Now* what are they doing?" —and Mr. da Souza's whispered replies.

Now he told me, "The old man wants to know what is the matter with my sister."

"I should have thought it was his job to diagnose the trouble."

"Oh, no. There are certain diseases—like appendicitis, for example —that they do not claim to cure. Can your psychiatrists cure them?"

"I suppose not."

"It is the same."

Mr. da Souza described his sister's experience to the old man, and explained that she suffered from alternate phases of utter withdrawal and great agitation. The old man nodded solemnly, asked a few questions, and then gave a signal to the musicians. The drummer began a strong, cheerful rhythm, the thin, sad sound of a flute joined in, and then, almost indistinguishable from the flute, the voices of the women singers rose. The dancing started quite briskly, each dancer coming out to the dance area alone to execute a few rapid turns and leaps, and then retiring to the side of the altar. There were six or seven of the dancers, all young men, who wore loose white trousers covered by calf-length skirts, and had bands of small bells strapped to their ankles. They were bare-chested, and their headdresses were made of red cloth, wound tightly over the forehead, with tassels of palm fiber hanging over the ears.

Soon the dancers appeared in twos and threes, and the dancing became faster and more acrobatic. They whirled around the clearing with such speed and in such intricate patterns of movement that it became impossible to distinguish one dancer from another. The drumming grew louder, the crowd more excited, but when I glanced over at Mr. da Souza's sister she was lying with her eyes still closed and her face now turned away from the dancing.

There came a moment when the rhythm of the drums changed and the dancers all appeared holding blazing palm-leaf torches. From time to time, as they continued their spins and turns, they would fling a whitish powder—gunpowder, I guessed—on their torches, making sudden sheets of flame. Some rubbed themselves with red-hot embers, some appeared with a torch in each hand and described wild circles of fire as they danced round the clearing. Still the figure on the bed lay motionless.

Abruptly the fire dancing came to an end. There was a consultation, conducted in low, worried voices, between Mr. da Souza and the old man. During this pause in the ceremony all the spectators were served with some rather nasty raspberry soda pop, and the orchestra drank palm beer. As I sipped my soda I kept watching the sister, who remained shrouded in her white sari and in her silent rejection of all the activity around her. I was suddenly very sorry for her. Clearly, she was sick. It must have been anything but soothing for her to listen to the relentless drums and to the gasps and shouts of the audience as the torches flared and the dancers stamped across the pavilion. Perhaps she had greater fortitude than I would have guessed possible, or perhaps she didn't hear any of it at all. From her expression, from her immobility, I couldn't tell; she might have been asleep.

When the performance resumed, two of the dancers appeared dressed as women. Throughout the action that followed, one retained the role of a Singhalese housewife, while the other was sometimes a friend, sometimes a neighbor or a servant or a mother-in-law, as the unfolding dance story required. Accompanied only by the singers, they went through a long pantomime, of remarkable precision, depicting the daily life, the duties, the joys of a Singhalese woman—the washing of clothes, the cleaning of the house, the peeling and preparing of vegetables, the cooking, the care of the children. At last the chores are done, and the housewife sits down before her mirror, combs and oils her hair, knots it carefully, makes herself beautiful for her husband. At this moment, the mood of the dance was broken by a gasp and a sudden struggling movement from the bed. The reedy singing of the women stopped. The dancers turned to stare at Mr. da Souza's sister. She sat up and swung her feet to the ground. She said something in a harsh, demanding voice. I nudged Mr. da Souza. Without looking at me, he said, "She wants to dance."

The old man hurried over and held a palm wand above the sister's head. Then the drums struck up again. The two pantomimists shuffled away, and another dancer, dressed in the male costume, appeared. He began to dance slowly in front of the sister. After a moment or two, she stepped forward, took her place behind the dancer, and started to follow his movements. The drumming gained speed and complexity, and the sister danced with it, leaving her partner and inventing movements of her own. She twisted away and circled the clearing. Her hair came down. She danced with increasing abandon, tossing her hair back when it got in her eyes. All of us—even the dancers—watched her in silence, not knowing quite what to expect. Slowly her movements became less frantic, and at last, breathless and shiny with sweat, she sank back on the bed.

It was by now well after midnight. The old man again talked with

Mr. da Souza, who then told me that it was time to bring on the eighteen demons. "They are terrifying," he said, "but you must not be distressed. They do good."

"Good demons?"

"No, they are bad, but so frightening that they scare away the other devils."

They were frightening, all right, and I was pleased to see that my child had gone to sleep, leaning limply against Francis. Even the thunderous roll of drums that announced the appearance of each demon failed to wake him. One by one, in black, green, or scarlet masks, in extraordinary costumes made of thick green leaves, with fangs, with great shocks of black hair, with talons or claws, with fierce, inhuman screams, the demons danced out, and eventually vanished into the enclosing darkness. Through it all the sister sat upright on the bed and watched; she trembled from time to time but otherwise showed no expression.

At last the performance ended, with more prayers and chanting. We got stiffly to our feet as the musicians and dancers started packing up their things. The sister was led back indoors. I looked at my watch, and was astonished to find that it was almost 3 A.M. Sleeping children were picked up, and the crowd dispersed in silence. We got back to the hotel just before dawn.

The next evening I hurried to the lighthouse, and found Mr. da Souza on the steps. When the children had become absorbed in their cricket game, he turned to me with his old smiling formality. "A fine, clear evening," he said. "We are nearly at the end of the rainy season."

"Will it get much hotter now?" I asked impatiently.

"It will get hot, but the sea becomes more beautiful. It will no longer be this muddy green."

"Mr. da Souza, I *must* ask you. Is she cured?"

He stared at the ground, frowning. "She is silent, but she goes about her business in the house," he said. "I think she is cured."

"Does the old man think so, too?"

"I think he may. He came to the house this morning to collect the rest of his fee, and we talked about my sister. He felt that the point at which she showed interest in the dance was very significant. You remember—how she ignored it all until the dancers were acting out the return of a husband to his wife at the end of the day. He prescribed"—Mr. da Souza smiled slightly at the little joke he was about to make—"I suppose you would call it 'treatment.' He said she should get married."

"Does she want to?"

"All women must want to get married," Mr. da Souza said, with a sigh. "I will have to arrange a marriage for her. I should have done so sooner, but I thought only of my own convenience and of Francis. And as a consequence she withdrew from her duties in my house. A woman's duties—the same duties—would appear different to her in her own house."

"You mean her illness was sort of a protest against her position in your house?"

He spread his hands in a helpless gesture. "At least, her illness drew attention to that position."

"But what will happen to you and Francis now?"

"I suppose I could remarry. My sister has often told me that I should, but I never listened. I thought that in saying this she was concerned for my welfare and happiness. I see now that she was also worried about her own. First, I will take her and Francis for a couple of weeks to the hills, to Kandy. When we return, I shall look for a husband for her."

"In that case, I probably won't see you again," I said. "We'll be leaving before you get back."

"Ah, I regret that." He paused as if he were formulating a difficult speech, and then said to me, with utter sincerity, "I must take this occasion, then, to thank you for your good advice. About psychiatry, I mean."

"Or devil dancing."

"Or devil dancing," he agreed, laughing.

# NINE

Our next extended journey took us to Russia. Faubion, who speaks Japanese, Chinese, Malay, French and Spanish, had also at one time learned Russian. He had studied it for what seemed to me rather eccentric reasons—he was interested in the music of Alexander Scriabin and apparently most of the relevant contemporary material about him was in Russian. The simplest thing, Faubion decided (his mind has its own weird logic), was to learn Russian and then try to get access to the unpublished music of Scriabin, to his diaries, letters, and reminiscences of his friends. Finances, the war, six years in the army, the occupation of Japan, the difficulties of getting a visa to Russia, and then again finances, slowed up his old dream of going to Moscow to find the material he wanted in Russian archives.

In 1957, after the "thaw" had started in Russia and it was possible for tourists to visit the country, we decided to join the increasing number of foreigners, attracted by curiosity and special interest, in seeing a nation that had for so long been inaccessible to casual travelers of our sort. In Moscow Faubion would be able to dig about to his heart's content in the Scriabin museum, both of us could write articles for magazines, Faubion could write his book about the Russian theater and dance, Jai could go to school and learn Russian. Faubion's findings are contained in his book *Broadway U.S.S.R.*, and mine in *My Russian Journey*. Jai has so far shown no urge to express himself in print.

I hadn't really known just what I expected of Russia. I told myself rather vaguely that I "simply wanted to go and see for myself."

An English friend of mine crystallized my attitude when she remarked, "I can see why you might want to go. It is just about the only place that is *abroad* any more."

We arrived in Leningrad, and both Faubion and I fell under the spell of that huge, lovely city, with all its faded elegance and its haunting reminders of the grandiose days of the czars when it was St. Petersburg. The palaces, the great houses, the imposing façades are still painted in the pale frivolous colors that the lost aristocracy fancied. The towers and domes and monuments, scattered across a hundred islands, still rise splendidly along the banks of the Neva River and the city's countless canals. And Leningrad is famous for its long-drawn-out evenings, a sentimental northern light that softens colors and is kind to evidences of decay and suits the city perfectly.

Of course we spent a lot of time sightseeing in Leningrad and walked for miles through palaces, cathedrals, museums. But one experience there seemed to me more impressive than anything else. It had the solid feeling of real life rather than of distant grandeur, and provided for us an unintentional excursion into modern Russian life.

Knowing that the Russians have a pleasing custom of preserving the house or apartment of a very distinguished person as an informal sort of museum—we had been shown enthusiastically through the early-nineteenth-century stylishness of Pushkin's apartment—I had asked Svetlana, our tourist guide, if we could see Dostoyevsky's apartment too. She had stubbornly tried to discourage us, and only when we equally stubbornly insisted had she taken us to a rather shabby part of town where, presumably, tourists seldom penetrated. She stopped the car on an undistinguished street corner and pointed to an apartment building. Its yellowish paint was chipped and peeling badly and large patches of plaster had been blasted off by shells during the war. She told us we couldn't go in because it wasn't a museum, and when I asked whether she could at least tell me which were the windows of the apartment where Dostoyevsky had lived, she shrugged but passed my question on to some children playing in the gutter. They simply stared at us with that particular cautious silence of slum children. Svetlana said, "There is nothing to see," in an I-told-you-so voice. And there the matter was dropped—except that Faubion and I were determined to find our way back there, without Svetlana, before we went on to Moscow.

The day we left Leningrad was moist and cold. Leningraders said that the summer was really over now. No more long mild evenings. Now autumn would spread, like the penetrating chill from the Neva, through the city. All afternoon I had been reading *The Insulted and Injured*, that early, inept, and curiously moving mixture of autobiography and fiction that Dostoyevsky had written nearly a century ago in St. Petersburg. When I came to passages like "he pointed to the foggy vista of the street, lighted by street-lamps dimly twinkling in the damp mist, to the dirty houses, to the wet and shining flagstones, to the cross, sullen, drenched figures that passed by, to all this picture hemmed in by the dome of the Petersburg sky," I had only to look out my hotel window to find an almost theatrical re-enactment of the scene. Although it wasn't actually raining, the Leningrad sky was soft with clouds and St. Isaac's golden dome was transformed by reflection to a somber metallic gray.

After tea Faubion and I walked to Dostoyevsky's apartment. It was already deep twilight, the premature evening of misty weather. When we again stood outside the building we could feel the damp seeping up from the canal at the end of the next block. The first trickle of people coming back from work had begun and there were customers at both the cigarette stall and, surprisingly, at the cold-drink stand. Three women in dark winter-looking clothes with woolen scarves over their heads and holding shopping baskets stood talking on the corner. They looked at us with curiosity, two foreigners idling about indeterminately on the sidewalk, and then went back to their gossip and news.

Imitating Svetlana, we stopped the first person who passed us on the pavement, a middle-aged woman with an occupied air. Faubion asked her whether she knew which was the apartment of Dostoyevsky.

She looked at us unbelievingly. "*Which* apartment?"

"Of Dostoyevsky. The writer."

"You are a foreigner?"

"Yes. American."

"I too am a foreigner. Czech. I know nothing of this." She smiled and added "Good evening" politely.

The entrance to the building was on the alleyway half blocked by the pile of lumber and building materials. "There is an alley, dark and narrow, shut in by huge houses. . . . The second house from the corner was under construction and was surrounded by scaffolding. The fence around the house came almost to the middle of the alley, and a footway had been laid round the fence." The place must have looked very much like this when Dostoyevsky wrote that passage, I thought.

We walked through the archway to a dank and messy courtyard. Firewood was stacked all across one side, partly covered with a length of tarpaulin. Next to it was a small shed or outhouse with a rotted door hanging unevenly from its hinges. Moisture had collected in shallow puddles between the flagstones. The children we had seen on our first visit were playing there, taking turns in climbing to the outhouse roof, jumping to the firewood, and then to the ground across a wide sheen of water. They stopped their game to stare at us, until we turned away uncertainly to examine the wooden board hung on a nail just inside the archway. It gave, in white painted letters, the names of the tenants and their apartment numbers, but that, of course, was no help to us.

We were trying to collect the courage to knock on the door of one of the apartments—any apartment—when the biggest of the children, the shaved-headed blond boy, came over to us.

"Foreigners?" he asked without smiling.

"Yes."

"Poles?"

"No," Faubion said, "I'm—"

"Hungarian?"

"No, American."

"Chewing gum?" the boy said hopefully.

"No chewing gum," Faubion said, sorry to disappoint the child.

But the boy was already busy unbuttoning his coat and fishing in the pocket of his shorts with a chapped and dirty hand. He produced a small, rather tarnished gilt-and-enamel badge, made like a lapel pin, and held it out to us on the palm of his hand. On the badge, in Russian characters, was inscribed "1957 Youth Festival U.S.S.R.," obviously a souvenir of the previous summer. "Foreign money?" he asked.

"I'm sorry. But we will buy it for rubles if you want."

"Rubles?" He turned down the corners of his mouth and put the badge away in his pocket. He looked resigned more than disappointed. While he was busy with the badge he said suddenly and casually, with his eyes averted, "You are searching still for the same apartment?"

"Yes."

"Second entrance, third floor, on your left." He raced away to join his companions, leaving us wondering. Had he expected a tip? If so, he hadn't allowed us time to give him one. Had he been unwilling to talk the first time we saw him because of the intimidating presence of Svetlana and the official-looking car? Had it just been the general caution of people who live in a cautious world? Shyness? And then, this time, was he just being kind? Had he been pleased that we had offered to buy his badge, even in rubles? But why had he approached us anyway? We never came to a satisfactory explanation of his behavior. It occurred to me much later that it is only in Russia that one searches so diligently for motives.

Inside the doorway marked "2" we found ourselves in a stone-floored hallway, colder than the evening outside. The stairs were uncarpeted stone too, with iron bars on each landing. On one landing a metal bathtub was propped against the wall with its four little claw feet sticking out toward the stairs. On the third floor two doors faced each other across the small hallway. Both were heavily padded and had strips of felt hammered along the edges to cover the cracks. We rang the bell of the door on the left.

All the way up Faubion had been composing sentences in his politest Russian. "Please forgive us for disturbing you, but is this the apartment that was at one time occupied by Fyodor Mikhailovich Dostoyevsky, the writer?" But when the door was opened to us by a gray-haired woman in a dark dress with a sweater over it, he could only blurt out, "Good evening—did Dostoyevsky live here?"

Understandably, she looked astonished. "*What* did you say?" she asked, and added as an afterthought, "Good evening."

The second time it came out sounding better, and she smiled. "Ah, Dostoyevsky. You are foreigners?"

"Yes. Tourists. And we are so sorry to trouble you."

"Ah, *tourists*. It is no trouble. Please come in. You are interested in Dostoyevsky?"

"We think him a great writer."

"Come in, please come in. Yes, this used to be his apartment."

She beckoned us through the outer and the inner door, equally padded, an arrangement like the light baffles of public buildings during wartime blackouts. I was suddenly aware of how drafty and freezing the Leningrad winter must be. She locked both doors behind us, and remarked pleasantly, "You would like to see this apartment where he lived? It is nothing very special."

A woman's voice from behind a closed door called out something to which our hostess replied, "Come here, come here," and, smiling at us, explained, "My sister—my younger sister."

The door on our left opened and a small round woman, dressed in black, emerged. She had a face like a bun, with bright, inquisitive raisin-colored eyes, and dark hair drawn into a knot on the back of her neck. "Foreigners," her sister said, as though only that one word would explain our presence. The four of us stood uncomfortably close together, packed between the padded black bench on one side of the foyer and a tall white-painted cupboard on the other. There was an old-fashioned wooden coatrack in one corner, and simply no room for any other furniture.

The older woman said, "I have often thought what kind of furniture Dostoyevsky had. This hall must have been empty—you can see that would be better. Really, there is only space for the waiting bench and the coatrack. Probably he had not much furniture to put here—he always had to sell things to pay doctors' bills, debts." She smiled at us rather apologetically. "I know all this because I have lived here so long—thirty years, even before I was married. When we first moved here there were still old people in the building who remembered Dostoyevsky. They are dead now, of course. But they used to tell us. Movers would come up the stairs. Another piece of furniture taken away. Another bill paid. He was very sick, you know. I was young when I heard these things, and it all seemed to me sad." She shrugged her shoulders. "Now . . ."

Now worse things have happened to all of us? I wondered. Or, now I have other things to think about?

But Faubion said politely, "Now he would have had free medical care?"

She laughed as though we all shared a secret together. "Yes. That is true."

With a rush of housewifely indignation she said, "You should have seen the place when we moved in! Dirt? Incredible! The people who had taken this apartment before us had done nothing to it. Of course, practically none of Dostoyevsky's things were here even when *they* came—even the books had been sold. Only this cupboard remained." She pointed to the tall, cheap cupboard in the hall. "It used to be in his bedroom. He kept his books in it. We had it painted white and moved here. There is so little space."

The younger sister opened the door behind her. "This was his room," she said in a soft, deprecating voice. "The coldest and darkest room in the building. This is where he lived." *The Insulted and Injured* had opened with the hero looking for a place to live: "All that day I had been walking about the town trying to find a lodging. My old one was very damp and I was beginning to cough rather ominously." We followed the sisters into his room. Smallish, with two narrow windows set close together in the wall opposite the door, it too looked crowded although there was actually not much furniture. Two iron beds, one under each window, a cupboard, a round table covered with a plush tablecloth, a couple of straight chairs. I walked over to the windows, squeezing past the table, and stared out at Dostoyevsky's view. The dingy courtyard, the dark thin little figures of the children playing, the Leningrad evening closing in.

Behind me one of the sisters switched on the light and said, "He worked here too, so I was told. He was in bed much of the time and had to do his writing here."

I turned away from the window to face the Victorian look of the room in the lamplight, the pink-flowered wallpaper, the tablecloth edged with little round bobbles. "Dostoyevsky's wallpaper was still here when we came to this apartment. It was a dark green, about this color." She indicated with her fingernail a fragment of leaf in the design of the present paper, a rather murky sage green. "But it was so badly stained and torn that we had to change it."

I could think of no questions to ask, could not even imagine the sick, tormented figure lying under that tidy white counterpane, writing away in the coldest, dampest room.

We crossed the tiny foyer to the door immediately opposite. This room was a bit bigger, with French windows opening on a narrow iron balcony that we had seen from the street. Here, too, there was a bed, but apparently the room was also used as a parlor—that is what it had been in Dostoyevsky's day—and there were three armchairs covered in white cotton and another round table. The wallpaper too was rather more formal, a plain, milky green the color of celadon, with a decorative border of rather fanciful urns. "The sun comes in here in the afternoons," the gentle voice of the younger sister said, "when we have some sun." We all smiled with her. Leningrad weather, like London weather, is always good for a mild crack.

While we were in this room the doorbell rang. The older sister hurried out to answer it, and we could hear fragments of a muttered conversation in the hall. Almost immediately our hostess returned with another woman of stocky build and slightly severe expression. She was still in her outdoor coat and scarf and was carrying a string bag filled with a bunch of onions, a large cabbage, a loaf of black bread and some packages wrapped in newspaper. She was introduced as "my older sister. This is her room."

In the awkward silence that followed I said, "How nice that the family is all together." When Faubion translated this, our hostess replied, without much interest, "Yes. We all lived here together once, when we were young. Now we all live here together again. Three old women."

"And in between?" my husband asked.

"In between, we married. And the war. All three husbands killed. Again we live together—like girls." She laughed to emphasize the absurdity of her description.

Back to the foyer and then into a thin sliver of a pantry next to the bedroom-parlor. Obviously part of the passageway had been partitioned off to make this pantry. The older sister was there unpacking her purchases. Eggs in a plastic bowl on the table, cookies on a blue china plate. There was a small electric hot plate on the table too, which transformed the narrow pantry into a makeshift kitchen. There was no proper kitchen and no bathroom. I supposed they must share those with other families somewhere in the building.

With a touch of eagerness the youngest sister led us through the pantry to curtained glass doors which opened into yet another bedroom. "My daughter's room," she said, almost whispering, and motioned us to follow her. She went directly to a baby's crib in the center of the room, and when we all stood round it, staring at the small pink child asleep in his closely wrapped shawls, she said, after an admiring moment, "My grandson."

I looked around at the rest of the room. Two large wardrobes were placed side by side, jutting into the room to form a kind of screen for the double bed in the corner. A desk and a bookcase. Two or three chairs. And the baby in his crib. "My daughter is a schoolteacher. Her husband too. They are not yet back from work." Rather timidly she asked, "Perhaps you will stay and meet them?"

"Oh, no," Faubion and I said together, suddenly aware of how long we had been there. He added, "We have already disturbed you far too much."

"But at least you will stay and have some tea with us?"

"No, really, we must go." We stepped back into the pantry.

"But *some*thing," the middle sister said, looking worried. She picked up the plate of cookies and handed them to us. We each took one and, since there wasn't room for more than one of us to sit at the pantry table, we all stood up nibbling cookies and smiling at each other with some constraint.

"Have we shown you what you came to see?" she asked.

"Yes, exactly," I answered firmly, lying shamelessly, for nothing could have held less of Dostoyevsky's atmosphere than this neat, cramped life, the quiet, the three old widows, and the sleeping infant.

"I have been wanting to ask you something." The first touch of diffidence came into her voice. "What is it that you find in Dostoyevsky's writing?"

Before I could answer she went on hastily, "I do not ask out of ignorance. I used to be a doctor, I am retired now. I get a pension of a thousand rubles a month." (I assumed that this was intended as an indication of her accomplishment during her career.) "My husband, before he was killed, was an engineer. So you understand that we are not uncultured. I have read Dostoyevsky—with particular care, since we live in his apartment—but still I must ask, what do you see in him? Why is he great?"

I couldn't think what to say, how to describe Dostoyevsky's calamitous power with words, his overwhelming sense of guilt and tragedy, the dark, dark world he lived in. At last I said, rather feebly,

"He wrote of such extraordinary things—such strange, unhappy people—"

She listened to Faubion's translation with growing bewilderment. "Extraordinary?" she said. "Strange? But Dostoyevsky wrote of everyday, *ordinary* things and people. When I finish a Dostoyevsky novel I forget it before I put the book down. What is there to remember? Now *Tolstoy*—a truly great writer. Who can ever forget Anna Karenina?" Anna Karenina, the rich, the aristocratic, the eternally romantic woman.

"To *us*," Faubion explained, "Dostoyevsky's world is extraordinary. And powerful. And remembered forever."

For the first time the oldest sister joined in the conversation. "You are foreigners," she said.

Faubion and I were silenced for a moment, hearing this familiar remark in an entirely new way.

At last the oldest sister continued. "Is it permitted to ask what country you come from?"

Faubion said, "I am American. My wife is Indian."

"America and India," she repeated wonderingly. "And you have come such a long way just to see *this* apartment?"

Moscow had quite a different flavor from Leningrad. A Leningrad acquaintance of ours had described it rather scornfully: "A confusion of houses—skyscrapers next to fifteenth-century wooden huts—a jagged skyline, nothing like the symmetry of our city. I think it is a mistake to have moved the capital to Moscow. The history is here—even the history of the Revolution. The beauty is here, more than anywhere in Russia. Let them have their factories in Moscow. We will always keep the culture."

As far as the looks of Moscow went, I found that I agreed with him. With the exception of the Kremlin and the inspired fantasy of St. Basil's in Red Square, Moscow is an ugly city, drab, colorless, ponderous. But we soon became used to it, and although we were encouraged to see the Soviet constructions and developments in places like Stalingrad and Kiev, we preferred to spend all our time in Moscow. We were perfectly willing to take Soviet achievements on faith; we just wanted to stay long enough in one place to get to know some of the people. It turned out to be much easier than we had been led to believe, because Russians seemed to be endlessly inquisitive about foreigners and would come up to us in restaurants, parks, theaters, on the street to ask questions. Admittedly we were a rather odd-looking group—one American, one Indian, one very pretty Negro girl (Jai's nurse), and one small boy dressed as a cowboy. But frequently, even after their initial curiosity had been satisfied, our Russian pickups became, we thought, more than just passing acquaintances, and in a few cases we really felt they were long-term friends. Accordingly, most of our evenings were spent at the theater, ballet or opera for our pleasure and for Faubion's book, and most of our days were studded with long conversations with strangers or with people we were gradually getting to know. All this was interspersed with more formal interviews with our "respectable" contacts—writers, actors, artists that the Ministry of Culture had arranged for us to see.

There was, however, one place in the Soviet Union other than Moscow and Leningrad that I did want to visit only because it sounded so romantic—Samarkand. With this in mind we arranged to end our stay in Russia in the province of Uzbekistan on the southern border in Asia. (One is liable to forget how much of Russia is Asia.) Even one glimpse of the piercing blue of Samarkand's domes and minarets, of the crumbling biscuit-colored walls, the great libraries and mosques of Timur's (Tamerlane's) capital would have justified the long journey from Moscow. We were lucky enough to have more than a week left before our visas expired, and we spent it all exploring the old, fabulous city.

From Uzbekistan, since we were only a short flight away from India, I decided to take Jai home to see his grandparents for a few months. The next two stories emerged from that return journey, and perhaps it is fitting that this collection should end where it began, in my own country and among my people and my family.

## *Stranded in Kabul*

Although I have always had a despairing and envious admiration of linguists, I have never had either the diligence or the ear to be Good At Languages myself. Only once in my life have I shone as an interpreter, and although I was enchanted with the sense of power it gave me and made all kinds of good resolutions, I don't suppose a comparable occasion will ever arise.

My husband and I, with our five-year-old son, had been spending three months in the Soviet Union. We had deliberately planned our trip to end in Uzbekistan, which shares a short stretch of frontier with India. From there it would be easy for me to travel home to India with my child to visit my parents, because a four-hour flight from Tashkent to Kabul, in Afghanistan, connects with an Indian airline flight from Kabul to Delhi.

My husband, who was returning to Western Europe, came to see us off at the Tashkent airport. In the chill light of daybreak, we watched the other passengers huddled beside their shabby suitcases. Just before we climbed aboard, my husband thrust a package of sandwiches into my hands, and two bottles of Narzan, an excellent Russian mineral water. Later I was very glad to have them because there were no stewards or hostesses on the plane, and no refreshments of any sort.

The plane was about half-full, so both my son and I could have window seats and watch Tashkent and its surrounding farms gradually shrink into a patch of muddy green in the vast expanse of desert, until the circling plane headed south and there was nothing before us but the distant mountains and the whitening morning sky. We made one stop before Kabul, at a small town on the Russian border. There the foreigners—a south Indian gentleman who introduced himself as Professor Iyengar, my son, and myself—were permitted to walk about in the thin winter sunshine of Central Asia, while the Russians were put through a meticulous examination of passports and documents. When we reassembled on the plane we found that only two of them were traveling on with us.

It is a short, but extraordinarily dramatic flight. The Hindu Kush is the wildest and most forbidding part of the Himalayas, so high that the plane flies between, not over, the mountains, and from the cabin you look *up* to see the snow-capped, treacherous peaks. Below you is a harsh and bony map of precipitous valleys and rocky ravines—a landscape utterly without comfort, and on too immense a scale to be anything but daunting. A sudden atmosphere of camaraderie and coziness flourished in the plane—we were even pleased to see the unsmiling member of the crew who came down the aisle handing out oxygen masks (with a special child's size for my son) to all the passengers. The cabin was not, of course, pressurized, and inevitably it was bitterly cold.

The Russians were defeating the cold with large gulps from a bottle of vodka that they passed between them. Professor Iyengar sat huddled in a brown tweed coat and smiled miserably at me whenever he caught my eye. The Russians, however, soon reached a point of expansive friendliness. They started to talk and joke with my son and to give him candies. "*Spasibo, bolshoye spasibo*," we repeated several times. Soon they generously offered me a swig of their vodka. I had learned through experience in Russia to expect a certain hearty fuss over children and also to listen for the familiar phrase that accompanied the offer of a drink—that a "blanket on the inside" was the best protection against the cold. When I heard it and nodded to show that I understood, a makeshift party quickly evolved.

Professor Iyengar was, as it happened, both a vegetarian and a teetotaler. He couldn't eat the sandwiches that I handed around because they contained sliced sturgeon and sausage, and shyly refused the vodka too. Instead he accepted a bottle of Narzan, which he drank in the Indian way, pouring the soda into his open mouth without allowing the bottle to touch his lips. The Russians were captivated with this performance, and all of us immediately imitated it with the vodka. Even though Professor Iyengar frequently retreated behind his oxygen mask with a reserved expression of private woe, our journey to Kabul had a festive air, intensified by the compound of exhilaration and heady unpredictability that the Russians felt about their first venture abroad. Professor Iyengar was equally eager to be taking this flight. His only previous experiences of "abroad" had, he told me, consisted of three very cold years at an English university and, recently, of ten even colder days in Moscow. To him the trip was a happy return to a reasonable climate—and home.

The Russians asked us innumerable questions, and this, really, was the beginning of my brief career as interpreter and linguist. Through much practice during my stay in Russia I had learned to recognize the most predictable questions that start a conversation with a foreigner, and with a shocking accent but a certain fluency had even mastered the replies. Where did I come from? India, I answered. And the gentleman? I turned to Professor Iyengar, slipping easily into the correct manner of an interpreter, and said, "They want to know where you come from."

"Madras," he said, in some surprise (an Iyengar can hardly come from anywhere else).

"Madras, India," I repeated with pride, for the Russians.

Smiling widely at both of us, they announced, "*Hindi-Russki bhai-bhai!*" and raised the vodka bottle. This is a phrase that every Indian hears with monotonous regularity in Russia. In Hindustani it means Indians and Russians are brothers. Evidently all Russians learned it when Prime Minister Nehru made his visit to the Soviet Union, and they have never forgotten it or missed an opportunity to display it. Professor Iyengar acknowledged the gesture soberly, and since I didn't know enough Russian to be able to explain that he spoke only Tamil, I replied, "*Hindi-Russki bhai-bhai!*" for both of us.

The stream of questions continued along well-worn lines. How long had we been in Russia? What had we been doing there? (To that, my part of the answer was easy, "*Touristi*," but it was quite beyond me to explain that Professor Iyengar had been invited as a member of a scientific conference. Recklessly, I said that he had been on a *Delegatsia Rabotnikov*—a delegation of workers, which would, I dare say, have annoyed the professor, but served to impress the Russians.) Did we like Moscow? ("*Da, da.*") What did we think of life in Russia? ("*Khorosho!*"–good!) and on and on. From time to time I added, "And you?" after my answers, and in this way learned that the Russians were from Sverdlovsk, that they were engineers (I think), and that they were going to work in Kandahar on some Russian project.

The questions and answers were interspaced in the normal Russian way, with nice simple toasts. We drank to everybody's health, to India, to the Soviet Union, to Nehru, to Khrushchev, to the younger generation as represented by my son, and, of course, to *druzhba i mir* (friendship and peace). It was so successful a party that none of us paid any attention to the gray drifts of cloud gathering on the peaks outside.

It was only after we landed in Kabul that we discovered that none of us would be continuing our journey that day. Kabul is set in a shallow saucer of land, surrounded by hills, and beyond them by the rugged, soaring mountains of the Himalayas, which are cut by very few passes. Planes, like the ancient armies of the Moguls, have to use these passes to enter and leave Afghanistan, and when the weather closes them, all traffic to Kabul stops. The Indian airline official remarked pleasantly that passengers were sometimes stuck in Kabul for three weeks, and offered us all a ride into town in the company's station wagon, to the "best hotel."

The Majestic turned out to be a dingy two-story block on the main street of Kabul. We climbed out of the station wagon, jumped over the open drain in the road, crossed a messy sidewalk, and entered the dark lobby of the hotel. There we stood, a disconsolate and diverse group with our luggage piled around us. Professor Iyengar looked quite gray with cold. The Russians, in their tight blue suits and squeaky brown boots, seemed impervious to the damp chill of the hotel. They looked around the lobby in silence, and then turned hopeful pink faces toward me. Clearly I had acquired the position of official interpreter and tourist guide, so I led our short procession into the manager's office.

To my great relief, he spoke English. He sat at a small, cluttered desk, sipping tea and smiling as I explained our predicament.

"By good chance," he said, "three best rooms are vacant."

He reached for keys and yelled something loud and indistinguishable. A tall, bearded Afghan in a brown woolen robe, tennis shoes, and a skullcap appeared at the door. The manager gave him the keys and some instructions in, I suppose, Farsi, the language of Afghanistan. He bowed politely to us in dismissal.

We all trailed upstairs after the Afghan, to the end of a stone-floored corridor. He opened a door and showed me one of the most cheerless rooms in my experience. Two narrow iron beds, covered with U.S. Army blankets, and the bare minimum of rickety wooden furniture gave the room a curiously institutional air. In the middle of the floor, dwarfing everything else, was a rusty iron stove. A fat pipe ran from the top of the stove across the room to a broken place in the window, and formed the chimney.

Beyond the beds there was another door. The Afghan tried its handle, then banged and rattled it with every sign of fury. At last there was an answering yell from a farther room, and the door was unlocked by a portly red-haired woman, tightly corseted under her black crepe dress. She started to say something angrily to the Afghan, but stopped when she noticed the rest of us. "*Pardon, madame*," she said to me, and then turned to leave, remarking over her shoulder, "*C'est ici la salle de bain.*" She pointed to a door the other side of the bathroom and added, "*Nous sommes là, en face, mon mari et moi. Je vous prie de laisser la porte ouverte quand vous avez fini.*"

I murmured, "*Merci, madame*," and then asked the Afghan (in English) if I could have some towels and soap. The woman paused at the door to her own room, interested. It was instantly clear to both of us that he didn't speak English. For the first time the woman smiled at me, and told me, as a fellow sufferer, that he didn't speak French either.

By this time Professor Iyengar and the Russians had joined us in the bathroom. The professor helpfully repeated my request in very slow basic English. The red-haired woman simply shrugged and kept insisting that it was all *inutile*. The Russians, standing patiently behind the professor, obviously hadn't an idea what was going on; they shifted their feet anxiously, all the friendly inquisitiveness of the plane evaporated. The Afghan was mercifully silent.

In moments of stress, I have noticed, I am apt to revert in thought or in speech to the language of my childhood. In Hindustani, and in a loud and edgy voice, I announced to the Afghan that all I wanted was a towel and a bit of soap. My small but dedicated audience watched the effect with a flattering and incredulous attention. The man smiled, showing yellow irregular teeth through his mass of beard and mustache. "*Ek dum, huzoor!*" (At once!) he said, and strode off in a purposeful way.

The rest of us were left staring at each other in the bathroom. At last the woman said wonderingly, in French, "You speak Farsi!"

"No, no—"

Professor Iyengar broke in thoughtfully "It is not really surprising. There must be many common words between Farsi and Urdu, and hence in Hindustani also. However, the grammar and possibly the pronunciation will present difficulties."

The Russians, sensing, I suppose, a change in mood, looked happier and attentive, and responded most cordially when the red-haired woman decided to introduce herself. "Her name is Mme. Haffar," I said, first in English and then in Russian. The Russians introduced themselves, we all shook hands, repeating each other's names politely and ignoring the incongruity of such formalities in a bathroom.

Mme. Haffar expressed herself enchanted to meet Russians. "Our countries are friends," she said to them, in French. She and her husband were Syrians. "Please tell them," she asked me.

"*Mme. Haffar Syrianka*," I said. "*Droog*," and then, suddenly remembering the plural of "friend," I amended it to "*Druzya*."

"Long live friendship," said one of the Russians—at least that's how I translated his remark.

"Always before," Mme. Haffar explained to me, "French has been sufficient for us as a language with which to travel in foreign countries. But here—" She opened her hands despairingly.

We were still talking in a clumsy, trilingual way, when the Afghan reappeared with a face towel and a piece of pink carbolic soap which evidently belonged to somebody else. By this time we were so pleased with our small success, and the feeling of solidarity that it gave us, that it occurred to none of us to stay behind when the Russians and Professor Iyengar were shown to their rooms across the passage.

Meanwhile, Mme. Haffar began asking about all the little mysteries and inconveniences that had been bothering her since she and her husband (with their two young sons) had moved into the hotel the week before. Were the stoves in the rooms never lighted? Did one pay extra for firewood? Were children half-price? Were meals in the hotel restaurant included in the charge for the rooms? She asked, she explained, because the hotel meals were inedible. But most of all she insisted on knowing why the door to the lounge was always locked.

I was thankful that the Russians, noisily accompanied by my child, had gone downstairs to bring the luggage up. In the long-drawn-out process of answering her questions I discovered that the Afghan's knowledge of Hindustani could, charitably, be described as fragmentary. His name was Salim, I learned. We soon fell into an odd form of communication that consisted almost entirely of nouns and imperatives. "*Aag?*" I would say, enunciating meticulously. "*Lakri?*" He looked at the stove in a bewildered way—he must have thought me strangely eccentric because any fool could see that there was neither fire nor wood in the stove. He shook his head.

"*Lakri lao! Aag jalao!*" I commanded in ringing tones.

"*Ek dum, huzoor,*" he replied briskly, and immediately answered Mme. Haffar's second question by holding out his hand in a gesture everyone understood. "*Paisa,*" he said. Luckily she had some Afghan currency to give him and kindly included us all in the purchase of wood. Before we let him go on his errand, we cleared up a few of the other problems. The price for the room included breakfast, and then one had to pay for one other meal in the restaurant, whether one ate it or not. The mystery of the lounge was less easily explained and took us on an excursion to the far end of the corridor where Mme. Haffar tried the door marked "Residents' Lounge," and triumphantly announced, "*Fermée à clef!*"

Salim shook his head regretfully. Impossible to open it, he told us. There was to be a party.

By the time we had sorted out our luggage and settled ourselves in our rooms, it was time for luncheon. Mme. Haffar declined our invitation, saying that she would wait for her husband and her sons, and the rest of us found our way to the hotel dining room feeling that after all this wasn't too bad a way to spend a day's delay. We were sheltered, we would be warm, and we were about to eat Afghan food for the first time.

Our mood began to change when we saw the dining room with

its view of a muddy courtyard and its quite repellent kitchen, where clouds of steam, a banging of pans, and a smell I didn't recognize announced that luncheon was ready. We sat at a large table covered with small disheartening maps made of gravy or grease, and examined the menu typewritten in English. There was nothing on it, except for tomato soup, that Professor Iyengar could eat—even the Afghan dish was "mutton pilau"—and he didn't want to risk "brown soup." It sounded as though it contained meat. I ordered "mutton cutlets with 2 veg." for myself and my son—it was the "2 veg." that attracted me because through most of Russia we had seen no green vegetables except the cabbage in cabbage soup. To the Russians I explained that there was *sup* and *kotlyety* (I didn't really feel that my Russian was being fully exploited), and they nodded cheerfully to both.

When the food arrived we saw that everything, even the soup, was covered with a layer of liquid, nasty-smelling grease. The Russians paid no attention to it, my son and I picked at floating pieces of meat, but Professor Iyengar looked both dejected and embarrassed and wouldn't touch his tomato soup until he inquired about the origin of the grease. With a certain gracious self-assurance, the waiter told us that everything was cooked with the best ingredients at the Majestic, so of course the fat came from the tail of the fat-tailed sheep. None of us had the heart to explain about the professor's vegetarianism, so we simply said that he had a weak stomach and could only eat plain boiled rice and raw tomatoes. To the professor this seemed to be only another tiresome, but expected, discomfort of "abroad." He told me not to worry about him, that he would fill up on fruit, for which Kabul was famous. "This valley used to be known as the orchard of Asia," he said. I avoided his eye when dessert turned out to be canned pineapple.

I spent most of the cold, overcast afternoon trying, unsuccessfully, to make my child take a nap while I huddled over the fire that Salim had built in the stove. I don't know what the others did, but whatever it was, by half past four the Russians were evidently too depressed to stay any longer by themselves without some kind of stimulation. They knocked on my door and after a good deal of talk and gesticulation, I gathered that they were asking me to help them get something to drink.

I stood in the passage, and in the manner that is usual in many Asian hotels summoned the room boy by yelling, "Salim! Salim!" Professor Iyengar's door opened. So did Mme. Haffar's. We waited nervously until Salim appeared from his cubbyhole at the end of the corridor. He took the order for "something to drink" for all of us, and soon returned with a large tray loaded with tea things. This wasn't precisely what the Russians had hoped for, but further questioning of Salim ended in the discovery that Kabul is dry. You can neither buy a bottle of alcohol nor order a drink in a public place. The Russians accepted cups of tea with fairly good grace, but it was clear from their expression that their stay in Kabul was becoming some inexplicable kind of nightmare.

While we were still sitting around the stove in my room, a stranger walked in. He seemed to be harried and relieved simultaneously, and a lot of rapid Russian talk followed in which I was well out of my depth. My friends from the plane were evidently insisting that something or other be explained to me. The stranger spoke Farsi as well as Russian, but no English. Salim was called back and a frenzied half hour began in which the stranger spoke to Salim in Farsi, Salim passed on his remarks to me in broken Hindustani, and I repeated them first in English to Professor Iyengar, who seemed very worried, and then in French to Mme. Haffar, who was simply inquisitive. The gist of this chaotic exchange proved to be fairly pedestrian. The stranger was an official from the Russian Embassy who had, as part of his job, to check on Russian newcomers to Kabul. He at last had tracked his compatriots down at the Majestic. Now he would escort them to the embassy, where they would presumably spend a jolly evening in less bizarre company.

But the real point of all this was that he had learned at the airport that no planes were expected to leave tomorrow or the day after. Even then, if the weather cleared, the backlog of traffic would probably hold us up for yet another day.

Feeling inexpressibly glum, the professor, my son, and I went for a walk after tea, sloshing along the littered pavements toward the murky river that winds through the city. Later, when we returned to the Majestic, cold, cross, muddy, and tired, we found that there was no hot water in the bathrooms. This involved me in a maddening exchange with Salim in which he insisted that hot water was unobtainable, while Mme. Haffar, relentlessly interested, punctuated the conversation with "*Qu'est-ce qu'il a dit?*" and "*Que voulez-vous, madame?*" and Professor Iyengar kept remarking, "To bathe is essential."

However, they pleased me with heartfelt congratulations on my ingenuity when at last I found a rather unorthodox solution to our problem. The way to get hot water, it turned out, was to order tea for twelve people *without* the tea leaves, milk, and sugar.

In the days that followed we saw a great deal of the Haffar family. M. Haffar was a round, bald, self-effacing man with beautiful manners. The two sons (twelve and eight) were charming, alert boys who took the lessons that their mother set for them every morning into their own room. Mme. Haffar would accompany us on rides in a pony cart around town, gazing at the undistinguished architecture and the more interesting stream of pedestrians. Most of the men wore robes and boots, the women were heavily veiled in tent-like black or white cotton burkas with only a strip of netting across the eyes to allow them to see. Some of the burkas were made of silk in subdued colors and occasionally, as a women stepped across a puddle, we would catch a glimpse of neatly turned ankles in sheer stockings and incongruously stylish shoes.

On these tours the conversation in our cart consisted of little more than painstaking inquiries from the Russians of how such-and-such was said in English (or French or Farsi or Hindustani), and my own efforts to increase my Russian vocabulary by reversing the process. Sometimes Mme. Haffar would interrupt with a brief spurt of comment in French. That ugly building over there, she would indicate with a wave of her hand, was the new Russian bread factory, or this road, fully paved, leading past the embassies to the airport, the only really good road in Afghanistan, also was built by the Russians. With a resigned acceptance of a nature that couldn't be changed, she added, "It explains itself, doesn't it? It can't be surprising that the American effort to improve relations with Afghanistan should fall into the shadow of the Russians. American aid to Afghan economy is always in invisible things—loans to the government, development projects—who can be grateful for that sort of thing when half of Kabul bicycles to work past the bread factory?" For once I was glad that my Russian was so limited.

In the afternoons, if it wasn't actually raining, the Haffar boys and my son used to play in the courtyard behind the hotel, otherwise they had to take their bat and rubber ball into the corridor. The lounge was always locked, always for a "party." Even when we discovered that any bedroom key opened the lounge door, Salim would never let us sit there because of the imminent beginning of a "party" (of which we never saw any sign).

Sunday was a relatively fine day—at least the rain held off and the clouds seemed to be thinning over the encircling hills. The Russians were to spend the day with their embassy friend, and the Haffars, Professor Iyengar, my son, and I hired a taxi to take us on a longish drive to the tomb of the Emperor Babur some miles out in the hills above the city.

When we returned to Kabul, M. Haffar included us all in an invitation to tea with a man that he called "the minister," by which I think he meant the government official in charge of his electrical plant. The gateway to the minister's house was in a slimy side street, and a muddy ditch, used as a sewer, ran along the outside wall. But as soon as we climbed out of the taxi and went through the gate, we were in an enchanting garden filled with winter flowers and the elegant tracery of bare fruit trees.

The minister, a good-humored man wearing an open robe over a Western business suit, waited for us in a tiny drawing room. He couldn't have expected this avalanche of strangers and children, but he received us without surprise. In English he asked Mme. Haffar and me to sit down, promised to send his wife to entertain us, and tactfully, in the proper Muslim way, led the men away to a separate part of the house. I had time only to wonder how they were going to talk to each other, and to glance quickly round the room at the beautiful faded carpets, the stiff dark furniture set against white walls between windows so small and so heavily screened that the room was always filled with a filtered twilight.

The minister's wife, a tiny, tidy woman, stepped into the room from a curtained doorway as though she had been waiting for a stage cue. She was exquisitely dressed in Western clothes that, to my untutored eye, looked like Paris models, nylon stockings, and very high-heeled pumps. She seemed painfully shy, sitting gracefully but uneasily on the edge of her chair and smiling in courteous silence at her guests. At last Mme. Haffar, with many gestures and a compelling expression, rashly announced that I spoke Farsi. I tried to say that this was entirely untrue, but my denials were lost in the soft, rapid flood of Farsi that the minister's wife directed toward me. I smiled and nodded, repeating here and there a word that I understood.

The tea brought in by a maid was a meal that remains in my memory as the most welcome and unexpected moment of our stay in Kabul. Tray after tray was produced, loaded with tiny aromatic cakes, improbably perfect bunches of grapes, mountains of apples, sliced sugared melons. There was a platter of small birds covered with a dark brown glaze. There were skewers of lamb and onions, hot little kebabs the size of coat buttons, candied cherries and ginger, some kind of milky sweet, and a number of dishes that I neither recognized nor, finally, had the appetite to taste. My son attacked the meal with an energy and concentration that I had never seen before, certainly not in the hotel dining room. We all watched, enthralled and unbelieving, while he ate five of the small grilled birds, leaving his plate piled with bones. The Haffar boys, meanwhile, were methodically emptying the bowls of fruit. There was no way of explaining this performance, and Mme. Haffar and I sat in helpless silence while the minister's wife appeared amused and at ease for the first time.

At some prearranged signal or inaudible summons, she rose, said good-by gently to all of us, and retreated through the curtained door. A second later, the men returned. When we reached the taxi we found that the back seat was covered with baskets of fruit, packages of the little birds, kebabs, and cakes. We were, of course, touched and delighted with these presents, but my attention was partly distracted from the generosity of the minister's wife by the sudden appearance of sunshine—watery and uncertain, but heralding a possibility of clearing skies and resumed plane schedules.

The next morning we all woke up to more assured sunlight and the distant blue of the mountain sky, and after breakfast there was an excited knocking on my door. As usual, Mme. Haffar and Professor Iyengar's doors opened at the same time as mine. The two Russians stood in the corridor excitedly telling me that they had received a message from the embassy. The plane from Kandahar was expected that morning, it would be returning—with them as passengers—after lunch. I repeated the news in English and in French, and finally to Salim, who was trotting inquiringly down the passage, in Hindustani.

I think the idea occurred simultaneously to Mme. Haffar and to me. Professor Iyengar, when we explained it to him, concurred, if not with enthusiasm, at least with his first really convincing smile. Mme. Haffar announced a holiday from lessons to her sons, and the boys (with a lot of unnecessary hushing and tiptoeing, having waited until Salim returned to his room) quietly opened the door of the lounge. They helped us carry in the fruit and the other delicacies that the minister's wife had provided, and set it out in an imposing array on the long table. I contributed two jars of caviar and a bottle of vodka that I had intended as presents from Russia to my family in India. Mme. Haffar added two packages of rather stale American cigarettes that she had bought, black market, in the bazaar. Professor Iyengar bashfully set out an old toffee tin filled with *supari* (areca nut) and cardamon seed which he had carried with him to Russia to salve recurrent bouts of homesickness.

At last we were ready to tap on the door of the Russians. They looked up from locking suitcases to see our delegation standing in the door. In my most formal tone I said, "*Ya vas priglashayu*," waving my hand to show that the invitation came from all of us. Mystified, they followed us to the lounge, where we threw open the door and stood back so that they could see the full splendor of the feast.

The excitement and the exclamations brought Salim scurrying into the lounge. He started to make his usual worried objections, but this time he faced a smiling and determined group. "But it *is* a party!" I assured him with triumph. "Look! Food. Drink. Guests. It *is* a party, so we stay in the lounge."

For a moment there was silence while Salim looked first apprehensive then resigned. "What's more," I continued bravely, "we will need glasses and plates, knives and forks and tea for the children and the professor."

At last Salim smiled too. "*Ek dum, huzoor*," he said, and we all felt it a moment of victory.

It was a magnificent party, and after two glasses of vodka I felt that my languages improved enormously. Now our list of toasts was longer too, because we drank to the airlines, Syria, and Afghanistan in addition to Russia, India, peace, friendship, the various national leaders, the younger generation, the whole world. The Russians were delighted with the fruit and the novel taste of areca nut and cardamon. Mme. Haffar remarked, "*Je me suis régalée!*" with her first bite of caviar. We spread it on bread (presumably from the Russian bread factory) provided by Salim. Cups and cups of hot tea and the fire we had lighted seemed to thaw Professor Iyengar. He emerged from his private veil of dejection and permitted himself to smell, but not to taste, the caviar, ate almost a whole bunch of grapes, and was persuaded, in the general gaiety, to recite a Sanskrit poem. He gave me a meticulous translation of it in English, and I passed on a looser one to Mme. Haffar in French. For the Russians all I could manage was "*Indiiskaya poema*," which scarcely seemed adequate to me, but appeared to satisfy them. Salim bustled about serving food, replenishing cups and glasses, sometimes glancing nervously toward the door. Our party broke up only when we heard the drone of the Kandahar plane.

This was my last appearance as an interpreter on such a lavish scale. The Russians hurried off to the airport, or so we thought. Actually, they must have found time to go to the bazaar because that afternoon Salim delivered two presents—one, a small American model of a plane, was for my son; the other was a football for the Haffar boys. Both cards said simply, "*Dosvidanya*"—"Good-by," or more literally, "Until we meet again."

I don't know whether the Haffars ever saw the Russians again, but the rest of us had no opportunity. The Indian plane came into Kabul the next day and left the same afternoon with Professor Iyengar, my son, and myself on board. For a couple of weeks, the toy plane was my only reminder of Afghanistan, but it was soon too battered and dented to be kept even as a souvenir. By now my son had quite forgotten the meaning of *dosvidanya,* and I have never had occasion to use the expression since.

# *Return to India*

During the three months that we were in the Soviet Union, I lost count of the number of times Russians asked us, "Don't you think our life here is very good?"

"Yes, very good," we always replied, politely refraining from adding, "for the Russians."

Inevitably the point would be pressed a little further. Life in the Soviet Union was not only good, we would be assured, but was getting better every day. Certainly on the evidence of the past few years this was no more than the truth. Usually after this kind of opening exchange, the Russians we met proved to be intensely inquisitive about life in America, my husband's country, and the questions ranged from the price of nylons to American intentions for nuclear war. Sometimes they even showed a faintly patronizing interest in my country, India.

On one such occasion I had a brief and uninspired conversation with a chance Russian acquaintance that I was to remember much later with quite a different feeling. A young man, noticing across a restaurant dining room that I wore a sari, came over to the table where my husband and I were sitting. "*Hindi-Russki bhai-bhai!*" he announced proudly.

"*Hindi-Russki bhai-bhai,*" I replied dutifully, and then, after the usual opening formalities, the young man started to ask me—or rather, to tell me—about life in India.

With my husband interpreting for us, he remarked, "The Indian people are very poor."

"Yes, they are."

"I have seen photographs. They have few clothes and many have no shoes."

"That's true."

"Most of them are uneducated."

"Yes."

"Many beggars on the streets."

"Yes."

"It must be very distressing to live in such a country."

"No—" I began, suddenly feeling homesick.

But the young man was finished with the subject of India. "In Russia we have a very good life . . ."

After our stay in Russia, I returned with my son to visit my family in India. We flew from Uzbekistan in the far south of Russia, over the magnificent expanse of the Himalayas to New Delhi. The plane arrived after dark and by the time we reached my uncle's house it was quite late at night and we were too tired to do much talking or to pay much attention to our surroundings.

The next morning, with my first glimpse of the newspapers, I was sharply aware not so much that I was in India as that I was out of Russia. One paragraph was enough to convince me. It ran, as I remember, something like this: "Yesterday the Prime Minister opened the debate in parliament on the Second Five-Year Plan with a two-hour speech in his usual diffuse style." I read, and reread, and *reread* the words "his usual diffuse style," remembering the monotonously reverential tone of all Russian newspapers toward all Russian leaders —the ones in favor, that is.

This was trivial enough as an incident, but in the course of that first day a number of other moments—equally minor, equally transient—began to acquire a collective force. I had offered to help with the household shopping, partly because I always enjoy bazaars and partly because I wanted to show my son a little of the city. We started in the fruit market, which I'm afraid my Russian friends would have found hopelessly disorganized. No orderly queues, no rationing, no fixed prices, no stern-faced women with string shopping bags waiting in line, dutifully reading signs saying, "Drink fruit juices. They are good for you."

To me an Indian bazaar is a source of endless delight and excitement. It is usually a series of plain wooden stalls on which are piled, with unconscious artistry, brightly colored fruits, vegetables, spices, gleaming silver jewelry, brilliant silks and cottons, or charming, grotesque, painted wooden toys. The vendors who can't afford a stall sit on the sidewalk outside the market, their baskets stacked behind them, their wives in vivid cotton saris crouching in the shade, and in front of them are spread carpets of scarlet chilies drying in the sun, small hills of saffron, turmeric, coriander, ginger, cinnamon—all the magical names from the old days of the spice trade with the Indies. With a worn stone mortar and pestle the vendor or his wife will grind your spices for you, blending them according to your particular taste, and weigh them in tiny brass scales strung on twine and balanced delicately in one hand. In all transactions you receive a pleasantly individual attention—nothing is standardized.

The vegetable and fruit and flower merchants are surrounded by baskets of purple eggplant, green peppers, strings of tiny silvery onions, heads of bitter Indian spinach, and a dozen Indian vegetables for which I don't even know the English names. I had forgotten about the profusion of fruit in India—it is only during the brief, intense summer that you see much variety of fruit in Moscow. In Russia, as winter approaches, all vegetables except for potatoes and the pervasive cabbage in soup, seem to disappear from the menus.

My son was enjoying himself, pouncing on the stacks of bananas —unobtainable in Russia—regarding with some suspicion the papayas and chikus which he had not remembered from his last stay in India. He prodded a pile of the tiny, sharp Indian limes to see if they would collapse, an action for which he would have been severely reprimanded in Russia. I was reminded of the evening when we had run into an official of the Ministry of Culture in the lobby of the Metropole, our hotel in Moscow. He had come to the hotel to buy a lemon. It seemed like an extraordinary place to come for such an item, but he explained that there were too few lemons in the winter, so that they were saved for the tourists and the foreigners and could only be obtained, if you were lucky, at an Intourist hotel.

Flowers. This was something I missed very much in Russia, where flowers are a real luxury. I can remember standing at a street corner in Russia, astonished by the sight of a flower woman sitting in the middle of a splash of color in those gray streets. The Russians stopped to look too. Not many of them bought the flowers—too costly—but a surprising number paused in the rush to get home from offices, factories, and shops in the shadowy autumn twilight just to feast for a moment on the rare color of a few stiff bunches of chrysanthemums on a street corner.

All around us, in Delhi, there were flowers. Yes, it is a tropical country and, yes, the climate makes this possible—but there was a personal pride and feminine joy in the countrywomen who tucked a marigold casually into their hair, who wove roses into small hoops to wear more formally around the knot of hair on the back of the head. I realized then that I had missed all this in Russia: the pleasure of women in being women, a sense of decoration, an unquestioned right of anyone to the small, cheap luxuries and gaieties.

But most impressive—to me anyway—are the people in an Indian bazaar. First of all, there is the inquisitiveness that often embarrasses foreigners. When you are engaged on an errand as prosaic as buying potatoes, in the course of the transaction your vendor may well ask you any variety of what my American friends would call personal questions. How old are you? How many children do you have? Only one? (A commiserating shake of the head.) Better hurry and have another before you are too old. Where do you live? Is your mother-in-law alive? Inevitably I made the comparison with Russia, where this kind of passing, interested exchange (between Russians) is so suspect. The right to express ordinary human curiosity about a fellow countryman came to seem like an unusual privilege.

Meanwhile the brisk, canny routine of bargaining would be going on, and the whole performance would be interspersed with jokes and cracks and comments. Next to me a man, bargaining for a basket of tangerines, remarked to the old woman standing behind the stall, "Clearly you believe in the soak-the-rich program." This was the popular description of India's new taxation policy. The woman looked amused and replied dryly, "Give me your income and I will gladly pay your taxes." And the bargaining went on without rancor—it was all very Indian, or rather, un-Russian.

We finished our shopping and summoned a boy to carry our purchases out of the bazaar—another small, cheap luxury.

On our way out of the market we had to pass the familiar barrage of beggars on the sidewalk and, as usual, gave them the small change left over from shopping. Even my son was struck with the contrast to Moscow. "Why are they asking for money, Mummy?"

"Because they are poor, darling."

"Why are they poor, Mummy?"

"India is a poor country, darling. Too many people and not enough food."

"We could give them some of our fruit."

"Well, that's what we've done in another way. We've given them some money to buy whatever they choose."

Then I was left wondering, as so often in the past, about the ethics of begging and giving. It is easy to win approval from foreigners by deploring two elements of Indian life—the caste structure and begging for a livelihood. The best that can be said about either of them is that it is gradually disappearing. However, it would be less than honest to pretend that social malaise is all that is involved in either system. The goals in the Hindu view of life are not the same as those of Russia or the Western world. Indeed, India's highest caste, the Brahmans, are traditionally sworn to poverty. Ambition, getting ahead, comfort, success are obstacles, not aims, in the Hindu concept of a good life. Enlightenment is reached, if it is reached, when you have detached yourself from worldly considerations and emotional drives of any sort, so it is not surprising that many of India's most respected "holy men" are, in fact, beggars, or perhaps live on unsolicited contributions from strangers, disciples, casual visitors.

What in the West is almost always a degrading occupation can, in India, be a high achievement. Not, of course, that all beggars are religious mendicants. Many are simply poor, or sick, or unemployed, or seeking a little extra income. If, to a Westerner, they are an embarrassment or raise guilt feelings about his own privileged life, to an Asian they are more likely to engender a down-to-earth recognition of conditions as they are and an urge to contribute in a small way to a social responsibility. This is combined with the knowledge that there is no society, including the Russian, in which privilege is unknown. Money, birth, education, accomplishment, something makes a class (or caste) structure. The Hindu view is not to rise to a higher level of privilege but to rise beyond the concern with privilege and levels altogether. It is hard enough to explain this attitude to a sympathetic, philosophic Westerner; it is impossible to describe to the average Russian, to whom spiritual values seem to be mysterious, unacceptable, or discredited.

Could the Indian government, like the Russian or the Chinese, abolish beggars with a sweeping compulsory measure? I suppose it could. Would the cost in undemocratic forcefulness be too high? I think it might. We are committed to raising the standard of living in India, but by different methods, at a different pace—a pace designed to preserve other important aspects of our life. Although a number of these thoughts occurred to me that day at the bazaar, luckily I hadn't the time to try to explain many of them to my son because he was thirsty and was more concerned with demanding a *limonad* of the sort he had liked in Russia. We stopped at a nearby coffeeshop.

An Indian coffeehouse, like an Indian bazaar, has its own peculiar atmosphere. It is a cheerful, unpretentious place in which to dawdle, encounter friends, talk, discuss, gossip. Students make fiery speeches to each other; women meet for a break in a morning's shopping; idlers stop by for a rest, to watch the world go by, to pick up a chance colleague. The actual drinking of coffee is the least important part of the whole affair. Looking around at the animated groups of uninhibited talkers at the tables, I couldn't help thinking that this particular sort of place doesn't exist in Moscow. There one can find restaurants (mostly rather expensive by any standard), or "Parks of Culture and Rest," or hotel dining rooms, and several varieties of bar ranging from the *pivnaya,* where as a rule you can't even sit down, where women are seldom seen, and where the customers walk to the bar, order a drink, down it, and leave all within the space of five minutes, to the *stolovoye,* which is considered more refined, more suitable for women, and where ordinary vodka is not served, though wines and brandy are brought to your table. But India is not a drinking country—not even in the states where there is no prohibition. The sight of drunks being thrown out of restaurants with the offhand ruthlessness that the Russians employ for such occasions is extremely rare in India.

Indians meet in public places for sociability, and though poor housing contributes, as it does in Russia, to the life of cafés and restaurants and street corners, still Indians do not meet for the dedicated purpose of getting drunk. They are incurable talkers. At the coffeehouse I found myself once again cozy and amused in the endless stream of comment, criticism, scandal, anecdote, and analysis that accompanies one's days in any Indian society. I like the idea that one can be interested, amused, or disapproving of the activities or remarks of one's neighbors, friends, and acquaintances, or of political figures, college professors, taxi drivers, and artists. I like the idea that one's concern, malicious or pleasant, in one's fellow countrymen cannot lead to their political harassment.

Listening that morning in the coffeehouse to the flurry of debate that rose from the students' tables about the latest political controversy, interspersed with the social chitchat of the ladies or the shop talk of secretaries, office workers, and clerks, I thought of the sad, sly exchanges we had shared with our Russian acquaintances. I remembered the way conversation with a Russian in a restaurant would stop cold whenever a waiter came to the table or strangers walked by. At first I was astonished to find that Russians are much more willing to talk than I had expected, that people will come up to you in parks, restaurants, on the street, drawn by curiosity to a foreigner, eager to ask and answer questions. But we soon learned, after hearing some deeply intimate confidences from Russians we scarcely knew, that our relations with them were very much in the nature of a shipboard romance. It can be intimate because it is so brief. "I can talk to you frankly," one of our friends said, not wistfully, merely as a statement of fact, "because you are in Moscow only a short time. Soon you will go and we will never meet again."

I remembered a waiter at the Metropole Hotel who had seen us so often in the dining room that one day he drifted unobtrusively over to our table to ask us in muttered conversation and scribbled notes about foreign writers. In return for whatever fragments of information we could give him, he told us about his favorite poet, Valery Bryusov. We had never heard of him, and then learned that he was banned in the Soviet Union. "You see," the waiter whispered, "he is a symbolist." In the rowdy air of the coffeehouse, it seemed incredible that there were places where poetry, even symbolist poetry, was considered too dangerous for the fragile human intellect.

After those early days in India, both the novelty of being at home and the continual contrasts with Russia began to wear thin. Soon I slipped back in the slow pace and familiar daily life of India. My son no longer noticed beggars. I no longer thought of a trip to the bazaar or the coffeehouse as an occasion. I even remembered the cold blue evenings of Moscow with some nostalgia as the Indian climate warmed up to its early spring. But once during that time I had reason to think of my trip to Moscow and of India as a nation with a shock of rediscovery. It was during the Independence Day parade that takes place in New Delhi every January 26.

It is an immense celebration and villagers from all the surrounding areas of the city had been walking into town or arriving in their bullock carts for days before. As the day grew closer all the open spaces of New Delhi were gradually filled with impromptu camps. Carts were unhitched, oxen grazed in the parks, the evening air was filled with the haze of open-air cooking fires for the scanty dinners of the travelers. On the streets you saw everywhere the brilliantly colored full ankle-length skirts and tight bodices of the village women. Each footstep (yes, barefoot, I would have had to admit to my Russian acquaintance) was emphasized by the metallic clink of silver anklets or toe rings. Every time a small child was hitched into a more comfortable position on his mother's hip, the sound of silver bracelets would accompany the movement. The fathers, proudly carrying sons on a tour of the city's sights or carefully washing their oxen at a public fountain, were less decorative but good-humored and ready for a festival. The streets were full of color and excitement and nobody checked the wanderings of the villagers as they looked around their capital.

In Russia you need a permit to travel even within the country, an identity card and an official permit before you may stay at a hotel. For most non-Muscovites, the only way to get to Moscow is to come, as a reward for outstanding service, on a brief "workers' tour" or as a member of some delegation. Chekhov's yearning phrase "To Moscow, to Moscow . . ." has just as intense a meaning now.

The day of the parade brought thousands of villagers and citizens of Delhi to the parade route, lining the roads in a dense, active crowd of mothers, fathers, children, babies, donkeys, oxen. Many families had their lunches tied up in pieces of cloth. Children clutched balloons or candy sticks. Little stalls selling nuts, tea, sweets, and fruit sprang up everywhere. I was lucky enough to have a seat on one of the bleachers outside the President's house, where the procession started, and next to me was an old man in a worn khaki sweater and army trousers. A faded patch on his arm said "Engineers." He was obviously a veteran, obviously now retired, and obviously he had never been higher in rank than the equivalent of a sergeant.

When the procession began with the arrival of the Indian President, the old man stood up to get a better view. All the pomp and ceremony of viceregal days surrounded the appearance of the President—the outriders, the cavalry escort, the great coach drawn by matched horses, guarded by lancers. Out of the coach stepped a small thin man in a brown *achkan* (the Indian jacket), narrow trousers wrinkled at the ankles, a Gandhi cap on his head. He looked embarrassed by the flashy display that surrounded him. Smiling shyly, he brought his hands together in a *namaskar*, the Indian greeting, and hurried to his place on the reviewing platform. This in no way discouraged the old man next to me. He raised his hands in a *namaskar* above the heads of the people around him. With tears streaming down his face, he yelled (apparently convinced that the President could hear him), "*Namaste ji! Jai Hind!*" and continued with such fervor that the rest of us near him suddenly found ourselves joining in a tribute from an Indian who had spent all his life in the British Army to an Indian who represented, at last, the fact that all this and India itself belonged to all of us.

The parade was splendid as such things go—a vast cavalcade of camels, elephants, ski troops, horsemen, the tough Gurkhas, the bearded colorful Sikhs—all the diversity and pageantry of India. But I am not really very keen on parades. They worry and depress me, and while this fantastic procession was going on, in my mind I had slipped back to the day of the fortieth anniversary of the Russian Revolution in Moscow. Another parade. Of a very different sort. There were no crowds lining the sidewalks—the streets had been cleared for security reasons. There was none of the good-humored pushing and shoving and wriggling of small children to get to the front where they could see best. Color? Pageantry? No, a few people in the factory workers' groups in the procession carried paper flowers, and one realized in a moment how seldom one saw color on the streets in Moscow, how rarely the drab grays and browns of the city were ever lightened by even so much as a pretty shop window. Mostly the Russian parade was grimly military, tanks and guns and huge rockets, and ranks and ranks of marching soldiers.

At the end of our parade the tribesmen from the Naga hills came by to do a dance in the street in front of the President. Predictably (it couldn't happen in Russia), they were late in getting started. Consequently, they clashed with the fly-past of the new Indian jets. Watching the two performances simultaneously, I could only think I would never have been able to explain to that anonymous Russian acquaintance of mine the appeal of Indian casualness, of the need for color, ease, humor—the joy of an Indian festival.

Poor and undernourished and undereducated, yes. But in India people turn out every election day in a larger percentage than anywhere else in the world to *choose* a government. They make a real holiday of it, decorating their oxcarts and dressing in their best clothes to go to the polls. Certainly one cannot pretend that there is nothing in India that needs to be changed, but somewhere in all this is a confidence and pleasure in being Indian, and in the country's ways. And, yes, those ways are very different from Russian ways.

Well, it never fails: one always sounds sentimental in trying to say things like this. Perhaps it is just as well that I never got a chance to explain to that remote young man in Moscow how I feel about India.

## *ABOUT THE AUTHOR*

Santha Rama Rau was born in Madras, India, in 1923, daughter of the Indian diplomat Sir Benegal Rama Rau. She went to school in England and in the United States, graduating from Wellesley College.

Her first book, *Home to India*, was published in 1945. Since then her travels have taken her back and forth across the world several times, her stories and articles have appeared in many magazines, and out of her experiences have come six other books: *East of Home*, *This Is India*, *Remember the House* (a novel), *View to the Southeast*, *My Russian Journey*, and *Gifts of Passage*. Her dramatization of E. M. Forster's novel *Passage to India* had an immediate success in London early in 1960 and plans for a Broadway production are under way.

In private life Miss Rama Rau is the wife of Faubion Bowers, also a writer and an authority on the Eastern theater and dance. They have a son Jai.

*Set in Linotype Janson*
*Format by Jacqueline Wilsdon*
*Manufactured by American Book–Stratford Press*
*Published by* Harper & Brothers, *New York*